This book explores what the Victorians said about the Stuart past, with particular emphasis on changing interpretations of Cromwell and the Puritans. It analyzes in detail the historical writings of Henry Hallam, Thomas Babington Macaulay, Thomas Carlyle and Samuel Rawson Gardiner, placing them in a context that stresses the importance of religious controversy for the nineteenth century.

The book argues that the Victorians found the Stuart past problematic because they perceived a connection between the religious disputes of the seventeenth century and the sectarian discord of their own age. Cromwell and the Puritans became an acceptable part of the national past, having been outsiders at the beginning of the century, only as the English state lost its Anglican exclusiveness. The tendency to accommodate Cromwell and the Puritans, particularly in the work of Gardiner, thus reflected a process of nation building that sought to remove sectarian divisions and which reached its climax as the Victorian age came to its close.

# THE VICTORIANS AND THE STUART HERITAGE

# THE VICTORIANS AND THE STUART HERITAGE

*Interpretations of a discordant past*

TIMOTHY LANG

*Dickinson College, Pennsylvania*

CAMBRIDGE
UNIVERSITY PRESS

Published by the Press Syndicate of the University of Cambridge
The Pitt Building, Trumpington Street, Cambridge CB2 IRP
40 West 20th Street, New York, NY 10011–4211, USA
10 Stamford Road, Oakleigh, Melbourne 3166, Australia

First published 1995

Printed in Great Britain by Antony Rowe Ltd, Chippenham, Wiltshire

*A catalogue record for this book is available from the British Library*

*Library of Congress cataloguing in publication data*
Lang, Timothy,
The Victorians and the Stuart heritage: interpretations of a
discordant past / Timothy Lang
p.    cm.
ISBN 0 521 48464 7
1. Great Britain – History – Stuarts, 1603–1714 – Historiography.
2. Historiography – Great Britain – History – 19th century.
3. Great Britain – Intellectual life – 19th century.
4. Great Britain – History – Victoria, 1837–1901. I. Title.
DA375.L35 1995
941.06'072041 – dc20    94–31974    CIP

ISBN 0 521 47464 7 hardback

WD

*For my parents*

# Contents

# Preface

Few periods in English history deserve the label "discordant" more than the seventeenth century. The Civil War and Glorious Revolution, the sectarian strife that pitted Protestant against Catholic, Anglican against Puritan, the national antipathies dividing England, Ireland and Scotland – all of these conferred on the age of the Stuarts a singular lack of harmony. But for the Victorians, it was discordant in another sense as well. The controversies of the seventeenth century had left deep divisions in English society which were still being felt long afterward. Victorian Whigs, Tories and radicals were as divided on the past as they were on contemporary politics. Dissenters sought inspiration in an earlier Puritanism, while some Anglicans looked longingly to the Stuart Church. The Cromwellian settlement still poisoned relations between Protestant England and Catholic Ireland. Indeed, no other period of the past intruded on the Victorian present so discordantly as the seventeenth century.

The purpose of this book is to explore how a number of Victorian historians approached the Stuart past, and to propose a thesis. The debate over the seventeenth century, I will argue, generated a body of politically engaged literature because it touched on one of the most controversial issues of the day – namely, the conflict between Church and Dissent, and to a lesser extent, between Protestantism and Catholicism. To be sure, the Victorian historiography of the Stuarts spoke to other matters as well, and I have no intention of reducing such rich material to a single theme. Important questions such as Parliamentary reform, democracy and the empire will be discussed as they arise. But it was the religious dimension that gave the debate, at least from the 1830s through the 1870s, much of its urgency. We are only now beginning to understand how preoccupied the Victorians were with religious controversy – and not just with the great struggle between belief and unbelief, but also with the sectarian disputes that made their mark on all fields of cultural endeavor as England slowly changed from an Anglican to a secular state. An examination of the Victorian debate over the Stuarts will deepen our awareness of the important role sectarian conflict played in Victorian culture.

This book will also demonstrate that the Victorians found the Puritan and Cromwellian episodes the most controversial aspect of the seventeenth century. The Civil War was a far more disturbing affair than the Glorious Revolution and, in contrast to William's assumption of the crown, the usurpation of Cromwell and the Puritans could have established truly frightening precedents. The Civil War also raised the most relevant questions for the Victorians. What was the role of Protestant Dissent in an officially Anglican society? Was it a subversive force, eroding the foundations of obedience much as the Puritans had done two centuries earlier, or was it a constructive movement embracing the ideals of toleration and liberty? How should the Establishment respond to the strengthening of Dissent that occurred during the Victorian years? Should it bolster the Anglican exclusiveness of the constitution, adopting a position that might be seen as Laudian, or should it act on principles of toleration and comprehension? What were England's mistakes in Ireland and what were their implications for contemporary policy?

Finally, I will identify a progression in the historiography of the Stuarts as it developed across the Victorian age. The Civil War, Commonwealth and Protectorate, episodes regarded in the early nineteenth century as a disruption in the nation's past, a disturbing interregnum, would become an acceptable part of that past by the century's end. This tendency to accommodate Cromwell and the Puritans, I will argue, was part of a larger process of nation building that was concerned with removing the divisions, particularly the sectarian divisions, in modern English society. As the barriers against Dissent were removed, as the English state lost its Anglican exclusiveness, so the Puritan past became integrated into a comprehensive national history.

Seventeenth-century themes impinged on all areas of Victorian culture, including literature, the arts, history and religion. Though I have written a book about historians, I hope my exploration of what these historians said and why they might have said it will interest scholars in other disciplines as well.

# Acknowledgments

This book began as a research project at Yale University. Frank Turner supervised my graduate work on the Victorian historiography of the Stuarts and has retained an interest in its future ever since. Peter Gay and David Underdown read an early draft and provided useful commentary. I hope this final version pleases them all. A graduate fellowship from the Yale Center for British Art enabled me to spend time in Britain conducting original research.

In the course of my work, many libraries in the United States and Britain treated me with generosity and kindness. I am particularly grateful to the librarians at the Yale Divinity School; Trinity College, Cambridge; King's College, London; Christ Church, All Souls College and the Bodleian Library, Oxford, for making manuscript material available to me. The interlibrary loan staffs at Denison University and Dickinson College have my gratitude for locating and procuring many hard-to-find volumes. A grant from the Denison University Research Foundation allowed me to spend a summer exploring the libraries of Britain.

One of the more pleasing aspects of my research has been sharing my thoughts with colleagues. Peter Blodgett, Bruce Thompson and Brian Ladd have for many years provided conversation, companionship and support. Richard Brent read an early draft of my chapter on Macaulay, while Rosemary Jann and Reba Soffer commented on an early version of the chapter on Gardiner. I thank them all for their remarks. David and Anne Leahy in London and Chris and Liz Walker in Cambridge opened their homes to me (sometimes for months on end) during my trips to England, making my visits there all the more pleasant. I would like to thank Dickinson College and my colleagues in the History Department for providing a congenial environment in which to bring this project to its close.

Ideas gain shape when they are spoken, strength when they are criticized. In countless conversations, my wife Lisa Lieberman has sharpened my arguments by listening and questioning. What is best in this book I owe to her.

# Politics, religion and history: David Hume and the Victorian debate

The Victorians wrote more on the Stuarts than on any other period in their nation's past. Considering how important religious controversy was to both the Victorian and Stuart periods, this preoccupation with Charles and Laud, Cromwell and the Puritans, James and William comes as no surprise. As they reflected on the contemporary conflict between Church and Dissent, the Victorians could not help but sense a parallel with the sectarian strife that had plagued the seventeenth century. Despite the Elizabethan insistence on uniformity, the Reformation had created a nation that was religiously plural, and the resulting conflict between Protestant and Catholic, Anglican and Puritan persisted well into the Victorian age. As Robert Southey pointed out in 1813, the Reformation may have been one of England's great "blessings," but it was a blessing bought at considerable cost. "The price we paid," Southey explained, "for the deliverance [from Roman Catholicism] was a religious struggle which, after more than a century, broke out into a civil war, which the termination of that war mitigated, but could not quell, and which has continued till the present day."[1] Britain, it seems, never thoroughly resolved its Reformation crisis until the close of the nineteenth century. As the Victorians wrestled with the problems of religious equality, they naturally turned to the Stuart past, producing a body of literature that was both scholarly and politically engaged.

For the generation that had witnessed the French Revolution,

---

[1] [Robert Southey], "History of Dissenters," *Quarterly Review*, 10 (October, 1813): 92–93. I have used two reference works – *The Wellesley Index to Victorian Periodicals, 1824–1900* (Toronto, 1966–1989) and *The Quarterly Review under Gifford: Identification of Contributors, 1809–1824* (Chapel Hill, 1949) – to determine the authorship of the many unsigned articles in the Victorian periodical press. Whenever the attribution for an unsigned article seems certain, I have placed the author's name in brackets.

I

the memory of Cromwell and the Puritans served as both a reminder and a warning: an assault on the nation's traditional institutions comparable to the destruction of the *ancien régime* in France had happened once before in England, and it could happen again if radicalism and Dissent were allowed to triumph. For conservatives like Southey, alarmed at the erosion of authority in the aftermath of the French Revolution, the special strength of England's constitution was its combination of ecclesiastical and political institutions. The union of Church and state ensured that religion conferred on the state that sense of awe which, as Edmund Burke had remarked in his *Reflections*, rendered it sacred and inviolable in the minds of the people. What troubled conservatives from Burke to Southey about the opposition to the Stuarts was that it had unleashed those forces which were now undermining the foundations of this confessional state. Cromwell and the Puritans had so thoroughly integrated political radicalism and religious dissent that their attack on the crown had led inevitably to the sub-version of the Established Church. For apologists of the Anglican constitution, the Puritan episode could never belong to the acceptable past, for this past, as Southey made clear in his essays and *Book of the Church*, must also be confessional. Within this Anglican framework, the lessons derived from Puritanism were wholly negative, emphasizing the evils that would result from the triumph of radicalism and Dissent.[2]

Nor were the critics of the Anglican constitution inclined to treat the Puritan past more sympathetically. While Dissenters, Whigs and radicals were predisposed to back the Parliamentary side in the Civil War, acknowledging its substantial contribution to the cause of political and religious liberty, they all, for one reason or another, chose to distance themselves from the example of Cromwell and the Puritans. For the Rational Dissenters, advocates of a reasonable Christianity shorn of its more fantastic elements, the religion of the Puritans seemed excessively enthusiastic and their politics correspondingly extreme. For moderate reformers like the Whigs, the opponents of the Stuarts had overstepped the limits of

---

[2] [Robert Southey], "Life of Cromwell," *Quarterly Review*, 25 (July, 1821): 279–347, "Hallam's *Constitutional History of England*," *Quarterly Review*, 37 (January, 1828): 194–260, "Lord Nugent's *Memorials of Hampden*," *Quarterly Review*, 47 (July, 1832): 457–519. Robert Southey, *The Book of the Church*, second edition (London: John Murray, 1824).

responsible conduct when, under the influence of Cromwell, they destroyed England's mixed constitution of king, Lords and Commons. Even the radicals, whose distrust of the crown and attraction to republicanism might have led them to look more favorably on the Puritan past, hurled some of the most bitter invective at the Protector. It was Cromwell, after all, who turned against the Commonwealth in order to satisfy his own ambitions, thus terminating prematurely England's republican experiment. No one, in the late eighteenth and early nineteenth centuries, was prepared to utter a good word in defense of Cromwell and the Puritans.

In the course of the Victorian age, England would gradually come to terms with its Puritan past, producing a shift in historical perspective that is all the more striking given the widespread antipathy toward Cromwell and the Puritans at the beginning of the nineteenth century. By Victoria's death in 1901, Cromwell had become a hero for many, and Puritanism had come to be regarded as one of the formative forces shaping the development of modern England. In his Ford Lectures, delivered at Oxford in 1896, S. R. Gardiner went so far as to call Cromwell the "most typical Englishman of all time."[3] Profound changes in the way a nation looks at its past must reflect deeper changes in the way it regards itself. This was certainly the case with England and the Puritans. By the close of the nineteenth century, established opinion had, for the most part, ceased to see the state as an Anglican stronghold resisting the disruptive forces of radicalism and religious dissent. As they abandoned their Anglican exclusiveness, the English came to appreciate the more constructive side to Puritanism. Cromwell's coming of age was thus closely connected to England's transition from a confessional to a secular state, a process that brought together religion, politics and the writing of history.

The story of this shift in historical understanding begins with David Hume, whose immensely popular *History of England*, published between 1754 and 1761, set the terms for much of the debate that followed in the early nineteenth century. Hume's *History* has been described as an Establishment history, one which

---

[3] Samuel Rawson Gardiner, *Cromwell's Place in History*, second edition (London: Longmans, Green and Co., 1897), 116.

used the past in order to support the existing Hanoverian regime. It aimed at encouraging political stability by alleviating the conflict between parties that derived from their partisan views of the past. If, as Paul Langford has recently suggested, eighteenth-century politics were the "politics of politeness" or the "pursuit of harmony,"[4] then the same can be said of Hume's *History*. It was very much a "polite" history since it demonstrated how Whig and Tory versions of the past could be harmonized and rendered acceptable to the national interest. Just as polite society refused, for the sake of harmony, to admit the ill-mannered, so Hume marginalized Cromwell and the Puritans, arguing that in the past their influence had been mostly destructive. To domesticate the Puritans would remain the achievement of the Victorians.

I

Hume, in his political writings, displayed a strong preference for stable, established regimes. He endorsed the Revolution of 1688 not so much because he believed the nation had been right to resist James II, but rather because the sixty or so years following the Revolution had brought peace, order and stability. Except for a small number of Jacobite malcontents, the English had grown accustomed to the Hanoverians, and Hume saw no reason to change what was already well established.[5] He also accepted the constitutional arrangement that had emerged from the Revolution, praising it as "singular and happy," even though he was aware of its drawbacks. In its favor, Hume pointed out that the eighteenth-century constitution had brought about the "most entire system of liberty, that ever was known amongst mankind" because it guaranteed the rule of law, protected the subject from arbitrary authority and secured property against encroachments by the state.[6] But at the same time he acknowledged that it was potentially unstable.

[4] Paul Langford, *A Polite and Commercial People: England, 1727–1783* (Oxford: Clarendon Press, 1989), 5–6.

[5] David Hume, "Of Passive Obedience" and "Of the Protestant Succession," *Essays Moral, Political, and Literary*, eds. T. H. Green and T. H. Grose, new edition (London: Longmans, Green and Co., 1882), 1: 463, 475–476, 479. See also Duncan Forbes, *Hume's Philosophical Politics* (Cambridge: Cambridge University Press, 1975), 96–97.

[6] David Hume, *The History of England, from the Invasion of Julius Caesar to the Revolution in MDCLXXXVIII*, new edition, with the author's last corrections and improvements (Philadelphia: Robert Campbell, 1795–1796), 4: 302, 6: 279–280.

The existence of court and country parties, representing the interests of the crown and Parliament, was a necessary and desirable attribute of England's mixed constitution. So long as these parties opposed one another moderately, each checking the excesses of the other, a beneficial combination of liberty and authority would result. But the risk was always present that political strife might upset the balance between parties and transform England into either an absolute monarchy or a pure republic.[7] Aware of this danger, Hume undertook to support the existing Hanoverian regime by formulating a view of politics that would encourage constitutional equipoise.

Scholars have recently noted that Hume's defense of the Revolution settlement shared much in common with the ideology of the Hanoverian court. Duncan Forbes has even described Hume's "philosophical politics" as an attempt to provide the Hanoverian Establishment with a rigorous intellectual foundation. When Hume, in his *History*, denied the existence of an ancient constitution, when he endorsed the benefits of commercial society, and when he defended the crown's right to influence Parliament through patronage, he was articulating a position that apologists for the court would have found congenial. But while we are surely correct to ally Hume with the court, we must also remember that he was never the partisan of a particular party. On some issues his stand resembled that of the country opposition – notably his anxiety over the public debt and his dislike of standing armies – and he was prepared to criticize both the Whig and the Tory parties. When he attacked the theories, fashionable among Whigs and Tories respectively, of an original contract and passive obedience, he was in fact demolishing the ideological props of both parties. Rather than act as a partisan, Hume chose to stand above parties in order to moderate the conflict between them, though this position was also favorable to the court since the Hanoverian regime would benefit most from the political stability that Hume hoped to encourage. Indeed, the call for an end to party

---

7 Hume, "That Politics may be reduced to a Science," "On the Independency of Parliament," "Whether the British Government inclines more to Absolute Monarchy, or to a Republic," and "Of the Parties of Great Britain," *Essays*, 1: 107–109, 119–122, 122–126, 133–137. Hume, *History of England*, 4: 284, 493–495, note LL. See also Forbes, *Hume's Philosophical Politics*, 184–186, 201–223.

strife was a familiar theme running through the court ideology of the period.[8]

As part of his effort to encourage political stability, Hume identified two related challenges to the permanence of the Hanoverian regime. In the first place, excessive strife between parties, especially when inflamed by dynastic or religious loyalties, appeared capable of upsetting a constitution which was balanced precariously between king and Parliament. Under any mixed monarchy, Hume believed, the political community would divide itself naturally into court and country parties. Contemporary Whigs and Tories, however, had departed from this ideal by allowing dynastic loyalties to distract them from their true court and country interests. The Whig allegiance to the Protestant succession and the Tory attachment to the Stuarts were aberrations due to the accidents of history which threatened to undermine stability.[9] The Jacobite uprisings of 1714 and 1745 were sufficient proof that dynastic concerns added an uncontrollable element to politics. Since these loyalties were rooted in opposing interpretations of the past, an objective account of the seventeenth-century struggle against the Stuarts would help ease tensions and return England's constitution to its original court and country purity. This, in part, was what Hume set out to do.[10] Describing the writing of his *History*, he made much of his desire to remain above "popular prejudices."[11] The result of these efforts was a narrative of the seventeenth century which demonstrated that the conflict between king and Parliament was largely inevitable and that the conduct of

---

[8]  The view that Hume's politics were "an attempt to give the established, Hanoverian, regime a proper intellectual foundation" has been developed most thoroughly by Duncan Forbes, *Hume's Philosophical Politics*, x, 91–101, 263–265. See also his "Politics and History in David Hume," *Historical Journal*, 6 (1963): 280–295, and his introduction to David Hume, *History of Great Britain: The Reigns of James I and Charles I* (Harmondsworth: Penguin Books, 1970), 7–54. Other scholars, often building on Forbes's insights, have also noted the similarities between Hume's political views and the court ideology of the mid-eighteenth century. See in particular: David Miller, *Philosophy and Ideology in Hume's Political Thought* (Oxford: Clarendon Press, 1981), 163–184. H. T. Dickinson, *Liberty and Property: Political Ideology in Eighteenth-Century Britain* (London: Weidenfeld and Nicolson, 1977), 132–138. J. G. A. Pocock, *The Machiavellian Moment: Florentine Political Thought and the Atlantic Republican Tradition* (Princeton: Princeton University Press, 1975), 493–498.

[9]  Hume, "Of the Parties of Great Britain," *Essays*, 1: 137–141.

[10]  Hume, "Of the Coalition of Parties," *Essays*, 1: 464, 469–470. Forbes, *Hume's Philosophical Politics*, 263–267. Dickinson, *Liberty and Property*, 100–101.

[11]  Hume, "My Own Life," *History of England*, 1: viii.

both sides was equally defensible, at least until Puritanism began to "poison" the Parliamentary cause.

The other potential source of instability according to Hume was fanaticism or enthusiasm. What made the conflict between political parties so dangerous was that they often became infected with a fanaticism which drove them beyond the bounds of moderate and responsible action. This had been the case with the Puritans under the Stuarts and with the Jacobites under the Hanoverians. By illustrating the menace inherent in enthusiasm, Hume's *History* in effect formed an argument against it. Like Edmund Burke later in the century, Hume considered the intrusion of the pulpit into politics as dangerous: "the religious spirit," he observed in his *History*, "when it mingles with faction, contains in it something supernatural and unaccountable."[12] Such had been the lesson of the English Civil War: once the Puritans emerged as the most powerful faction in the Commons, it was only a matter of time before fanaticism and subversion triumphed over moderation and constructive reform. That the rise of Puritanism as a political force had led to the anarchy of the Civil War and Cromwell's usurpation was no accident. Hume's *History* thus confirmed the maxim that fanaticism in politics, if not restrained, must always culminate in despotism.[13]

Hume started his *History* at that point in the narrative where "the misrepresentation of faction began chiefly to take place."[14] Historians had conventionally seen the reign of James I as the beginning of the conflict that would finally end with the Glorious Revolution. Hume was no different; only, where others had written as partisans, Hume presented justifications for the conduct of both the king and Parliament. He based his celebrated defense of the Stuarts on a rejection of those arguments which appealed to an immemorial constitution in order to defend the rights and liberties of the subject. The only constitution operative when James came to the throne, Hume insisted, was that of the Tudors, and under those princes the English monarchy had become nearly absolute. The courts of High Commission and Star Chamber, which exercised arbitrary jurisdictions, the crown's frequent appeal to martial law, the absence of the right to habeas corpus, the monarch's ability to

---

[12] Hume, *History of England*, 4: 257.   [13] Ibid., 5: 302.
[14] Hume, "My Own Life," *History of England*, 1: viii.

intimidate juries and other powers of prerogative had conspired to obstruct any plan of regular liberty. Even Parliament's traditional privilege of approving all taxation was frequently violated by the use of forced loans, benevolences, ship money and other arbitrary impositions. The dispensing power, which enabled the king to set aside any act of legislation, had further weakened the position of Parliament. Reviewing the extensive power of the Tudors, Hume concluded that "the most *absolute authority* of the sovereign . . . was established on above twenty branches of prerogative, . . . every one of them, totally incompatible with the liberty of the subject."[15] On the basis of the precedent set by the Tudors, and by Elizabeth in particular, James was entitled to rule absolutely. Far from being an enemy of the constitution, he was, according to Hume, actually preserving that constitution as it had previously existed.

As James was following in Elizabeth's footsteps, his subjects, drawing on the Renaissance revival of classical antiquity, were developing new ideas of liberty that would soon challenge his absolutism.[16] The urgency with which the Commons opposed their sovereign, Hume argued, was due in large measure to their recent prosperity. James, no longer able to finance the affairs of state from his own income, looked to the nation as a source of revenue. But the Commons, jealous of their property and animated by their new "spirit of freedom and independence," were reluctant to surrender their wealth to a monarch not known for his frugality. Here was the source of the conflict between crown and Parliament: the prosperity of the early seventeenth century had given rise to new ideas about politics, stressing the liberty and independence of the subject and necessitating a new arrangement in government. To protect the rights of the nation, it was now necessary to limit the royal prerogative and secure the rule of law.[17] Hume emphasized that the Commons, in challenging the authority of the king, were innovators who "less aspired at maintaining the ancient [Tudor] constitution, than at establishing a new one, and a freer, and a better" one at that.[18] For Hume, then, the tension between James and his Parliaments was in a sense unavoidable. The king was as justified in keeping to Elizabethan precedent as the Commons were

15  Hume, *History of England*, 4: 164–173, 177, 312–316.
16  Ibid., 4: 209–212.
17  Ibid., 4: 229–231, 493–495, note LL.        18  Ibid., 4: 232–233.

in responding to the new economic realities and the spirit of the age. In the struggle that was certain to come, Hume concluded, either "no party or both parties would justly bear the blame."[19]

The constitutional contest which began under James culminated under his successor. Charles I adhered firmly to the idea of absolutism that his father had inherited from Elizabeth, while the Commons remained protective of their wealth and, enlivened "with a warm regard to liberty," used the crown's need for revenue as a means to restrain the royal prerogative.[20] Under these conditions, the conflict between king and Parliament intensified until cooperation between the two became impossible. As he chronicled these disputes, Hume continued to insist that the conduct of both parties was defensible, if not always exemplary: the king's violations of liberty, though often dangerous and unwise, conformed to past practice, while Parliament's attempt to limit the royal prerogative, though unprecedented, was necessary for establishing the rule of law. Discussing the five knights, whom Charles had imprisoned for their refusal to support the forced loan of 1626, Hume provided a defense of both parties. Charles, he pointed out, was acting no differently than his predecessors, who had always detained their subjects arbitrarily, even though the practice was a clear violation of the law. The five knights, on the other hand, by challenging the king's right to imprison at will, were forcing him to comply with the law.[21] Discussing the Petition of Right, Hume similarly made the case for both sides. Because it circumscribed the royal prerogative, the Petition was a forward-looking contribution to the growth of liberty. But the king's reluctance to recognize the Petition was also understandable since emergencies were likely to arise that would require him to violate the very liberties he was asked to concede.[22] When Charles finally chose to dispense with Parliament altogether, he did so, Hume concluded, because it was the only way to preserve the constitution he had inherited against the innovations of the Commons.[23]

The Long Parliament completed the revolution that the Petition of Right had initiated. Although Hume's treatment of the Long Parliament was mostly hostile, he did not dismiss its accomplishments entirely. He saw its early acts, especially the Triennial Bill

---

[19] Ibid., 4: 282–285.  [20] Ibid., 4: 345–348.
[21] Ibid., 4: 360–367.  [22] Ibid., 4: 378–384, 386.  [23] Ibid., 4: 395–396.

and the abolition of the courts of High Commission and Star Chamber, as important steps toward limiting the king's prerogative and establishing the rule of law. "In short," he wrote,

> if we take a survey of the transactions of this memorable parliament, during the first period of its operations, we shall find that, excepting Strafford's attainder, which was a complication of cruel iniquity, their merits in other respects so much outweigh their mistakes, as to entitle them to praise from all lovers of liberty. Not only were former abuses remedied, and grievances redressed: Great provision, for the future, was made by law against the return of like complaints.[24]

What disturbed Hume most about the Long Parliament was not its attempt to establish legal government in England, but rather its willingness to forgo moderation, a trait he attributed to the steadily increasing influence of Puritanism. That the fanaticism of the Puritans discredited the Parliamentary cause, Hume made abundantly clear:

> It may be worth observing [he wrote], that all historians, who lived near that age, . . . represent the civil disorders and convulsions as proceeding from religious controversy, and consider the political disputes about power and liberty as entirely subordinate to the other . . . So entire was the subjection into which Charles was now fallen, that, had not the wound been poisoned by the infusion of theological hatred, it must have admitted of an easy remedy. Disuse of parliaments, imprisonments and prosecution of members, ship-money, an arbitrary administration; these were loudly complained of: But the grievances which tended chiefly to inflame the parliament and nation, especially the latter, were the surplice, the rails placed about the altar, the bows exacted on approaching it, the liturgy, the breach of the sabbath, embroidered copes, lawn sleeves, the use of the ring in marriage, and of the cross in baptism. On account of these, were the popular leaders content to throw the government onto such violent convulsions: and, to the disgrace of that age, and of this island, it must be acknowledged, that the disorders in Scotland entirely, and those in England mostly, proceeded from so mean and contemptible an origin.[25]

In his *History*, Hume chronicled the transition in English government from the arbitrary kingship of the Tudors to the limited monarchy of the Hanoverians in which the establishing of the rule of law and the liberty of the subject played a crucial role. Had the Parliaments of the early Stuarts acted with moderation to achieve

---

[24] Ibid., 5: 24–25, 44–46.
[25] Ibid., 5: 20. See also ibid., 5: 63–64, 93–94, 475, note DD.

legal government, it appears likely that Hume would have had no quarrel with them.[26] But Puritanism soon permeated the Parliamentary cause, giving it the strength to challenge the king's authority, but at the same time infusing the movement with an enthusiasm that would prove fatal in the end.

Hume viewed the Puritans, both the Presbyterians and Independents, as little more than fanatics. Their theology was absurd and their pretense to Godliness was mere hypocrisy, disguising the most base motives. Puritanism, Hume contended, broke society apart by annihilating those sentiments that restrained self-interest. Deluded into thinking they were serving a higher cause, the Puritans abandoned the values that normally regulated civilized behavior. Bound by neither shame nor duty nor honor, the saint "was at full liberty to gratify all his appetites, disguised under the appearance of pious zeal." Puritanism, Hume concluded, "loosened all the ties of morality, and gave entire scope, and even sanction, to the selfishness and ambition which naturally adhere to the human mind."[27] In both England and Scotland, Puritanism had led inevitably to turbulence, sedition and the subversion of legitimate authority. The Puritans may have challenged the king in order to limit his prerogative and defend the rights of Parliament, but in the process they raised an army in which the more extreme Independents came to predominate. In disregard for precedent and legality, the Independents, hoping to establish a republic, purged the Commons of their Presbyterian rivals, executed the king – for Hume, the most atrocious of their crimes – abolished the monarchy, and turned out the House of Lords.

Hume found the statesmen of this Commonwealth narrow-minded and incompetent, preoccupied with maintaining their own power and consequently unqualified to settle the affairs of the nation.[28] Nor did Hume consider it surprising that their failures at government should terminate in the dictatorship of Oliver Cromwell, the only exceptional one among them. "By recent, as well as all ancient, example," he reflected, "it was become evident that illegal violence . . . must inevitably end at last in the arbitrary and despotic government of a single person."[29] Hume's portrayal of

---

[26] Ibid., 5: 15.
[27] Ibid., 4: 258, 319, 427, 495, note LL, 5: 94, 201, 475, note DD.
[28] Ibid., 5: 288.     [29] Ibid., 5: 302.

Cromwell was overwhelmingly hostile, stressing the Protector's ambition and duplicity. Cromwell, Hume alleged, was a "frantic enthusiast" and the "most dangerous of hypocrits." He was a "great master of fraud and dissimulation," an "artful and audacious conspirator," pursuing "by artifice and courage" a carefully laid plan to achieve his own "unlimited authority."[30] At other times, Hume described Cromwell as an incredible combination of contraries. He was at once absurd and wise, despotic and just. Cromwell's words, for instance, were full of "obscurity, confusion, embarrassment," and yet his actions were "decisive and judicious." Indeed, Hume continued, the discrepancy between "the sagacity of his actions and the absurdity of his discourse" constituted the "most prodigious contrast that ever was known."[31] Once Protector, Cromwell devised policies that were as fair as his appointment of honest judges, as despotic as the imposition of the major generals, and as foolish as Barebone's Parliament, a "preposterous" assembly made up of the "very dregs of the fanatics."[32] In the end, Hume's portrait fails to convince because the contrasts are too sharply drawn. Unable to see Puritanism as anything but hypocrisy, and failing to appreciate the sincerity of Cromwell's piety, Hume lacked the insight which the Victorians would use to make sense out of Cromwell's otherwise inexplicable career.

With its attack on Cromwell and the Puritans, Hume's *History* furnished conservatives in the period after the French Revolution with ample material for a historical defense of the Anglican constitution. For Hume, as for them, the social function of religion was to promote political stability by inculcating values of obedience. Anglicanism, with its fondness for the monarchy, its "attachment to ceremonies, to order, and to a decent pomp and splendor of worship," was admirably suited for this task.[33] Whereas seventeenth-century Puritanism had subverted established authority and led to anarchy, Anglicanism under Laud's direction had tended in the opposite direction. Hume was no friend of Laud, considering the Archbishop a fanatic who had done more harm than good, but he saw the merit in Laud's emphasis on ceremony. Had Laud's ideas, Hume implied, been implemented with the "cool reflection of a legislator," they would have made the Church more

---

[30] Ibid., 5: 161, 205–206, 256, 278, 299, 306.    [31] Ibid., 5: 308, note †, 318, 341, note *.
[32] Ibid., 5: 308–310, 320–321, 331.    [33] Ibid., 4: 495, note LL, 5: 1.

attractive to the "rude multitude," and religion would have carried out more effectively its task of instilling obedience.[34] For conservatives in the late eighteenth and early nineteenth centuries, alarmed at the breakdown of order in France and fearing the same in England, the lesson of Hume's *History* was unmistakable: the preservation of the Anglican Establishment and the proscription of Dissent were the necessary preconditions for maintaining social order at home.

## II

Hume's account of the Stuart past was part of an effort to encourage moderation in the politics of Hanoverian England. By alerting his readers to the dangers inherent in fanaticism, he made a strong argument for removing religious controversy from politics. He also hoped to ease the animosity between Whigs and Tories by demonstrating that as far as their "*historical* disputes" were concerned, each of the contending parties "was justified by plausible topics; that there were on both sides wise men, who meant well to their country; and that the past animosity between the factions had no better foundation than narrow prejudice or interested passion."[35] This was the purpose behind Hume's *History*. To label that work Tory was thus largely misleading; like his other political writings, its allegiance was to the Revolution of 1688 and the Hanoverian succession. But despite its aims, Hume's *History* became known as a Tory production. As Whigs and radicals in the late eighteenth and early nineteenth centuries began to assail the Hanoverian Establishment, they turned their attention to the work that had provided that regime with such an elegant historical foundation. Historians like Catharine Macaulay, John Millar and Charles James Fox challenged Hume's defense of the Stuarts in order to strengthen the case for the opposition. But while they all supported Parliament in its struggle against the king, and while some even sympathized with the republicans of the Commonwealth, not one was prepared to initiate a full-scale reassessment of Puritanism. Indeed, after the outbreak of the French Revolution, defenders of the Establishment like Edmund Burke extended

[34] Ibid., 4: 407–408, 5: 170.
[35] Hume, "Of the Coalition of Parties," *Essays*, 1: 464–465.

Hume's critique of Puritanism to cover contemporary radicalism and Dissent as well. Nor would any historian alter significantly Hume's characterization of Oliver Cromwell as an ambitious and hypocritical fanatic. To see something constructive in England's Puritan and Cromwellian past would become the task of the Victorians.

The perception, common after the French Revolution, that radicalism and Dissent posed a serious challenge to the Hanoverian Establishment ensured that the Puritan past would remain problematic for the rest of the eighteenth century. Radicals and Dissenters were likened to the Puritans as the excesses of the Interregnum seemed a powerful portent of what would happen should the regime's opponents triumph once again. For apologists of the Establishment, then, the seventeenth century provided a context for understanding contemporary radicalism and Dissent as well as a rhetorical strategy for combating them. In his *Reflections on the Revolution in France*, for instance, Edmund Burke enlisted the Stuart past in the defense of the Hanoverian regime. Replying to the Unitarian Richard Price, who had referred to the events of 1688 in order to encourage radical politics, Burke appropriated the Glorious Revolution for the Establishment, presenting an interpretation that was intended to discredit a radicalism that he felt was now shared by Whigs, Dissenters and French Revolutionaries. The legitimacy of England's institutions, Burke affirmed in his *Reflections*, lay in their antiquity. England's "ancient constitution" had grown over the centuries as each new generation added its wisdom to that of its predecessors, modifying existing institutions and practices without destroying their essential integrity. The Glorious Revolution had maintained this constitution in defiance of a king who was intent on subverting it. "The Revolution," Burke asserted, "was made to preserve our *antient* indisputable laws and liberties, and that *antient* constitution of government which is our only security for law and liberty." The Revolution of 1688 had initiated nothing new and Richard Price was mistaken to argue that it had confirmed the nation's right to impose a government of its own devising.[36]

---

[36] Edmund Burke, *Reflections on the Revolution in France, and on the Proceedings in Certain Societies in London Relative to that Event*, ed. Conor Cruise O'Brien (Harmondsworth: Penguin Books, 1969), 117–122. For Burke's traditionalism, see J. G. A. Pocock, "Burke and the

To strengthen his case, Burke drew two historical parallels. In the first, he coupled the Glorious Revolution with the Restoration, arguing that in both instances England had found itself without a king and that both times it had found a solution to the problem in the traditional principle of hereditary succession. To associate the Revolution with the Restoration was to deprive the events of 1688 of any tendency toward innovation. In the second place, Burke attacked the radicalism of Dissenters like Price by emphasizing their ties to an earlier Puritanism. What bothered Burke most about Price's sermon was that he heard within it the voice of seventeenth-century Puritanism, complete with its distinctive blend of religious enthusiasm and political democracy. Behind Price's claim that England now enjoyed the right "to choose [its] own governors; to cashier them for misconduct; and to form a government for [itself]," Burke saw the same principle at work which had led the nation once before to put its king to death. Within Burke's rhetoric, Richard Price became indistinguishable from the Reverend Hugh Peters, the Puritan divine who had preached approvingly of the king's execution.[37] When he was done, Burke had reversed Price's use of the past. The Glorious Revolution remained a great legitimating event, but the principles it sanctioned were conservative, and the radicalism of Dissenters like Price stood discredited by its association with the excesses of the Civil War and Commonwealth.

In his attack on the French revolutionaries, Burke used an argument that closely resembled Hume's criticism of the Puritans. The revolutionaries, Burke maintained, by substituting the rights of man for tradition, had destroyed the values that he associated with chivalry, and in the process had severed the bonds that held society together. "The age of chivalry is gone," Burke proclaimed: "Never, never more, shall we behold that generous loyalty to rank and sex, that proud submission, that dignified obedience, that subordination of the heart, which kept alive, even in servitude itself, the spirit of an exalted freedom."[38] Just as Hume's Puritans, under the illusion of Godliness, had indulged their appetites, so Burke's revolutionaries, under the illusion of liberty, had unleashed

Ancient Constitution: A Problem in the History of Ideas," *Politics, Language and Time: Essays on Political Thought and History* (New York: Atheneum, 1971), 202–232.
[37] Burke, *Reflections*, 94–100, 106, 157–159.   [38] Ibid., 170–175.

their destructive passions. In both instances the ideal was as false as its effects were pernicious. The Puritan's Godliness was as far removed from true religion as the revolutionary's freedom was from true liberty. In both cases the false ideal had undermined those values that were necessary for preserving order. The consequence was, in England as in France, an orgy of destruction.

If spokesmen for the Establishment debased Puritanism in their war against radicalism, opposition writers did not treat it much better. Even when they were inclined to judge favorably the opponents of the Stuarts, these Whig and radical historians limited their praise to particular aspects of Puritanism rather than endorsing the movement as a whole, and they certainly fell far short of initiating a complete rehabilitation of the Puritan and Cromwellian past. An adversary of the Hanoverian regime like the Scotsman John Millar, whom Francis Jeffrey once described as a "decided whig" with republican sympathies,[39] provides a case in point. Millar was not especially alarmed at the growth of contemporary radicalism, nor was he averse to seventeenth-century radicalism, displaying throughout his *Historical View of the English Government*, published posthumously in 1803, a fondness for republican schemes of government. Though Millar acknowledged that Puritanism could lead to political excess, he did not linger on the fact, and he never used Puritanism, after the fashion of Hume or Burke, as an argument against radical politics. Instead, he concentrated on what he found most constructive in the religion of the Presbyterians and Independents, noting the liberal tendencies in each. The Independents in particular, he remarked, were the first to develop a modern concept of toleration. Denouncing religious establishments as "a kind of persecution," they became spokesmen for "religious freedom" and the "rights of private judgment." All denominations, according to their principles, should be regarded as equals and the community should be "encouraged to follow the dictates of reason and conscience." As a political party, the Independents inclined toward republicanism, their belief that the congregation should appoint the clergy finding a counterpart in

[39] [Francis Jeffrey], "Millar's *View of the English Government*," *Edinburgh Review*, 3 (October, 1803): 158–159.

the democratic principle that the community should elect all political officers.[40]

To point out the liberal potential in Independency, however, hardly amounted to a rehabilitation of England's Puritan past, for what seemed promising in theory became corrupt in practice. Millar conceded that the early Puritans, regardless of their principles, were as intolerant as any other denomination. He further noted that before they could fulfill their promise and create a truly popular government, they had fallen under the domination of Oliver Cromwell, "an extraordinary genius, utterly devoid of all principle," who used the Independents to destroy the monarchy and introduce "an odious species of despotism." Cromwell's character, Millar wrote, was "universally known," implying that his assessment of the Protector would not deviate from the norm established by Hume. Millar's Cromwell was an enthusiast, inelegant and rude, incapable of expressing himself clearly, yet able to act decisively and with cunning shrewdness. Originally sincere in his religious beliefs, he soon became a hypocrite, hiding his base ambitions behind a carapace of piety. "Certain it is," Millar concluded, "that the consummate hypocrisy of Cromwell was the great engine by which he procured the confidence of his whole party, and obtained an ascendancy over all their movements." The execution of the king was inexpedient, the republic set up after his death was imperfect, based as it was on an inadequate representation, and its one lasting effect was to prepare the ground for Cromwell's usurpation and despotism.[41]

The most radical challenge to Hume's interpretation of the seventeenth century came from Catharine Macaulay. A republican whose *History of England* appeared between 1763 and 1781, Macaulay intended her work to rescue England's republican past from the aspersions cast on it by Hume and others. As expected from an outspoken critic of Hanoverian corruption, she praised the opposition to the Stuarts, defended the right of Parliament to wage

[40] John Millar, *An Historical View of the English Government, from the Settlement of the Saxons in Britain to the Revolution in 1688* (London: J. Mawman, 1803), 3: 126, 130–133, 140–141, 290–291. For Millar, see Duncan Forbes, "'Scientific' Whiggism: Adam Smith and John Millar," *Cambridge Journal*, 7 (1953–1954): 660–670, and William C. Lehman, *John Millar of Glasgow, 1735–1801: His Life and Thought and His Contributions to Sociological Analysis* (Cambridge: Cambridge University Press, 1960).
[41] Millar, *Historical View*, 3: 144–147, 298–301, 323–325, 328–329, 331–341, 360–362.

war on the king, and vindicated the Commonwealth, pointing out that it had abolished a "tyranny of more than five hundred" years, created a republic rivaling those of the ancients, and asserted England's prominence in the world. Its administration was "just and impartial," its management of the nation's resources was skillful and frugal, and its deliberations showed no signs of corruption. Seeking a cause of the republic's failure, Macaulay targeted Oliver Cromwell. His rise to power, she explained, echoing Hume, was a result of his duplicity, selfishness and ambition, and his rule was far from exemplary: he imposed a military dictatorship, governed arbitrarily, ignored Parliamentary practice, violated the principles of justice, and persecuted at one time or another every religious denomination.[42]

When she examined the seventeenth century's religious controversies, Macaulay, like Millar, tended to focus on the constructive side of Puritanism. In answer to Hume, she pointed out that the Puritan opposition to Laud's innovations was far from frivolous given the close connection of Church and state, and like Millar she admired the Independents for their early understanding of toleration.[43] And yet, despite the approving tenor of these observations, there is little indication that either Macaulay or Millar ever intended to rehabilitate Puritanism outside of its immediate connection with republicanism or the political opposition to the Stuarts. Neither historian, for instance, addressed the issue of Puritan piety, and until someone did, Hume's charge that Puritanism was a form of hypocrisy concealing selfish ambition could not be answered. Indeed, there is some evidence that Macaulay was as uneasy with Puritanism as was Hume, considering religious enthusiasm to be incompatible with republican virtue. Cromwell, who destroyed the Commonwealth in order to satisfy his ambition, was for Macaulay an "enthusiast of the first form" with a "highly puritanical" religious faith, whereas disinterested public servants like Sir John Eliot were not.[44] Above all, Macaulay and

---

[42] Catharine Macaulay, *The History of England from the Accession of James I to the Elevation of the House of Hanover*, third edition (London: Edward and Charles Dilly, 1769), 1: v–xxi, 3: 39–41, 4: 406–409, 5: 91–103, 196–198, 203. For a biography of Macaulay, see Bridget Hill, *The Republican Virago: The Life and Times of Catharine Macaulay, Historian* (Oxford: Clarendon Press, 1992).

[43] Macaulay, *History of England*, 2: 54–55, 4: 251–254.

[44] Ibid., 2: 77–78, 4: 159.

Millar understood Puritanism more narrowly than would their Victorian successors. They tended to speak most often of Independents and Presbyterians, religious factions important because of their support for one political party or another. When they used the term Puritan, it designated little more than the broader category encompassing the two denominations. To see in Puritanism a larger social or cultural movement embodying the spirit of the age was simply beyond them. To describe Puritanism, after the fashion of Carlyle, as "the last of all our Heroisms," to find in Puritanism an explanation for the Civil War or to view it as one of the formative forces in English history would have been inconceivable to any eighteenth-century historian.

The Puritan and Cromwellian past would remain an uncomfortable topic from the period of the French Revolution until well into the opening decades of the nineteenth century. The apparent similarities between Puritanism and radical Dissent, between the Civil War and the French Revolution were too close to admit the Puritans into the acceptable past. When in the 1790s Charles James Fox, the leader of the Whigs, turned to history in order to restore the credibility of his party, he was careful to dissociate it from the disturbing aspects of the Civil War. His *History of James the Second*, published posthumously in 1808 and recognized as a statement of Whig principles, made no mention of Puritanism and blamed Cromwell for the excesses of the 1640s, thereby removing from the Parliamentary opposition the responsibility for executing the king. Rather than founding the reputation of the Whigs on the uncertain heritage of the 1640s, Fox turned to the unimpeachable Revolution of 1688, planning a history that would have appropriated the Revolution for the opposition by demonstrating that the real danger to the constitution had always emanated from the crown.[45] Even after Waterloo and the collapse of the French Revolution, Cromwell and the Puritans continued to represent a dangerous precedent. When Henry Hallam attempted in the 1820s to reconsider what it meant to be a Whig, he too kept his distance from them. Like Hume, Hallam abandoned the Long Parliament after its initial period of reform, believing that it had succumbed to irresponsible passion. Like Fox, he chose to construct his

---

45 Charles James Fox, *A History of the Early Part of the Reign of James the Second* (Philadelphia: Abraham Small, 1808), 4, 7, 10–11.

moderate Whiggism, a compound of the party's Burkean and Foxite traditions, on the legacy of the Glorious Revolution.

During the next fifty years, however, these historical perceptions would change considerably. One of the Victorians' great historiographical achievements was to reverse the prejudice against Cromwell and the Puritans. Already by the 1820s the young Thomas Babington Macaulay, writing in the Whig *Edinburgh Review*, had placed Cromwell on a par with Washington, challenging Fox's judgment that Washington was the greater statesman because he had refrained from imposing a military dictatorship when placed at the head of a victorious revolutionary army. By the 1840s, Thomas Carlyle's *Letters and Speeches of Oliver Cromwell* had refuted Hume's verdict that the Protector's collected utterances would make the most nonsensical book ever. By the 1880s, Samuel Rawson Gardiner, building on a generation of scholarship, had described Puritanism as a great moral force, one of the two formative influences in English history. The cumulative effect of this shifting opinion was, by the 1890s, to transform Cromwell into something of a national hero, his statue now prominently displayed outside the Houses of Parliament. The reasons for this change in historical perception are not hard to find: as the century progressed, the circumstances that had once made the memory of Cromwell and the Puritans seem so dangerous largely disappeared. The revolutionary threat, which had alarmed Burke and others, steadily diminished as the reform acts of 1832, 1867 and 1884 laid the groundwork for English democracy. Nor were sectarian controversies as vehement as they had once been. The Dissenters had become increasingly integrated into English society – most of their outstanding grievances had been redressed by the 1880s – and Anglicans began to regard unbelief as a greater menace than Christian Dissent. In these changed circumstances the Puritan past took on new meaning.

England's acceptance of its Puritan and Cromwellian heritage was one manifestation of its transition from an Anglican to a secular state. Beginning with the repeal of the Test and Corporation Acts in 1828 and Catholic emancipation in 1829, measures which broke open the Anglican constitution, and continuing through most of the century, England gradually relinquished its Anglican exclusiveness. As the character of the state changed, so the conviction that the nation's history must legitimate an official Anglicanism gave way to an interpretation of the past that was more broadly national. The writing of history was part of this process. Early in the century, Whigs like Hallam and Macaulay used the past in order to argue the case for granting political equality to Catholics and Dissenters. In their historical writings, they reversed the rhetoric uttered by those defenders of the Anglican constitution who had regarded religious uniformity as a necessary precondition for political stability. The lessons of the Civil War, Macaulay pointed out, demonstrated that intolerance, and especially the use of coercion to ensure uniformity, had actually led to rebellion. At about the same time, Dissenting historians began to stress the positive impact which Puritanism had made on the development of modern England.

Opponents of Protestant Dissent had typically alluded to the excesses of the Puritans in order to expose the destructive potential within all forms of religious or political nonconformity. In the decades after Waterloo, however, Dissenters began to acknowledge their own history and to use it more constructively, emphasizing the Puritan contribution to the development of political and religious liberty. Major histories written by Dissenters like William Godwin, John Forster and Robert Vaughan presented Puritanism as an important force behind the emergence of a liberal England that was now able to accommodate sectarian diversity. As the foundations of the Anglican constitution began to collapse after the repeal of the Test and Corporation Acts, Dissenters used the Puritan past to legitimate religious reform, interpreting it as the culmination of the liberal tendencies inherent in England's Protestant heritage. In the process, they affirmed the efforts of the Puritans, and by association themselves, to bring these liberal tendencies to fruition. Within this interpretive framework, Cromwell came to epitomize the religiously inspired activist who tried his best in unfavorable circumstances to create a society founded on religious toleration and civil liberty. To make their case, Dissenters drew heavily on Carlyle's edition of Cromwell's *Letters and Speeches*, a work which they believed had finally put to rest the accusation that Cromwell was an ambitious hypocrite.

The accommodation of Dissent during the nineteenth century was part of a larger process of nation building that had as one of its aims the removal of sectarian divisions. The writing of history contributed to this process since the religious controversies which threatened to obstruct national politics had originated in the seventeenth century. To construct an interpretation of the past that was national instead of sectarian therefore became a liberal imperative. Macaulay's history of the Glorious Revolution and Gardiner's many volumes on the Civil War, books which defined the contours of the Stuart past for generations to come, presented interpretations stressing the inclusion of all religious parties. Out of Gardiner's work in particular emerged a vision of the past emphasizing the equal contributions that both Puritan and Anglican had made to the building of modern England. This liberal reworking of the past finally brought Cromwell and the Puritans into the realm of the acceptable.

# CHAPTER I

# Henry Hallam and early nineteenth-century Whiggism

When the Duc de Broglie, visiting London amid the excitement over the first Reform Bill, wanted advice on how to judge the impending measure, he sought out the Whig historian Henry Hallam. He was, Broglie thought, "the greatest living publicist in England, if not the greatest she had ever possessed," a clear sign of how easily reputations rise and fall.[1] In the years before 1832, Hallam was known for two considerable works of history, a *View of the State of Europe during the Middle Ages* and the *Constitutional History of England*, published in 1818 and 1827.[2] Recent scholarship had paid little attention to Hallam. His books are long and dull, falling easily into Carlyle's category of "dry-as-dust." And yet they repay scrutiny, especially for the insights they provide into the ideological debates of the period after Waterloo. For Hallam's two most important works were part of a wider effort to reconstruct the Whig party following the death of Charles James Fox in 1806.

I

The Foxite opposition to Pitt during the French Revolution and the wars against Napoleon imparted to the Whigs a political tradition emphasizing constitutional balance and aristocratic government. Central to this tradition was the notion that England possessed a balanced constitution in which the aristocracy, dominating both houses of Parliament, would play the pivotal role. Though constitutional balance could be upset by either the crown or the people,

---

[1] *Personal Recollections of the Late Duc de Broglie, 1785–1820*, trans. and ed. Raphael Ledos de Beaufort (London: Ward and Downey, 1887), 2: 514.
[2] Hallam wrote one other major work, an *Introduction to the Literature of Europe, in the Fifteenth, Sixteenth, and Seventeenth Centuries*, 4 vols. (London: John Murray, 1837–1839), an examination of which lies outside the scope of this chapter.

the Foxites were inclined to fear encroachments by the king and his ministers, a distrust of royal influence that explains their long-standing commitment to economical reform as a way of restricting patronage and preserving constitutional equipoise. As the crown became less sinister in the opening decades of the nineteenth century, however, this preoccupation with the constitution and corruption began to appear behind the times. The Foxite belief in aristocratic government was likewise open to the charge of anachronism. The Whigs had always clothed their aristocratic exclusiveness in the rhetoric of popular sovereignty. The rights of the people, they asserted, required protection, but not by means of the public's direct participation in government. The Whig magnates, who had secured these rights from the crown at the Glorious Revolution and whose landed independence and historic role in government would ensure moderation, had an obligation to act on behalf of the people. Believing that the principal threat to constitutional balance emanated from the crown, the Foxites were willing to prop up the constitution's popular side by granting reasonable concessions. With the growth of radicalism, however, the aristocracy's claim to be acting in the people's interest lost much of its appeal as the middle and working classes became intent on using their own power to acquire more extensive rights.[3]

Fox's death removed the one personality capable of keeping the Whigs together, and after 1806 the party began to lose coherence. To distinguish themselves from the Tories, the Whigs had usually presented themselves as friends of the people. But the emergence of an energetic radical movement in the years after Waterloo made this strategy increasingly problematic. In the first place, the Whigs had done little to substantiate their commitment to reform. Their accomplishments during the Ministry of All the Talents had been disappointing – apart from the abolition of the slave trade in 1806, no significant reforms had been passed – which made their boast of

[3] For the Foxite tradition in the early nineteenth century, see: Peter Mandler, *Aristocratic Government in the Age of Reform: Whigs and Liberals, 1830–1852* (Oxford: Clarendon Press, 1990), 13–22. Richard Brent, *Liberal Anglican Politics: Whiggery, Religion, and Reform, 1830–1841* (Oxford: Clarendon Press, 1987), 28–36. Leslie Mitchell, *Holland House* (London: Duckworth, 1980), 39–50. Abraham D. Kriegel, "Liberty and Whiggery in Early Nineteenth-Century England," *Journal of Modern History*, 52 (1980): 253–278. J. R. Dinwiddy, "Charles James Fox and the People," *History*, 55 (1970): 353–359. Austin Mitchell, *The Whigs in Opposition, 1815–1830* (Oxford: Clarendon Press, 1967), 7–24.

being a popular party sound increasingly hollow.[4] In the second place, the rise of an active radicalism made it difficult for the Whigs to embrace a legitimate reform program without alarming conservatives in the party. This was particularly true of Parliamentary reform. Grey, leading the Foxites after 1806, believed the best way to defeat the radicals would be for the Whigs to win the public's confidence by promoting some degree of Parliamentary reform. But every time he endorsed such a measure, no matter how cautious, he risked losing the support of conservatives. If, on the other hand, he abandoned reform in order to appease his party's right wing, then he risked driving the more progressive Whigs into the ranks of the radicals. The result was an indecisive leadership that satisfied no one and failed to give the party direction.[5]

Encumbered with a Foxite legacy whose relevance for the new century was far from certain, and burdened with a weak leadership, the Whigs grew steadily ineffective after 1806. Eventually the party would reassert itself. Taking advantage of the disruption in English politics caused by the reemergence of the Catholic issue in 1826, the Whigs would attain office in 1830 and carry the first Reform Act in 1832. Historians may differ over which groups were responsible for reconstructing the party, but they agree that the Whigs experienced an ideological reorientation in the decades before 1830. William Thomas has suggested that by 1815 a number of "professional men" had joined the party alongside the aristocrats and were beginning to make their influence felt. Politicians like Brougham, Mackintosh, Romilly, Horner and Jeffrey, embracing the new science of political economy and often trained in the Scottish universities, were more liberal than their aristocratic patrons. They were lawyers or businessmen who urged the Whigs to become responsive to interests outside Parliament in order to gain a more democratic following in manufacturing and commercial areas. They were willing to work with moderate radicals like Burdett in an effort to make the party truly popular but still distinct from extremists like Cobbett, Cartwright or Hunt.[6]

---

[4] A. D. Harvey, "The Ministry of All the Talents: The Whigs in Office, February 1806 to March 1807," *Historical Journal*, 15 (1972): 645–648.

[5] E. A. Smith, *Lord Grey, 1764–1845* (Oxford: Clarendon Press, 1990), 36, 179–189, 204–221.

[6] William Thomas, *The Philosophic Radicals: Nine Studies in Theory and Practice, 1817–1841* (Oxford: Clarendon Press, 1979), 46–57. Biancamaria Fontana, *Rethinking the Politics of Commercial Society: The Edinburgh Review 1802–1832* (Cambridge: Cambridge University

Hallam's work as a historian should be placed in the context of this attempt to revive and redirect the Whig party in the decades before 1830. Though he never sat in Parliament, preferring the pursuit of literature to active politics, his *Middle Ages* and *Constitutional History* were both political works that addressed the crisis of identity facing the Whigs. His allegiance to the party has never been questioned. A frequent visitor to Holland House and Bowood, he could count among his friends many prominent members of the party. Echoing generations of Whigs, Hallam once said that his standard in politics was a "well-ordered liberty," order ensuring the absence of anarchy, liberty the absence of tyranny.[7] Like most Whigs, he supported the repeal of the Test and Corporation Acts, Catholic emancipation, reform of the Irish Church, reductions in taxation in order to ameliorate the condition of the people and restore their confidence in Parliament, and the abolition of West Indian slavery and the slave trade.[8] We can also place Hallam more precisely among the "professional men" of the party. Like many of them, he was trained in the law, practicing as a barrister on the Oxford circuit, and he was a recipient of

Press, 1985), 112–185, and John Clive, *Scotch Reviewers: The Edinburgh Review, 1802–1815* (Cambridge, Mass.: Harvard University Press, 1957), have examined the role of the *Edinburgh Review* in articulating the liberal ideology of these professionals. Though his argument has a different emphasis, see Peter Mandler's observations on the tension between liberal and Foxite principles in the Whig party before 1830. *Aristocratic Government*, 36–64.

In a series of articles, Ellis Archer Wasson has discounted the influence of these professionals on the reconstruction of the Whig party and has focused attention instead on a group of young aristocrats – Milton, Tavistock and Althorp – who embraced Parliamentary reform in the years after Peterloo. Richard Brent has recently extended Wasson's argument by stressing the importance of religion and placing a number of liberal Anglicans, of whom Lord John Russell was the most prominent, alongside Wasson's Evangelical young Whigs. Though Wasson and Brent have shown that the picture may be more complicated than the one drawn by Thomas and others, they have not eliminated the importance of the "professional men" and the *Edinburgh Review* in shaping Whig ideology. Ellis Archer Wasson, "The Great Whigs and Parliamentary Reform, 1809–1830," *Journal of British Studies*, 24 (1985): 434–464, "The Spirit of Reform, 1832 and 1867," *Albion*, 12 (1980): 164–174, "The Coalitions of 1827 and the Crisis of Whig Leadership," *Historical Journal*, 20 (1977): 587–606. Brent, *Liberal Anglican Politics*, 36–64.

[7] *Dictionary of National Biography*, s.v. "Hallam, Henry (1777–1859)." Francis Horner to Hallam (22 July 1815) and Hallam to Francis Horner (26 July 1815), *Memoirs and Correspondence of Francis Horner, M.P.*, ed. Leonard Horner (Boston: Little, Brown and Co., 1853), 2: 261, 263.

[8] Hallam to John Whishaw (28 April and 2 June 1828), *The "Pope" of Holland House: Selections from the Correspondence of John Whishaw and His Friends, 1813–1840*, ed. Lady Seymour (London: T. Fisher Unwin, 1906), 320–321, 322–324. Hallam to Francis Horner (19 March 1816), *Memoirs of Francis Horner*, 2: 317–318.

aristocratic patronage. During the Ministry of All the Talents, when Lansdowne was chancellor of the exchequer, Hallam was appointed a commissioner of stamps, a sinecure that freed him from his legal career and enabled him to devote his time to scholarship.[9] Finally, Hallam was friendly with other professionals, particularly Francis Jeffrey and Francis Horner – who considered Hallam "one of *us*" – and like them he was an early contributor to the *Edinburgh Review*, writing on history, literature and politics.[10]

Placing Hallam among these Whig professionals serves as a reminder that, taken as a group, their views were not uniform, but encompassed a wide variety of positions. They were not all staunch advocates of reform, like Brougham or Whitbread, or necessarily at odds with the older Foxites within the party. For, on the issue of Parliamentary reform, Hallam became increasingly cautious as the new century opened. Lacking the necessary evidence, we can only guess at the reasons for his emerging conservatism.[11] But it seems plausible that the excesses of the French Revolution and the encouragement which events in France had given to radicalism in Britain and Ireland had the same effect on Hallam as they had on others of his generation, making him wary of widening the franchise.

Whatever Hallam's views on the French Revolution, he soon became a resolute opponent of Bonaparte, believing that the war against France was vital to Britain's security and expressing displeasure at the Treaty of Amiens.[12] Hallam's aversion to Napoleon and radical reform became most apparent in his reaction

---

[9] *DNB.* Frederic Boase, *Modern English Biography*, s.v. "Hallam, Henry."

[10] Francis Horner to Hallam (2 August 1805), *Memoirs of Francis Horner*, 1: 304. For Hallam's contributions to the *Edinburgh Review*, see the *Wellesley Index to Victorian Periodicals, 1824–1900*, ed. Walter Houghton (Toronto: University of Toronto Press, 1966–1989), 1: 922.

[11] Writing to his friend Webb Seymour in 1802, Hallam noted that in the interval since 1798, when they had both left Oxford, his political opinions had diverged from Webb Seymour's. Since Webb Seymour went on to take up residence in Edinburgh, become immersed in Scottish philosophy, extend his patronage to liberals like Francis Horner and help found the *Edinburgh Review*, we can assume that his politics remained fairly liberal. Hallam's position, it seems fair to conclude, must have become conservative relative to Webb Seymour's. Hallam to Lord Webb Seymour (27 May 1802), Lady Guendolen Ramsden, *Correspondence of Two Brothers: Edward Adolphus, Eleventh Duke of Somerset, and His Brother Lord Webb Seymour, 1800 to 1819 and After* (London: Longmans, Green and Co., 1906), 60.

[12] Hallam to Miss Hallam ([24 May 1802]), Henry Hallam papers, Christ Church, Oxford, 9: 10. Hallam, "Biographical Notice of Lord Webb Seymour," *Memoirs of Francis Horner*, 1: 478.

to the anti-aristocratic eulogy of the Spanish people that Brougham and Jeffrey published in the *Edinburgh Review* in 1808. Occasioned by the Spanish insurrection against French domination, the article called for "radical improvements" in the English constitution and expressed the hope that events in Spain would revive the reform movement in Britain just as the French Revolution had in 1789. Brougham and Jeffrey ended their tribute to Spanish democracy with the suggestion that Britain negotiate with Bonaparte in order to secure the best possible terms for the insurgents, a recommendation that would have led to a victory for revolution in Spain and precluded the total defeat of France. Hallam, finding the political tenor of the article objectionable, eventually severed his connection with the *Review*.[13] After the Hundred Days, when some Whigs were inclined to treat Bonaparte as the legitimate choice of the French nation, Hallam argued strenuously for the restoration of the Bourbons.[14]

Hallam's response to the Hundred Days provides a good indication of his position in the party since Napoleon's return to France in 1815 nearly split the Whigs along lines similar to those of 1794. Foxites like Grey and Holland, liberals like Horner and Althorp, radical Whigs like Whitbread all opposed a resumption of the war against France and the restoration of the Bourbons after Waterloo. Hallam's dislike of Bonaparte and his championing of the Bourbons would have allied him with the Grenvilles, who would throw their support behind the Tories in 1817, and the conservative Fitzwilliam, one of the most uncompromising opponents of Parliamentary reform in the 1820s.[15] Indeed, Hallam's arguments in favor of the Bourbons resembled those of William Elliot, a recipient of Fitzwilliam's patronage. According to Hallam, the only way to achieve "tranquillity and permanence of government" in France would be to "preserve the hereditary title of her sovereign." As he explained: "The moral securities of government are strict religious

13 [Henry Brougham and Francis Jeffrey], "Don Pedro Cevallos on the French Usurpation of Spain," *Edinburgh Review*, 13 (October, 1808): 215–234. For the controversy which the article generated, see Clive, *Scotch Reviewers*, 110–113. For Hallam's response, see Peter Clark, *Henry Hallam* (Boston: Twayne Publishers, 1982), 7–8.
14 Hallam to Francis Horner (26 July 1815) and (19 March 1816), *Memoirs of Francis Horner*, 2: 264–265, 318–319.
15 L. Mitchell, *Holland House*, 247–259. A. Mitchell, *Whigs in Opposition*, 82–92. E. A. Smith, *Whig Principles and Party Politics: Earl Fitzwilliam and the Whig Party, 1748–1833* (Manchester: Manchester University Press, 1975), 346–372.

principles of obligation, sober and steady habits in domestic life, and the point of honour in keeping promises. All these are miserably weak in France; and I see no means so likely to restore them, as the habit of paying obedience to government as legitimate, and even as prescriptive." Whereas liberals and radicals spoke the language of self-determination, referring to the right of the French people to choose their governors, Hallam spoke of order based on religion and submission to prescriptive authority, a Burkean rhetoric pleasing to conservatives.[16]

In the years after 1806, then, as others within the party began to orient the Whigs toward popular reform, Hallam urged caution. Aware of how easily revolution could lead first to anarchy and then to despotism, he warned that in England reform must proceed slowly, in conformity with the nation's longstanding traditions. Reviving in his histories the notion of the balanced constitution, he would demonstrate that good government depended on a delicate balance, maintained by an aristocratic Parliament, which the Tories' encouragement of executive power and the radicals' advocacy of democracy threatened to upset. Here was an argument in favor of the unreformed constitution which would clearly distinguish the Whigs from their adversaries on both the right and the left. Without opposing reform on principle, it set limits on the kinds of change that were acceptable. So long as a given reform could be shown to enhance the public good without disrupting constitutional balance, then it should be encouraged. True to this reasoning, Hallam's histories provided powerful arguments in support of Catholic emancipation and the repeal of the Test and Corporation Acts. But a measure such as the Reform Act of 1832, Hallam thought, should be resisted because it would tilt the constitution too much toward the side of democracy.

II

The most important ideological characteristic of Hallam's two works of history was their reassertion of a Foxite constitutionalism. One idea, more than any other, sustained his political and historical thinking: "The government of England," he wrote in the

---

[16] Hallam to Francis Horner (26 July 1815), *Memoirs of Francis Horner*, 2: 264. For Elliot's position, see A. Mitchell, *Whigs in Opposition*, 91.

opening sentence of his *Constitutional History*, "in all times recorded
by history, has been one of those mixed or limited monarchies."[17]
According to this formula, England enjoyed a mixed government of
king, Lords and Commons, in which the right to govern was shared
equally among the estates of the realm. The constitution's three
components operated in balance, each checking the excesses to
which the others were prone, and performing specific functions
defined by law and past practice. As long as the constitution
remained in equilibrium, good government would prevail, but once
the balance was disrupted, tyranny or anarchy would triumph.
Underlying this argument was the conviction that power was
naturally rapacious and dangerous to liberty unless checked and
balanced. Taken together, these ideas formed the celebrated
doctrine of the separation of powers, which had entered England's
political vocabulary long before Hallam published his *Constitutional
History*. Charles I had referred to the balanced constitution in order
to warn Parliament that any attempt to govern without his
participation would result in disorder and imbalance. After the
Restoration and throughout the eighteenth century, the doctrine
became a frequent assumption of both country and court polemics.
Country writers, challenging the court's use of patronage, argued
that placemen, pensions and standing armies destroyed the
equilibrium of the constitution by undermining the independence
of the House of Commons. Apologists for the court, on the other
hand, pointed out that the system of patronage was a necessary
check on the power of the Commons. By the early nineteenth
century, the doctrine of the balanced constitution was such a well
established component of political debate that it provided
the Whigs with an easy justification for their efforts to restrict the
power of the crown.[18]

---

[17] Henry Hallam, *The Constitutional History of England from the Accession of Henry VII to the Death
of George II* (New York: W. J. Widdleton, 1871), 1: 17.
[18] For the formulation and heritage of this theory in both its British and American contexts,
see: Isaac Kramnick, *Bolingbroke and His Circle: The Politics of Nostalgia in the Age of Walpole*
(Cambridge, Mass.: Harvard University Press, 1968), 137–169. J. G. A. Pocock, *The
Machiavellian Moment: Florentine Political Thought and the Atlantic Republican Tradition*
(Princeton: Princeton University Press, 1975), 361–366, 401–407. Bernard Bailyn, *The
Ideological Origins of the American Revolution* (Cambridge, Mass.: Harvard University Press,
1967), 34–77. Stefan Collini, Donald Winch and John Burrow, *That Noble Science of Politics:
A Study in Nineteenth Century Intellectual History* (Cambridge: Cambridge University Press,
1983), 55–57.

Also important for Hallam's political thinking was his belief that the true end of government was to promote the public good. To one trained in English law, the precept that good government meant legal government was self-evident, and this was the liberal principle that Hallam saw prevail in England after the Revolution of 1688. The purpose of law, he argued, was to protect the freedom of the subject, to guarantee his right to property and expression and to secure him against arbitrary arrest and imprisonment. For a nation to prosper, then, its government must abide by laws such as these, which respect the rights and privileges of the people. Like other Whigs, Hallam identified the nation's interests with Parliament; through its representatives in the House of Commons, England made its needs known, and to ensure that the administration met these needs, the king and his ministers must be held accountable to the Commons. Any monarchy that saw itself as absolute and claimed a divine sanction or indefeasible right, placed itself above the law and beyond the reach of Parliament, and was thus incompatible with the public good. In essence, this had been the case with the Stuarts. During the seventeenth century, Hallam argued, those kings had attempted to render their authority absolute, and only with the Glorious Revolution and the resulting alteration in the line of succession was the power of the monarch made subordinate to the law and dependent on the House of Commons. By granting the crown to William of Orange, the Convention Parliament made it clear that "the rights of the actual monarch" emanated from "the parliament and the people." What the nation gave, it could take away; if William or his heirs ever violated the fundamental rule of government and acted against the public good, then the nation, through its representatives in Parliament, could revoke his title to the throne.[19]

Hallam based his interpretation of the Stuart past on the premise that a mixed monarchy, in which the rights of Parliament were clearly defined, had existed in England long before the seventeenth century. In his *Middle Ages* he sought the origins of this constitution, entering into a controversy that had once generated considerable excitement, especially as it concerned the House of Commons. During the seventeenth century the contest between king and Parliament had made it imperative to determine on what

[19] Hallam, *Constitutional History*, 3: 94–96.

historical grounds, if any, the Parliamentary cause stood. Wishing to uphold the claims of the House of Commons, theorists of the common law had appealed to the ancient constitution, arguing that the Stuart kings had no right to deprive Parliament of its privileges since these had existed unaltered from time immemorial. After the Revolution of 1688, references to the ancient liberties of Englishmen, to their immemorial constitution and free Anglo-Saxon institutions became a frequent strategy in the opposition writings of Bolingbroke and others. During the late seventeenth century, however, the royalist historian Robert Brady sought to refute these arguments by demonstrating that the origin of the modern Parliament, with its Lords and Commons, was not rooted in England's Anglo-Saxon past, but was a more recent occurrence. Denying altogether the existence of the ancient constitution, he asserted that England's feudal kings had virtually created Parliament after the Conquest when they summoned to their councils not only their tenants in chief, but representatives of the counties and boroughs as well. Whatever privileges the House of Commons may have enjoyed, he reasoned, it did so only with the king's consent.[20]

By the time Hallam's *Middle Ages* appeared, more than a century later, this controversy over the origins of the constitution had lost much of its urgency. Where radical thinkers had once appealed to the ancient constitution, demanding a restoration of the democracy which they found in an idealized Anglo-Saxon past, they were now more likely to base their polemics on theories of natural rights or Benthamite utilitarianism.[21] Since political controversy had moved away from such purely historical questions as which came first, Parliament or king, Hallam believed he could deal impartially with England's medieval past. In general, he followed the lines of Brady's

---

[20] For a discussion of this controversy, see J. G. A. Pocock, *The Ancient Constitution and the Feudal Law: A Study of English Historical Thought in the Seventeenth Century* (Cambridge: Cambridge University Press, 1957). See also Kramnick, *Bolingbroke and His Circle*, 127–136, 177–181, and Alan Craig Houston, *Algernon Sidney and the Republican Heritage in England and America* (Princeton: Princeton University Press, 1991), 70, 75–77. For the continuation of the controversy into the eighteenth century and beyond, see R. J. Smith, *The Gothic Bequest: Medieval Institutions in British Thought, 1688–1863* (Cambridge: Cambridge University Press, 1987).

[21] For radical uses of the Anglo-Saxon past, see Christopher Hill, "The Norman Yoke," *Puritanism and Revolution: Studies in Interpretation of the English Revolution of the 17th Century* (New York: Schocken Books, 1964), 50–122.

argument, dispensing with the ancient constitution and placing the beginnings of Parliament after the Conquest.[22]

Hallam began his *Middle Ages* with an investigation into the Anglo-Saxon past and, though impressed with the continuities in English history, he made no mention of either the ancient constitution or the immemorial rights and liberties of Englishmen. He stated explicitly that the Witenagemot was not equivalent to the modern Parliament since there was no system of representation and since the "inferior freemen" played no role in its affairs. Nor could he uncover sufficient evidence to suppose that the county courts involved trial by jury. He refused to believe that the Anglo-Saxon past represented a golden age prior to the establishment of feudalism in which all Englishmen lived as equals, concluding that "much of the intrinsic character of the feudal relation" was probably present in Anglo-Saxon England, "though in a less mature and systematic shape than it assumed after the Norman conquest."[23] With arguments such as these, he discredited what remained of the radical rhetoric which had attempted to justify reform on the grounds that it would return the nation to its original constitutional purity.

Having dismissed the ancient constitution as apocryphal, Hallam then located the origins of its modern counterpart in the age of the Plantagenets. The granting of Magna Carta represented "the first effort towards a legal government," and in the early nineteenth century it was still "the key-stone of English liberty." It guaranteed the personal property and liberty of all freemen by protecting them against arbitrary arrest and spoliation, and in this provision Hallam saw the principle of habeas corpus. The Magna Carta further implied that Parliamentary consent was necessary for all forms of taxation, although eighty years would pass before this practice gained explicit recognition in the Confirmation of the Charters enacted by Edward I.[24] The dominant feature of England's nineteenth-century constitution was its successful combination of king, Lords and Commons, and Hallam traced the origin of this arrangement to the reigns of Henry III and Edward I. The earliest indisputable examples of county and borough representation

---

[22] Henry Hallam, *View of the State of Europe during the Middle Ages*, seventh edition (Paris: Baudry's European Library, 1840), 2: 58, 79–80.
[23] Ibid., 2: 4–23.    [24] Ibid., 2: 37–39, 56–58.

occurred under Henry III, and his successor, Edward I, continued
the practice on a regular basis. By the time of Edward III, both
houses had made clear that it was illegal for the king to raise money
or alter the laws without their consent, and the Commons had
established its right "to inquire into public abuses, and to impeach
public counsellors."[25] From then on, the rights and privileges of
Parliament had steadily grown. Englishmen of the early nineteenth
century, Hallam concluded, enjoyed few "essential privileges" or
"fundamental securities against arbitrary power" that were not
already in existence by the first of the Tudors.[26]

Hallam rarely spoke theoretically about the process of history,
but at one moment in the *Middle Ages* he entered into a dispute with
the Scottish historian John Millar which provides some insight into
his views on how institutions, especially the law, grow and change.
At issue was the Anglo-Saxon practice of frank-pledge, a custom
whereby the friends and relatives of an accused person were held as
sureties in order to guarantee that the accused would stand trial
and, if convicted, comply with the terms of his sentence. In this way,
Anglo-Saxon law made the community responsible for the conduct
of each of its members. To account for the origin of this practice,
the philosophical Millar had proposed that all societies, Anglo-
Saxon or otherwise, developed according to a universal plan and
that customs such as frank-pledge were characteristic of one stage
in this process. To corroborate his theory, he had described the
customs of various other societies, hoping to prove that they too
used procedures resembling frank-pledge. Hallam, however,
rejected Millar's universal plan as mere speculation. Frank-pledge
for him was uniquely Anglo-Saxon, having evolved over many years
as the English kings attempted to deal with the problems posed by
their rude and barbarous subjects. An initial practice of making the
accused post bail was gradually modified as new circumstances
arose until the fully developed custom of frank-pledge emerged. As
each new modification was shown to work, it became part of
the custom, and in this manner England's laws came to embody the
collective wisdom and experience of many generations.[27] When

---

[25] Ibid., 2: 56, 58–70, 75–82, 86–98.     [26] Ibid., 2: 205.

[27] Ibid., 2: 15–18. John Millar, *An Historical View of the English Government, from the Settlement of
the Saxons in Britain to the Revolution in 1688* (London: J. Mawman, 1803), 1: 189–199. For
Millar, see Duncan Forbes, "'Scientific' Whiggism: Adam Smith and John Millar,"
*Cambridge Journal*, 7 (1953–1954): 660–670, and William C. Lehman, *John Millar of Glasgow*,

Hallam referred to the law in these terms, he was hardly saying anything new. Seventeenth-century legal thinkers like Coke or Hale had long before worked out a theory of the common law which ascribed its value to the combined wisdom of the judges and lawyers who had created it, and these ideas received further elaboration in the eighteenth century when Burke, in his *Reflections on the Revolution in France*, argued that England's political institutions were superior because they were deeply rooted in tradition, having grown over the ages as each new generation added its experiences to those of its predecessors.[28] Hallam's *Middle Ages* thus represented the continuation into the nineteenth century of a tradition of political thinking based on a respect for the historical process that stretched back, through Burke's *Reflections*, well into the seventeenth.

In an early letter to his friend Lord Webb Seymour, Hallam once remarked that he had rejected the type of philosophy commonly practiced in Scotland for a more English way of thinking. Years later, answering Webb Seymour's accusation that his *Middle Ages* was a work lacking philosophy, Hallam replied that in fact there was philosophy in his history, even though Webb Seymour, with his Scottish leanings, had not recognized it as such.[29] Considered in light of his criticisms of Millar, these comments suggest that Hallam deliberately rejected those universalist notions of development favored by the Scottish historians, preferring instead a view of the historical process rooted in the English tradition of the common law. Such a choice was perfectly consistent with his own legal training and suggests that Hallam, eschewing the more radical approach of Millar, was attempting to put forth an alternative Whig account of the English past which was compatible with the conservative traditionalism of thinkers such as Burke.

*1735–1801: His Life and Thought and His Contributions to Sociological Analysis* (Cambridge: Cambridge University Press, 1960). For the developmental views of the Scottish historians, see J. W. Burrow, *Evolution and Society: A Study in Victorian Social Theory* (Cambridge: Cambridge University Press, 1966), 10–16.

28 For an analysis of the relationship between the seventeenth-century common law theorists and Burke, see J. G. A. Pocock, *The Ancient Constitution and the Feudal Law*, 36, 171–173, 241–243, and the same author's "Burke and the Ancient Constitution: a Problem in the History of Ideas," *Politics, Language and Time: Essays on Political Thought and History* (New York: Atheneum, 1971), 202–232.

29 Hallam to Lord Webb Seymour (27 May 1802, and 5 November 1813), *Correspondence of Two Brothers*, 59, 124.

What bothered Hallam most about the Scottish historians was their emphasis on "general principles" rather than on "matters of fact." Millar, he complained, "display[ed] a fault too common among the philosophers of his country, that of theorising upon an imperfect induction, and very often upon a total misapprehension of particular facts."[30] In this spirit, Hallam felt called upon to correct the errors which William Robertson had made in his *History of Charles the Fifth*. Hoping to draw a simple causal connection between the growth of commerce and the emergence of political liberty, Robertson had attributed – mistakenly Hallam thought – the independence of Europe's cities to the prosperity generated by the Crusades and to the deliberate policies of kings who were seeking a force capable of offsetting the power of the barons.[31] Nor did Hallam accord much merit to the kind of general propositions found in the historical sections of Adam Smith's work. In the *Wealth of Nations*, for example, Smith had attributed the emergence of good government and liberty to the salutary influence of the towns on the countryside. It was the rise of commerce that broke the arbitrary power of the great barons by encouraging them to spend their wealth on luxuries rather than on maintaining military establishments. Hallam, however, approached the issue from an entirely different direction. Whereas Smith's argument was economic and universal, specifying neither time nor place, Hallam's was institutional and rooted in the uniqueness of England's past. For Hallam, it was the peculiarities of English feudalism, which lacked the military character of its continental counterpart, the development of the common law, the "civil equality of all freemen below the rank of peerage," and the "subjection of peers themselves to the impartial arm of justice" that accounted for the growth of political liberty in England.[32]

In an earlier context Burke had warned against using abstract reasoning in making political judgments. He had reprimanded English supporters of the French Revolution for evaluating its accomplishments abstractly and for ignoring those "circumstances" that "render every civil and political scheme beneficial or noxious

---

[30] Hallam to Lord Webb Seymour (27 May 1802), ibid., 59. Hallam, *Middle Ages*, 1: vii.

[31] Compare Hallam, *Middle Ages*, 1: 148–150, with William Robertson, *The History of the Reign of the Emperor Charles the Fifth* (Philadelphia: J. B. Lippincott, 1884), 1: 32–34, 36–38.

[32] Adam Smith, *The Wealth of Nations*, ed. Andrew Skinner (Harmondsworth: Penguin Books, 1980), 508, 512–514. Hallam, *Middle Ages*, 2: 52–56, 3: 172–177.

to mankind." For Burke institutions could be judged correctly only when seen in their particular settings, and political change would be welcome only if it respected those arrangements which had been established by tradition and were known to work. It was their disregard for historical circumstances that had enabled the revolutionaries in France to discount past practices and impose their truly radical alternatives.[33] Hallam recognized the same tendency toward abstraction in the writings of the Scottish historians, and in his own works paid particular attention to "circumstances." Hallam certainly would not embrace all of Burke's judgments – indeed, his interpretation of the Glorious Revolution differed considerably from Burke's – but adopting a Burkean empiricism, he endorsed a Burkean belief in tradition and distrust of unnecessary innovation.

III

In his *Constitutional History*, written between 1818 and 1827, Hallam turned to England's Tudor and Stuart past. The years that he spent writing his *History* saw an intensification of the movement for constitutional change that gave an added urgency to his work. The economic distress afflicting the country after 1818, the public reaction to the Peterloo Massacre, and the Queen Caroline affair aroused popular reformers and prompted more Whigs than ever before to opt for some degree of Parliamentary reform. In 1819, 1821, 1822 and 1823, Lord John Russell brought the issue before the Commons. In Ireland, the founding of the Catholic Association organized popular Catholicism, raised the specter of insurrection, and made Catholic emancipation the most urgent political problem after 1825.[34] As the reform movement focused increasingly on constitutional change, the Stuart past gained in relevance since the aristocratic and Anglican exclusiveness which reformers found objectionable in the constitution had in large part emerged out of the crises of the seventeenth century. The repeal of the Test and Corporation Acts in 1828 and Catholic emancipation in 1829 would

---

[33] Edmund Burke, *Reflections on the Revolution in France*, ed. Conor Cruise O'Brien (Harmondsworth: Penguin Books, 1981), 90–91, 106, 117–125, 152–153.

[34] Austin Mitchell, "The Whigs and Parliamentary Reform before 1830," *Historical Studies, Australia and New Zealand*, 12 (1965): 22–42. G. I. T. Machin, *The Catholic Question in English Politics, 1820 to 1830* (Oxford: Oxford University Press, 1964).

remove disabilities that owed their existence to the sectarian controversies of the seventeenth century, and the Reform Act of 1832 would alter a system of representation that had remained largely undisturbed since the 1670s. Interpretations of the Stuart past, of which Hallam's was one of the most important, would figure in the political rhetoric of the period as polemicists debated the historical assumptions on which the constitution had stood for more than a century and a half.

When Burke, in his *Reflections*, discredited reformers and Dissenters by associating them with both the French revolutionaries and the Puritan radicals who had overthrown the monarchy of Charles I, he set the tone for much of the Tory rhetoric in the decades to come. What alarmed Burke most about Richard Price's sermon commending the French Revolution was that he heard within it the voice of seventeenth-century Puritanism. Behind Price's claim that England had established the right in 1688 to choose its own governors Burke found the same principle at work that had once led the nation to execute its king.[35] Robert Southey's essays defending the Anglican constitution kept this rhetoric alive throughout the early nineteenth century.[36] Writing on the eve of the Reform Act, the Tory polemicist John Wilson Croker alluded to the misfortunes of the Civil War in order to alert the nation to the dangers at hand. The desire for constitutional change, he warned, was "as old as the Great Rebellion." The reformers of the 1830s were nothing less than the direct descendants of the revolutionaries of the Long Parliament. They were "the ultra-whigs, the dissenters, the republicans, and all that party which derives its origins from the reign of Charles I, and which, on every occasion that has since successively offered, has shown itself hostile to the monarchical and ecclesiastical parts of the constitution." Were they to triumph again, Croker predicted, England should expect the worst: "they never will be satisfied with any thing short of expelling *once more* the bishops, the lords, and the monarch."[37] Behind all this rhetoric lay

---

[35] Burke, *Reflections*, 94–100, 157–159.
[36] [Robert Southey], "History of Dissenters," *Quarterly Review*, 10 (October, 1813): 90–139, "Life of Cromwell," *Quarterly Review*, 25 (July, 1821): 279–347, "Hallam's *Constitutional History of England*," *Quarterly Review*, 37 (January, 1828): 194–260, "Lord Nugent's *Memorials of Hampden*," *Quarterly Review*, 47 (July, 1832): 457–519.
[37] [John Wilson Croker], "Friendly Advice to the Lords," *Quarterly Review*, 45 (July, 1831): 512, and "State of Government," *Quarterly Review*, 46 (November, 1831): 303. For a more extended discussion of the parallel between the 1640s and 1830s, see [John Wilson

Hume's celebrated defense of the Stuarts, which Francis Jeffrey considered the "great support of . . . *sincere* Tory opinions."[38]

Radicals, on the other hand, drew sustenance from England's seventeenth-century republican tradition. Catharine Macaulay, answering Hume, had published between 1763 and 1781 a *History of England* that praised the Parliamentary opposition to Charles I and admired the Commonwealth established after his execution.[39] William Godwin extended this tradition into the 1820s with his *History of the Commonwealth*, which is instructive for its coupling of republicanism and Dissent. Godwin, raised as an Independent and educated in the Dissenting academies, remained within the tradition of rational Dissent long after he had abandoned his Christian belief. The purpose of his history was to rehabilitate England's republican and Dissenting traditions by writing an account of the Commonwealth that would judge the period fairly. For Godwin, republicanism was the political expression of seventeenth-century Independency, and by showing what was constructive in one tradition he demonstrated what was praiseworthy in the other. These divided loyalties help to explain the ambivalence that characterized his appraisal of Cromwell. As a republican, he could not accept the fact that Cromwell's ambition had put an end to the Commonwealth and destroyed the benefits that republican government might have conferred on England. But as a Dissenter, he was drawn to Cromwell as the greatest historical figure whom the Dissenters ever produced. Where establishment polemicists such as Burke or Croker had denied Dissent a constructive role in the nation's past, Godwin demonstrated the legitimacy of the Dissenting tradition by showing what was admirable in the aspirations not only of the Commonwealthmen, but of Cromwell as well.[40]

Croker and John Gibson Lockhart], "The Revolutions of 1640 and 1830," *Quarterly Review*, 47 (March, 1832): 269–300.

38 [Francis Jeffrey], "Brodie's *Constitutional History*: Corrections of Mr. Hume," *Edinburgh Review*, 40 (March, 1824): 99–100.

39 Catharine Macaulay, *The History of England, from the Accession of James I to the Elevation of the House of Hanover*, third edition (London: Edward and Charles Dilly, 1769). For the survival of the republican tradition across the eighteenth century, see Caroline Robbins, *The Eighteenth-Century Commonwealthman: Studies in the Transmission, Development and Circumstance of English Liberal Thought from the Restoration of Charles II to the War with the Thirteen Colonies* (Cambridge, Mass.: Harvard University Press, 1959).

40 William Godwin, *History of the Commonwealth of England, from Its Commencement, to the Restoration of Charles the Second* (London: Henry Colburn, 1824–1828).

Hallam's *Constitutional History* can be read as a contribution to this debate over the Stuart past. As in his earlier work, the doctrine of the balanced constitution provided the organizing principle. The mixed constitution that had emerged from the Middle Ages, he argued, was imperfect and rarely achieved equilibrium during the sixteenth or seventeenth centuries. It was a "monarchy greatly limited by law, but retaining much power that was ill calculated to promote the public good, and swerving continually into an irregular course, which there was no restraint adequate to correct."[41] In his *Constitutional History*, Hallam examined the agonizing struggle between king and Parliament out of which grew the mechanisms and habits necessary to bring the actual practice of government into conformity with the law.

In his consideration of this struggle, Hallam was the partisan of neither the Stuarts nor the extreme Parliamentarians, but understood that each party had at one time or another overstepped its legal bounds and disrupted the constitution's balance. Under the Tudors and early Stuarts the monarchy was the primary offender. Charles carried the arbitrary practices of Elizabeth to such lengths that only the vigorous resistance of Parliament saved the constitution from ruin. The Long Parliament briefly returned the constitution to equilibrium by limiting the power of the crown, but then destroyed what it had achieved as it encroached on the king's legitimate authority, led the nation into civil war, overthrew the constitution, and created a republic. After the Restoration had reestablished a government of king, Lords and Commons, the later Stuarts threatened to subvert the constitution once again in their attempt to render their authority absolute. The Glorious Revolution, in a sense the culmination of Hallam's *History*, finally put an end to this chronic instability. By setting the king beneath the law and making him responsible to Parliament, the Revolution successfully combined "hereditary monarchy" with "security of freedom" in such a way that "neither the ambition of kings shall undermine the people's rights, nor the jealousy of the people overturn the throne."[42] A constitutional arrangement guaranteeing the equal participation of both monarch and Parliament had finally been achieved.

The beauty of Hallam's approach to England's constitutional

---

[41] Hallam, *Constitutional History*, 1: 282.    [42] Ibid., 3: 94–95.

development was that it enabled him to challenge the interpretations of the Stuart past made popular by Hume on the one hand, and by radicals such as Catharine Macaulay or Godwin on the other. Like most Whigs, Hallam read Hume as a Tory apologist for the royal prerogative who had defended the unconstitutional conduct of James I and Charles I on the pretext that they were merely continuing the practices of government which their predecessors had established. Henry VIII and Elizabeth had ruled as absolute monarchs and the fact that their Parliaments willingly supported them proved to Hume that absolutism was the accepted form of government in the sixteenth century. If there was a constitution in existence when James I came to the throne, then for Hume it was the absolutism of Elizabeth. According to this interpretation, the early Stuarts were defending past practice and the Parliamentarians, contrary to the orthodox Whig view, were the innovators attempting to subvert what was already established.

In his *Constitutional History* and *Middle Ages*, Hallam took Hume to task. The point of these books was to show that a mixed constitution had developed in the course of the Middle Ages which the Tudors and early Stuarts had frequently and willfully transgressed. Where Hume, in his approach to the Middle Ages, described the actual conduct of the Plantagenets, noting how often they violated the law and concluding that England's medieval kings were absolute in practice, if not in name, Hallam pointed to the steady growth of the laws protecting the subject and limiting the king's authority. Although Hallam agreed with Hume that medieval society lacked the means to enforce all its laws, he nevertheless spoke of the "real, though imperfect, liberty" of his ancestors.[43] England's laws were present in the statute books, the legal boundaries to the royal authority established during the Middle Ages were thus real, and Hume was wrong to imply that they were not. Nor did Hallam accede to Hume's claim that absolutism was generally accepted during the seventeenth century. He agreed with Hume that Elizabeth was a powerful and often arbitrary monarch. But he emphasized that she frequently overstepped the constitution and he rejected outright Hume's claim that the nation had willingly submitted to her. Elizabeth's Parliaments defended their right to participate equally in the governing of the nation and they

---

[43] Hallam, *Middle Ages*, 2: 170–172.

resisted her "high assumptions of prerogative." The Elizabethan Parliament, Hallam concluded, was not "so servile and submissive an assembly" as Hume had made it out to be, and the Tudor monarchy, like the Plantagenet, was "greatly limited by law" in principle, if not always in practice.[44] James and Charles may have continued to govern in the spirit of Elizabeth, but in so doing they violated the constitution and met with a justified resistance from Parliament.

Hallam's *History* also offered an alternative to those interpretations of the Stuart past that praised indiscriminately the actions of Parliament. Hallam was no democrat and frowned upon the republican ideal of government by Parliament alone. Popular assemblies, he once warned, "when inflamed by passion," were likely to ignore justice and moderation.[45] As an illustration of this observation he pointed to the Long Parliament which at first "effected more for [England's] liberties, than any that had gone before," but then "ended by subverting the constitution it had strengthened, and by sinking . . . beneath a usurper it had blindly elevated to power." Hallam initially praised the Long Parliament for placing much-needed restraints on the power of the crown. The Triennial Act, the condemnation of ship-money and the abolition of the courts of Star Chamber and High Commission were laudable measures in which he could find nothing at all innovative. They were the last in a series of confirmations of the rights and liberties of Englishmen that stretched from Magna Carta through the Petition of Right.[46] But Hallam's praise for the Long Parliament ended here. The assembly soon succumbed to passion, encroached on the king's lawful authority until civil war became unavoidable, and violated the constitution, the privileges of the Lords and the rights of the people. "These great abuses of power," Hallam reflected, " . . . would make a sober man hesitate to support them in a civil war, wherein their success must not only consummate the destruction of the crown, the church, and the peerage, but expose all who had dissented from their proceedings, as it ultimately happened, to an oppression less severe perhaps, but far more sweeping, than that which had rendered the star-chamber odious." By 1642, on the eve of the Civil War, Hallam considered Charles more likely to preserve

[44] Hallam, *Constitutional History*, 1: 230, 248, 263, 266–267, 281–282.
[45] Ibid., 1: 355.   [46] Ibid., 2: 96–104.

the constitution than the Parliamentarians: "Law, justice, moderation, once ranged against him, had gone over to his banner."[47]

Critical, then, of both the Stuarts and the Commonwealthmen, Hallam's *History* championed the Whiggism that triumphed with the Glorious Revolution. There was for Hallam a crucial distinction between the revolutions of 1648 and 1688: whereas he condemned the regicides for destroying England's mixed constitution by abolishing the monarchy and the House of Lords, he praised the statesmen of 1688 because they successfully met the challenge posed by James II and in doing so not only preserved, but also strengthened that mixed constitution. By altering the succession and establishing that the power of the crown derived from Parliament, the Whigs at the Revolution discredited those doctrines of indefeasible right and passive obedience that had exerted such a pernicious influence in the past.[48] As they emerged from the *Constitutional History*, the Whigs appeared as responsible statesmen, neither republicans nor upholders of absolute monarchy, who stood for liberty under law and within the confines of England's mixed constitution. Hallam provided them with a long and honorable pedigree which had the effect of legitimating them in the present by rooting them in the past. Their principles had prevailed not only at the Glorious Revolution, but during the opening moments of the Long Parliament as well.

For Hallam, the trademark of the Whigs was their tendency to favor moderate reform. The Tories, he explained, considered the constitution an "ultimate point" from which they would never deviate, while the Whigs "deemed all forms of government subordinate to the public good, and therefore liable to change, when they should cease to promote that object." But there were limits to acceptable change, for the Whigs rejected "all unnecessary innovation." They welcomed liberty of the press and freedom of inquiry. Advocates of toleration, they supported the Dissenters and abhorred the "haughty language of the Church."[49] Here was the Whiggism that Hallam celebrated in his *Constitutional History*. It informed as well his own approach to the political problems confronting England in the early nineteenth century.

Between 1808 and 1827, the years when Hallam was occupied with his two works of history, there were few problems more pressing

---

[47] Ibid., 2: 104, 137–149.    [48] Ibid., 3: 93–103.    [49] Ibid., 3: 194–196.

than relations between Church and state, especially as the demands of the Roman Catholics and Protestant Nonconformists grew stronger and the role of the Anglican Establishment came into question. In general, the Whigs were the friends of both Catholics and Dissenters. Arguing that religion was an inadequate reason for excluding a sizable portion of the community from the political process, they made Catholic emancipation and repeal of the Test and Corporation Acts standard policies. But their advocacy of religious freedom rarely amounted to an outright rejection of the Established Church. Like most of their contemporaries, the Whigs believed that religion was vital to a moral society and that it was the state's responsibility to promote it. A national church, they reasoned, broad enough to meet the spiritual needs of the majority, would best achieve this aim. Not surprisingly, the Whigs often criticized those High and Low Churchmen who would narrow the doctrines of the Anglican Church and exclude many Protestants who might otherwise have been members.[50]

On matters of religious policy, Hallam took the Whig position. He believed strongly in freedom of inquiry and disliked all forms of ecclesiastical tyranny. One of his earliest publications was a strident defense of John Leslie, professor of mathematics at the University of Edinburgh, whose appointment to the position had been challenged, unsuccessfully as it turned out, by the Edinburgh clergy on the grounds that he held atheistical beliefs. Demonstrating how the churchmen had misconstrued Leslie's opinions and accused him unjustly, Hallam not only protested an instance of clerical persecution, but emphasized the necessity of freeing philosophical speculation from clerical domination.[51]

Hallam was also a firm advocate of Catholic emancipation, and in an early article for the *Edinburgh Review* he made his views clear: the penal laws were unjust, served no useful function and ought to be repealed. Recognizing that Catholic emancipation was mostly an Irish problem, he turned to the history of England's dominion in Ireland to explain why the laws were originally framed and why they

[50] G. F. A. Best, "The Whigs and the Church Establishment in the Age of Grey and Holland," *History*, 45 (1960): 103–118.

[51] [Henry Hallam], "A Statement of Facts Relative to the Election of a Mathematical Professor of the University of Edinburgh," *Critical Review*, 5, third series (July, 1805): 242–252. For the authorship of this article, see Francis Horner to Hallam (2 August 1805) and Hallam to Horner (9 August 1805), *Memoirs of Francis Horner*, 1: 302–305.

were no longer necessary. The English supremacy, he pointed out, was an "unjust usurpation," the most severe consequence of which was the arbitrary imposition of the Reformation on an unwilling nation. For Hallam, as for many Whigs, the sole justification of the Established Church rested on the condition that it represented the religious beliefs of the majority, and on this ground the Irish Church stood condemned. Ireland had never been a Protestant country and would probably never become one. The Anglican religion, in Hallam's opinion, was an "anomalous system," suitable only to England, which had never prospered anywhere else: not in Scotland, America, or Ireland. In so far as the penal laws were designed to create Protestant converts, they had failed and would continue to do so. Nor could Hallam find reason to fear Catholic participation in the politics of his own country. As long as England itself remained Protestant, a Catholic majority in Parliament would be impossible, and even were Catholics to dominate the court, as they had in the reign of James II, they could do little harm since the constitution following the Revolution of 1688 was protected by annual sessions of Parliament, the Mutiny Act and "popular sentiment and long habits of freedom."[52]

In his *Constitutional History*, Hallam continued to ponder the question of Church and state, noting in his preface that much of the book was taken up with religious matters precisely because they were "most important in their application to modern times."[53] In this work of history, then, he presented his most mature thoughts concerning the policies which governments ought to pursue toward those who dissent from the established religion. His genuine aversion to ecclesiastical tyranny was evident throughout. He deplored the Elizabethan persecution of the Catholics, the Laudian attack on the Puritans and the exclusion of the Dissenters after the Restoration. Such policies were not only unjust, they were inexpedient. Religious intolerance, he reflected, no matter how violent or extreme, would never change a person's beliefs. At best it would make him a hypocrite, outwardly conforming to the established practices while inwardly remaining true to his faith. At worst it would turn him against the state which had set out to oppress

---

[52] [Henry Hallam], "Sir J. Throckmorton on the Catholic Question," *Edinburgh Review*, 8 (July, 1806): 313–314, 315–316, 319–320.
[53] Hallam, *Constitutional History*, 1: vii.

him. "It is my thorough conviction," Hallam wrote, "that the persecution . . . carried on against the English catholics, however it might serve to delude the government by producing an apparent conformity, could not but excite a spirit of disloyalty in many adherents of that faith." If religious oppression led naturally to rebellion, then only toleration would guarantee subjects loyal to the crown. "If a fair and legal toleration," he reflected, " . . . had been conceded in the first part of Elizabeth's reign, she would have spared herself those perpetual terrors of rebellion which occupied all her later years."[54]

Hallam used England's seventeenth-century past not only to argue for toleration, but to urge as well the subordination of the Church to the state. He believed in the rule of law and for this reason objected to the intrusion of religion into politics. His study of England's history amply illustrated that whenever religious parties were allowed to predominate, fanaticism triumphed over legal government. In particular, his *History* demonstrated that when religious motives were permitted to influence the judicial process, respect for the law was sacrificed while persecution and intolerance prevailed. To ensure the rule of law, then, Hallam recommended the subordination of the Church to the state, for only the secular magistrate was sufficiently free from religious zeal. This Erastian ideal he found best realized in the Anglican arrangement of his own day, where "every sentence of the spiritual judge [was] liable to be reversed by a civil tribunal."[55] In contrast to High Churchmen and Dissenters, Hallam advocated an Anglicanism which was comprehensive, tolerant, and law-abiding. This was a moderate position, agreeable to the Whigs, and to justify his claim that it was the legitimate voice of the Established Church, Hallam stressed its honorable heritage. He singled out the work of Hooker, whose *Ecclesiastical Polity* justified a broad church by teaching that within Christianity ritual observances and forms of ecclesiastical government were variable, and he laid a similar emphasis on Chillingworth, the English founder of the "latitudinarian school of theology." Despite what the Dissenters might argue, Hallam pointed out, Cromwell and the Independents never practiced the toleration they preached; it was in fact the "Anglican writers,

[54] Ibid., 1: 130, 172.     [55] Ibid, 2: 194, n. 3.

the school of Chillingworth, Hales, Taylor, Locke, and Hoadley, that rendered [toleration] victorious."[56]

In addition to Catholic emancipation, the Whigs' other constitutional cause during the 1820s was Parliamentary reform and on this issue Hallam was at odds with the more progressive members of his party. He was not opposed in principle to changes in the electoral system. When in 1828 the Whigs brought in a bill to transfer two representatives from Penryn to Manchester, Hallam declared that he was "delighted" with the measure.[57] But the comprehensive Reform Bill introduced by Russell in March, 1831, Hallam found unacceptable.[58] The most explicit explanation of why he viewed the bill with disfavor appears in the memoirs of the Duc de Broglie. An Anglophile and a friend of many prominent Whigs, Broglie recorded in his *Personal Recollections* a conversation between Hallam and Lord Lansdowne concerning the shortcomings of Russell's proposal. What struck Hallam most about the bill was its extent. To a historian who saw England's political development as a Burkean exchange between past and present, Russell's proposal seemed to disregard precedent, vested rights, and the "wisdom of our ancestors." A plan as innovative as this, he feared, would set in motion a sequence of reforms which would culminate in universal suffrage and the abolition of both the monarchy and the House of Lords. Hallam further observed that the king had already lost most of his real influence, possessing now only a "moral authority," and that the Lords were in a similar state of decline. The power of government thus rested almost entirely with the House of Commons and if the Reform Bill were to pass, then the "middle classes" would come to dominate not only the Commons, but the government as a whole. Ideally, Hallam argued, the "three powers" of monarchy, aristocracy and democracy ought to balance one another in Parliament. The English constitution owed its stability in the past to this balance and a properly framed reform bill should aim to strengthen, not destroy it. The Duc de Broglie recorded this conversation more than thirty years after the event, and he acknowledged that across the interval some ideas of his own may

---

56 Ibid., 1: 216–219, 2: 77–79, 197.
57 Hallam to John Whishaw (28 April 1828), *The "Pope" of Holland House*, 321.
58 Hallam to Lord John Russell, draft letter (20 July 1831); Hallam papers, Christ Church, Oxford, 7: 7–8. *Memoirs, Journal, and Correspondence of Thomas Moore*, ed. Lord John Russell (London: Longman, Brown, Green, and Longmans, 1853–1856), 6: 221.

have colored his account.[59] Be that as it may, a reading of the *Constitutional History* reveals that Hallam did reason in much the manner Broglie described.

The final section of Hallam's *History*, which described the growth of the constitution through the reign of George II, ended on a note of uncertainty. His account of the seventeenth century had shown clearly that constitutional balance was at best a precarious condition, and when he went on to survey the developments of the eighteenth century, he discovered powerful forces, both political and economic, which threatened to undermine the balance achieved in 1688. Owing to the economic prosperity which England experienced during the eighteenth century, the "democratical influence" in Parliament, the "commercial and industrious classes," had increased, and although the House of Commons was still primarily aristocratic throughout the reign of George II, this trend had continued into the nineteenth century.[60] For Hallam, however, the strength of the Commons lay to a great extent in its aristocratic makeup. The Commons, he wrote, should not "follow with the precision of a weather-glass the unstable prejudices of the multitude." Its function was to steer "a firm course in domestic and external affairs, with a circumspectness and providence for the future, which no wholly democratical government has ever yet displayed." Only a "middle position between an oligarchical senate and a popular assembly" would guarantee the Commons its "dignity and usefulness."[61] Although Hallam never commented on those constitutional developments which occurred after the death of George II, the inference seems certain that he considered the influx of this "democratical" element into Parliament an unwelcome event, and reasoning such as this may account for his opposition to the Reform Act of 1832: an extensive widening of the franchise would only add to the decline of aristocratic influence in the House of Commons.

IV

Although a work of considerable scholarship, Hallam's *Constitutional History* was also engaged literature, addressing the political

[59] *Recollections of the Duc de Broglie*, 2: 515–523.
[60] Hallam, *Constitutional History*, 3: 289–291.        [61] Ibid., 3: 230.

controversies of the 1820s. It was at once a forceful statement of Foxite principles, emphasizing that the purpose of government was to promote the public good, insisting on the rule of law, and displaying a fundamental loyalty to the English constitution in Church and state. Hallam expressed these views in a history that was neither Tory nor republican. He rejected the interpretation of Hume, which saw validity in the absolutism of the early Stuarts, and of the republicans, which set out to vindicate the radicalism of the Commonwealth. Challenging Hume's attempt to use an alleged Elizabethan absolutism in order to defend the policies of James I and Charles I, Hallam made clear his opposition to an unrestrained executive and his healthy respect for the rights and liberties of Englishmen. Criticizing the Long Parliament for its excesses, he further demonstrated his aversion to republican schemes of government and to those popular radicals who continued to draw sustenance from the "good old cause." Applied to contemporary issues, Hallam's Whiggism cautioned moderation. In matters of religion, he urged a latitudinarian Anglicanism, subordinate to the law and the civil authorities, and displaying toleration toward those Protestant Dissenters and Roman Catholics who still found it impossible to worship within the Established Church. But he opposed extensive measures of Parliamentary reform, fearing that a widening of the franchise and an alteration in the representation such as the Whigs would carry in 1832 might disturb constitutional equipoise by diluting the aristocratic composition of the Commons.

Coming at a time when progressives, responding to popular pressure, were encouraging the Whigs to embrace Parliamentary reform, Hallam's histories provided a set of principles that conservatives in the party would have found attractive since their reassertion of a Foxite constitutionalism, their Burkean traditionalism, and their belief in aristocratic government established comfortable limits to constitutional change. No wonder, then, that the young Viscount Milton, having decided that only Parliamentary reform would restore social harmony and rebuild the people's confidence in aristocratic leadership, deemed Hallam's interpretation of the Civil War too favourable to the royalist cause.[62] For those Whigs frustrated with Hallam's conservatism, there were

---

[62] Wasson, "The Great Whigs," 442.

other interpretations of the English past available. Lord John Russell had used his *Life of William Lord Russell* and *Essay on English Government* to direct the Whigs away from their customary preoccupation with the crown and toward an endorsement of popular issues.[63] In 1825 Macaulay published his celebrated essay on Milton, and three years later he was asked to review Hallam's *Constitutional History* for the *Edinburgh*. The differences between Hallam's and Macaulay's approaches to the past reflect clearly the division in the party between those anxious about the future, and those eager for reform.

Macaulay agreed for the most part with Hallam's interpretation of the Reformation and, like Hallam, used arguments drawn from England's Tudor and Stuart past to encourage Catholic emancipation and relief for Dissenters.[64] But despite this large area of agreement, the two parted company over Parliamentary reform. Macaulay, growing impatient with Hallam's conservatism, closed his review by arguing vigorously in support of reform. The period of English history beginning with the Tudors and ending with the reign of George II was a distinct epoch in the nation's past dominated by the contest between king and Parliament. By the mid-eighteenth century, Macaulay pointed out, Parliament had secured its rights and privileges, the modern constitution had been established, and the conflict between parties had temporarily abated. But this political stability was deceptive, for a new contest was emerging between the unenfranchised nation and the ruling oligarchy: "The conflict which commenced in the middle of the eighteenth century," he observed, and "which still remains undecided . . . , is between a large portion of the People on the one side, and the Crown and the Parliament united on the other."[65] Given the development of English industry and commerce, given the rise of a politically responsible middle class and an increasingly discontented working class, some degree of Parliamentary reform was rapidly becoming necessary. England's governing elite in the 1820s thus faced a situation analogous to that which had confronted James I: either it could follow in the path of the Stuarts, oppose

63 Brent, *Liberal Anglican Politics*, 40–64.
64 [Thomas Babington Macaulay], "Hallam's *Constitutional History*," *Edinburgh Review*, 48 (September, 1828): 100–112.
65 Ibid., 162–165.

constitutional change and plunge the nation into civil war; or it could learn from the events of the seventeenth century, reform itself peacefully and avoid revolution by bringing the middle class into the political community. "We know of no great revolution," Macaulay reflected, "which might not have been prevented by compromise early and graciously made."[66]

Much of Hallam's hesitation over Parliamentary reform was based on an analogy between the 1640s and his own age: the Parliamentarians in the Civil War had invalidated their cause by destroying the balance of the constitution and the nineteenth-century advocates of Parliamentary reform, he feared, were threatening to do the same. As part of his own polemic, then, Macaulay threw his support behind the opponents of the Stuarts, vindicating the Long Parliament and insisting that the Civil War had been, in fact, necessary and justifiable. To substantiate his claim, he used an argument concerning the growth of standing armies that was found in the work of John Millar and that echoed those eighteenth-century opposition writers who had stressed the dangers that armies posed to free republics. In his *Constitutional History*, Hallam had argued that the leaders of the Commons overstepped their legal bounds and upset constitutional balance when in 1642 they attempted to deprive the king of his right to summon the militia.[67] In his response to Hallam, Macaulay used an entirely different line of reasoning to exonerate the Parliament and defend its decision to control the army. Most of the states of Europe, he pointed out, had enjoyed free constitutions so long as they were defended by militias drawn from the people. But with the rise of professional armies in the sixteenth and seventeenth centuries, the monarchs of the continent acquired the means to subvert the liberties of their subjects and render their authority absolute. England, however, had avoided this unfortunate development because, as an island, it had no need for a standing army until the reign of Charles I, when the rebellions in Scotland and Ireland had made one necessary. Only then did a professional military threaten the nation's free constitution. Seen within this context, the struggle between the king and Parliament was over control of the army. For Macaulay as for Millar, England remained free at a time when

---

[66] Ibid., 168–169.     [67] Hallam, *Constitutional History*, 2: 127–136.

the other states of Europe were becoming absolute monarchies precisely because it refused to give up its army to Charles.[68]

In accepting the Civil War as necessary for the defense of freedom, Macaulay was drawing near to the radical tradition of Catharine Macaulay and William Godwin that Hallam had explicitly rejected. Where Macaulay was comfortable embracing those reforms which would bring the middle class prominently into the political community and wrote history that spoke to the ideological needs of the Victorians, Hallam's preoccupation with the constitution seemed to owe more to the late eighteenth century. The doctrine of the balanced constitution, so central to his interpretation, was already obsolete by the time he was writing, and the *Constitutional History* was the last major study of the seventeenth century to use it as an explanatory device. As works of erudition, Hallam's histories would survive well into the nineteenth century, until they were surpassed by the scholarship of the great Victorians – Stubbs and Freeman on the Middle Ages, Froude and Creighton on the Reformation, Macaulay and Gardiner on the Stuarts. As an expression of ideology, they were eclipsed by the Reform Act of 1832, which changed irrevocably the constitution that Hallam had hoped to preserve.

---

[68] Macaulay, "Hallam's *Constitutional History*," 124–133. See also John Millar, *Historical View of the English Government*, 3: 113–125. For a discussion of the Scottish influences on Macaulay's thinking, see J. W. Burrow, *A Liberal Descent: Victorian Historians and the English Past* (Cambridge: Cambridge University Press, 1981), 41–48, and John Clive, *Macaulay: The Shaping of the Historian* (New York: Alfred A. Knopf, 1973), 77, 105, 107, 124. For the standing army controversy in its Scottish context, see John Robertson, *The Scottish Enlightenment and the Militia Issue* (Edinburgh: John Donald, 1985).

# CHAPTER 2

# Thomas Babington Macaulay and Victorian religious controversy

Macaulay's immensely popular *History of England* has received greater critical notice than perhaps any other book of its kind written during the Victorian period. And yet, despite all this attention, few commentators have appreciated the extent to which these five volumes, published between 1848 and 1861, can be read as a liberal response to the religious disputes that dominated English politics from the passing of the Reform Act in 1832 to the furor over "Papal aggression" in the early 1850s.[1] Macaulay himself certainly

---

[1] References to religious matters are so pervasive in Macaulay's *History* that it is surprising scholars have made so little of them. But such is the case. Macaulay's two most recent biographers, Owen Dudley Edwards, *Macaulay* (New York: St. Martin's Press, 1988), and John Clive, *Macaulay: The Shaping of the Historian* (New York: Alfred A. Knopf, 1973), pay scant attention to the sectarian dimension of early Victorian politics and consequently do not relate Macaulay's work to it. Clive also ends his biography with Macaulay's return from India in 1838 and does not deal at all with the issues behind the writing of the *History*. Jane Millgate, *Macaulay* (London: Routledge and Kegan Paul, 1973), is concerned primarily with questions of literary technique. Even her chapter on Macaulay's treatment of the Irish question does not place his position on Ireland and Catholicism in the larger context of his overall approach to sectarian politics. Other recent studies which are mainly interested in Macaulay's general contribution to English literary culture, Rosemary Jann, *The Art and Science of Victorian History* (Columbus: Ohio State University Press, 1985), 66–104 and A. Dwight Culler, *The Victorian Mirror of History* (New Haven: Yale University Press, 1985), 20–38, are all but silent on the topic of religion. J. W. Burrow, *A Liberal Descent: Victorian Historians and the English Past* (Cambridge: Cambridge University Press, 1981), 11–93, notes early on that the conflict between Church and Dissent made the Stuart past especially relevant to the Victorians, but then chooses to pursue other themes in his discussion of Macaulay. Joseph Hamburger, *Macaulay and the Whig Tradition* (Chicago: University of Chicago Press, 1976), is one scholar who does deal with Macaulay's position on religious controversy, but his approach is considerably different from, though not necessarily incompatible with, mine. Hamburger argues that Macaulay saw politics as the art of "trimming" between the extremes of "revolution" and "repression." Religion, Hamburger goes on, provided Macaulay with one model for comprehending political extremism, with Puritanism, for example, becoming analogous to radicalism. But, as I will argue, Macaulay also understood politics in terms of a conflict between Anglicanism, Dissent and Catholicism, which was just as important for the Victorians as their fear of revolution. The great Victorian essayists – Stephen, Morley,

knew that his book would be read in this way. On the publication of his first two volumes in 1848 he noted in his journal: "I expect . . . furious abuse both from the ultra Evangelicals and from the Tractarians, nor shall I be sorry to be so abused." Several days later he remarked: "It is odd that I have not yet seen a single line – encomiastic or vituperative – on the religious disquisitions which fill so many pages of the book, and which, I should have thought, must have excited the indignation of all sects, Papists, Churchmen, Puritans, and Quakers. But this I suppose is still to come."[2] Macaulay's *History* did eventually arouse considerable controversy, and much as he anticipated it was not over his interpretation of the Revolution's secular achievement. To interpret the events of 1688 and 1689 as a defensive and prescriptive revolution which finally put an end to the conflict between crown and Parliament without altering the fundamental laws of the kingdom was almost commonplace by the mid-nineteenth century and could be found in the works of Henry Hallam and Sir James Mackintosh. Reading Macaulay's *History* in 1848, the year of continental revolutions, Tories as well as Whigs would have found reassuring his conviction that England had avoided an uprising in 1848 precisely because it had experienced a "preserving revolution" in 1688.[3] It was not his comments on the constitution so much as those "religious disquisitions" that would prove controversial in the end.

Histories of the Stuart past generated so much discord during the nineteenth century in part because the Victorians saw a parallel between the religious controversies of the seventeenth century and the sectarian strife of their own age. Few problems troubled Victorian politics as persistently as religious dissent. The repeal of the Test and Corporation Acts in 1828 and Catholic emancipation in 1829 may have dispelled the myth that Britain could remain religiously uniform, but they left many subsidiary issues

    Gladstone and others – gave us an incomplete image of Macaulay which all of the works
    mentioned above have helped to revise. Now that historians have started to recapture the
    religious context of Victorian politics it is time to place Macaulay within it.
 2  Macaulay, Journal (7 and 12 December [1848]). I would like to thank Dr. Robert Robson
    for making his typescript of Macaulay's journal available to scholars. Both journal and
    typescript are in the library of Trinity College, Cambridge.
 3  *The Works of Lord Macaulay*, Albany edition (London: Longmans, Green and Co., 1898), 3:
    281–284, 288.

unresolved. With the rise of Protestant Dissent in England and Scotland and the increasingly well-organized Catholic challenge to the Protestant Establishment in Ireland, discussions about Laud and the Puritans, Cromwell and Charles, James and William easily became ideologically charged. Where High Anglicans and Tractarians might seek inspiration in the churchmanship of Archbishop Laud or the Nonjurors, Dissenters from the traditional denominations – Congregationalists, Baptists, Presbyterians – invariably traced their beginnings back to seventeenth-century Puritanism. As Dissent became more vocal in the 1830s and 1840s, historians like the Congregationalist Robert Vaughan and the Unitarian John Forster produced a body of scholarship that emphasized the contribution which Puritanism had made to the growth of civil and religious liberty in England. Though speaking from a position outside the mainstream of English Dissent, Thomas Carlyle presented in his powerful but idiosyncratic edition of Oliver Cromwell's *Letters and Speeches* an image of Cromwell as a Christian hero, sincere in his Puritan faith, that would inspire generations of Nonconformists to increased political activity.

The admission of Dissenters and Catholics into the political community forced the Whigs to rethink the role of the Established Church in what was now acknowledged to be a religiously plural society. With the doctrine of the Anglican constitution no longer appropriate, new principles had to be found to replace those which posited Anglican Christianity as the basis for civil government in England. Macaulay's essays of the 1820s and early 1830s made important contributions to this debate, and his *History of England* was a powerful expression of the religious latitudinarianism characteristic of mid-Victorian Whiggism. Just as the Glorious Revolution could be interpreted as having finally brought to an end the century-old conflict between king and Parliament, so the events of 1688 and 1689 could be seen as having established the principles of religious liberty that would make England a truly tolerant nation. In his *History*, Macaulay would celebrate an undogmatic Protestantism that he would attribute to William III, and he would provide a historical justification for admitting Dissenters into the political community as full members. He would acknowledge that the great tragedy of the Revolution had been its treatment of the Catholic population of Ireland, and by contrasting England's mistakes in Ireland to the successful religious settlement in Scotland, he would indicate what steps should be taken to rectify the Irish situation. Finally, replying to High Churchmen and Tractarians, he would defend the Erastianism that lay at the heart of the English constitution in Church and state.

I

Historians have only now come to appreciate the importance of religion, particularly sectarian controversy, in shaping the politics of the 1830s and 1840s. In his study of the religious aspects of early nineteenth-century Whiggism, Richard Brent has recently drawn attention to a strong liberal Anglican tendency that emerged in the 1820s and became prominent in the Whig party after Melbourne formed his second government in 1835. Led by Russell and Althorp, these liberal Anglicans set out in the 1820s to transform the Whigs into a popular party by endorsing those reforms advocated by the middle classes such as widening the franchise and granting concessions to Catholic and Protestant Dissent. On religious matters their position was latitudinarian and Erastian. They supported the Church of England, believing that it had an important role to play in the traditional areas of devotion and education, and thought that its association with the state should remain intact. But they were also sympathetic to Dissenters. They were willing to accommodate non-Anglicans and remove their grievances providing it would not threaten the well-being of the Anglican Establishment to do so. Thus they commuted the tithe in England, a reform which did not affect the financial standing of the Church in any meaningful way, but were not prepared to abolish Church rates once the Dissenters made the attack on Church rates the first salvo in a campaign toward disestablishment. In the 1830s they extended the right to grant degrees to the nondenominational London University, provided for the civil registration of births, marriages and deaths and enabled Dissenters to be married according to their own rituals. They reduced the size of the Protestant Establishment in Ireland, bringing it more closely into conformity with the number of its communicants, and endorsed the principle that its surplus revenue should be used for nonsectarian purposes benefiting the entire Irish nation. They embraced measures to open Oxford and

Cambridge to Nonconformists and proposals for a state-funded system of nondenominational education.[4]

Between 1825, when he began writing for the *Edinburgh Review*, and 1834, when he departed for India, Macaulay shared similar concerns with the liberal Anglicans. Though not a liberal Anglican in a doctrinal sense, he too was interested in making the Whigs a popular party, in broadening the base of British politics, and in challenging the Anglican exclusiveness of the constitution. Though he spent considerable time cultivating social ties among the leading Foxites and owed his seat in the Commons to Lansdowne's patronage, his political sympathies were close to those of Russell and Althorp. When the issue of whether or not Parliament could use the excess revenue of the Irish Establishment for nonsectarian purposes finally split the Whig party in 1834, allowing the liberal Anglicans to gain the ascendancy, Macaulay was prepared to throw his support behind Russell and Althorp.[5] By the end of 1833 he had suspected that a split in the Whig party was imminent and it was in part to avoid its unpleasant consequences that he accepted a position on the Supreme Council of India. Macaulay was afraid that if he chose to stay in England and weather the political storm, then he would have to sever the ties he had formed with the leading Foxites in order to remain consistent with his political principles, which were more liberal than theirs. As he explained to his sister: "my political prospects are very gloomy. A schism in the ministry is approaching ... If I remain in office I shall, I fear, lose my political character. If I go out and engage in opposition I shall break most of the private ties which I have formed during the last three years. In England I see nothing before me, for some time to come, but poverty, unpopularity, and the breaking up of old connections." Escape to India, he hoped, would enable him to avoid all of this: "By accepting the post which is most likely to be offered to me, I escape for a short time from the contests of faction here. When I return I find things settled, – parties formed into new combinations, – new questions under discussion. I shall then be able, without the scandal of a violent separation, and without

---

[4] Richard Brent, *Liberal Anglican Politics: Whiggery, Religion, and Reform 1830–1841* (Oxford: Clarendon Press, 1987), 8–9, 25–28, 36–40, 60–62.

[5] For the controversy over Irish appropriation and the dominance of the liberal Anglicans in the Whig party after 1835, see ibid., 16, 65–103.

exposing myself to the charge of inconsistency, to take my own line."[6]

Once in India, safely removed from English domestic politics and yet well informed as to their progress, Macaulay made clear exactly what his course of action would have been had he remained in England. He would have backed the reformers and, if necessary, would have broken his ties with the Foxites and conservative Whigs. "My judgment is this," he wrote to his friend Thomas Spring Rice: "The strongest party, beyond all comparison, in the empire is what I call the *centre gauche*, the party which goes further than the majority of the present ministry, and yet stops short of the lengths to which [the radicals] Hume and Warburton go." He associated the *"centre gauche"* with the political principles of Althorp, and advised Spring Rice: "Stick to the *Centre Gauche*. Gain their confidence. And you may do what you please. This is the game that I would have tried to play, if I had remained in England."[7] To propose that Macaulay allied himself with those Whigs loyal to Althorp and Russell is not to argue for an identity of interests or principles. As will become clear, Macaulay, far more than the liberal Anglicans, was hoping to free liberalism from its religious preoccupations and was able to envision a society founded on purely secular grounds. In practice, however, this divergence of opinions may not have been as significant as it seems. Macaulay was always acutely aware of the limits that circumstances placed on political activity. He knew that England, Scotland and Ireland were overwhelmingly Christian, and that in England, at least, the Established Church was popular enough for any attempt to sever its ties with the state to meet considerable resistance. The problem confronting Macaulay was not how to create a secular polity, but rather how to liberalize the Christian and Anglican polities that were already in existence.

That Macaulay should have backed Althorp, Russell and the liberal Anglicans in the 1830s is hardly surprising. Like them, he had always embraced popular causes. The list of measures he

[6] Macaulay to Hannah Macaulay (17 August 1833), *The Letters of Thomas Babington Macaulay*, ed. Thomas Pinney (Cambridge: Cambridge University Press, 1974–1981), 2: 300–301.

[7] Macaulay to Thomas Spring Rice (11 August 1834), ibid., 3: 74–75. The ministry that Macaulay referred to was essentially Grey's original government of 1830. Though the conservative Whigs – Stanley, Richmond, Ripon and Graham – resigned from the cabinet in May, 1834, and Grey followed in July, Macaulay did not hear of this shake-up until after he had written to Spring Rice.

endorsed while campaigning in 1832 for the representation of Leeds reads like a catalogue of progressive Whiggism. The abolition of slavery, free trade and the revision of the Corn Laws, the secret ballot and an ending of intimidation in elections, strict government economy and reduced taxes, the removal of all remaining religious disabilities, measures to regulate child labor, abolition of government sinecures, reform of municipal corporations, and the removal of stamps on newspapers – all of these were causes popular with the middle-class electorate.[8] His early polemical efforts in the *Edinburgh Review* were similarly aimed at transforming the Whigs into a more widely based party by appealing to Dissenters, Catholics and the middle class, while at the same time absolving the Whigs from the charge of radicalism. He criticized the Tories for their Anglican and aristocratic exclusiveness, and he argued for the repeal of the Test and Corporation Acts, Catholic emancipation and Parliamentary reform. And yet Macaulay was hardly a radical. Despite the unmistakable influence of utilitarian ideas on his own thinking, he considered the Benthamites dangerously radical.

As part of his effort to articulate a popular Whiggism, Macaulay used his early essays on the Tudor and Stuart past, written between 1825 and 1832, to shift the focus of Whig rhetoric from the Glorious Revolution to the Civil War. The interpretation of the seventeenth century that emerged from these occasional writings thus departed considerably from the historiographical tradition represented by Hallam, which generally deplored the excesses of the Civil War. In the essay on Milton, Macaulay argued vigorously that any justification for the deposition of James in 1688 could be used to legitimate Parliament's decision to wage war against Charles in 1642. In his review of Hallam's *Constitutional History*, he used a different argument to make a similar point. Had Parliament not seized control of the army, Macaulay asserted, then Charles would have followed the example of continental rulers and used his soldiers to render the monarchy absolute. It was the Civil War that preserved liberty in England, not the Glorious Revolution, and Macaulay belittled the revolutionaries of 1688 because they called in a foreign army to do what the nation should have done by itself.

---

[8] See the descriptions of Macaulay's election speeches in the *Leeds Mercury*, 16 June, 8 September, 1 December and 11 December 1832. Macaulay to Joseph Lees ([2] August 1832), *Letters*, 2: 162–167.

This shift in rhetorical emphasis was significant. The Revolution was essentially an aristocratic event, and Whigs had routinely referred to it when making the claim that the aristocracy, because it had wrested popular rights from the crown in 1688, was able to defend the interests of the people. The Civil War, on the other hand, was regarded as a genuinely popular movement, and by embracing it Macaulay sanctioned the right of the people to participate in the political process. In his essay on Burghley, published just after the passing of the Reform Act, Macaulay vindicated popular politics when he judged the Elizabethan monarchy a good government precisely because the threat of rebellion ensured that the queen, who lacked a standing army, would respond to the public interest.[9]

Macaulay's legitimation of the Civil War brought him close to the republican tradition of Catharine Macaulay and William Godwin, whose volumes on the Commonwealth had started to appear in 1824. But Macaulay was not a radical, and like other members of his party he wanted to affirm the respectability of the Whigs by distancing them from both popular and Benthamite radicalism. In his essays on Milton and Hallam, for example, he displayed little enthusiasm for England's republican past. He revealed the errors committed by the Commonwealthmen, and reserved his praise for Oliver Cromwell, a figure whom radicals chastised for destroying the republic established on the king's execution.

The ambition of Oliver [Macaulay explained] was of no vulgar kind. He never seems to have coveted despotic power. He at first fought sincerely and manfully for the Parliament, and never deserted it, till it deserted its duty. If he dissolved it by force, it was not till he found that the few members who remained . . . were desirous to appropriate to themselves a power which they held only in trust, and to inflict upon England the curse of a Venetian oligarchy. But even when thus placed by violence at the head of affairs, he did not assume unlimited power. He gave the country a constitution far more perfect than any which had at that time been known in the world. He reformed the representative system . . . He gave the Parliament a voice in the appointment of ministers, and left to it the whole legislative authority.

9 [Thomas Babington Macaulay], "Milton," *Edinburgh Review*, 42 (August, 1825): 325–334, "Hallam's *Constitutional History*", *Edinburgh Review*, 48 (September, 1828): 124–133, 159, "Nare's *Memoirs of Lord Burghley* – Political and Religious Aspects of His Age," *Edinburgh Review*, 55 (April, 1832): 280–285.

"He will not lose," Macaulay boasted, "by comparison with Washington."[10] Whereas the Commonwealthmen were guilty of many excesses, Cromwell received Macaulay's approbation because he tried to restore a moderate, just political order. It was not the republicans' zeal for liberty that impressed Macaulay so much as Cromwell's attempt to balance freedom and order in the aftermath of the Civil War.

Macaulay's treatment of the two parties that fought the Civil War reveals further his concern to dissociate the Whigs from the republican tradition. Though inclined to favor the Parliamentarians and oppose the royalists, he was also aware that the Cavaliers possessed some attractive qualities that the Puritans lacked. Macaulay certainly took the Puritans seriously – their religiosity was sincere and had enabled them to achieve much in the cause of liberty – and yet he was aware of their limitations: they discouraged literature and learning, were ostentatious and lacked "eloquence." They remained fanatics and were inclined toward intolerance.[11] On the other side, Macaulay could not avoid viewing "with complacency" the "character of the honest old Cavaliers," despite his hatred of the Stuarts. These royalists may have been mistaken in their politics, but "they possessed, in a far greater degree than their adversaries, those qualities which are the grace of private life." Their virtues were "courtesy, generosity, veracity, tenderness, and respect for women. They had far more both of profound and of polite learning than the Puritans. Their manners were more engaging, their tempers more amiable, their tastes more elegant, and their households more cheerful."[12]

In his essays on Milton and Hampden, Macaulay portrayed his subjects as great men precisely because they were neither Puritan nor Cavalier, but combined what was best in both parties. Milton, like the Puritans, took up the cause of liberty. He shared their religiosity and enjoyed the strength which that gave them. But he avoided their excesses – their "frantic delusions, their savage manners, their hideous jargon, their scorn of science, their aversion to pleasure" – because he tempered that religiosity with the "estimable and ornamental" qualities of the Cavaliers. Combining

---

[10] Macaulay, "Milton," 335. For a similar eulogy of Cromwell, see "Hallam's *Constitutional History*," 143–145.
[11] Macaulay, "Milton," 337–341.     [12] Ibid., 341–342.

the Puritans' quest for liberty with the Cavaliers' love of intellect, Milton fought for the "most valuable" of freedoms – freedom of thought. In the model of political conduct that Macaulay was advocating here, the struggle for liberty was thus moderated by an aristocratic sense of decorum. "Though [Milton's] opinions were democratic, his tastes and his associations were such as harmonize best with monarchy and aristocracy."[13]

Macaulay made a similar case for Hampden. Although a "celebrated Puritan," his creed was of a unique variety. "He was a man," Macaulay wrote, echoing his characterization of Milton, "in whom virtue showed itself in its mildest and least austere form. With the morals of a Puritan, he had the manners of an accomplished courtier." Intellect and discernment, moderation and prudence, polish and eloquence, humanity and charity, valor and resolution were all qualities which Macaulay attributed to Hampden. These characteristics were distinctive of the "gentleman" and they "distinguished him from most of the members of his sect and his party." Taken together, they made him the ideal citizen: independent and free from personal ambition, he took his civic duties seriously, even to the point of bearing arms in defiance of tyranny and defense of liberty. Hampden was, Macaulay wrote, "the only man who united perfect disinterestedness to eminent talents – the only man who, being capable of gaining the victory for [England], was incapable of abusing that victory when gained." Had Hampden survived the Civil War, Macaulay ventured to surmise, the excesses of the Commonwealth might never have taken place.[14] Like Milton, Hampden was the model of political conduct: mannered, moderate, disinterested, and dedicated to the public good.

Macaulay's historical essays, then, provided him with the means to express his support for those movements that would culminate in the repeal of the Test and Corporation Acts, Catholic emancipation and Parliamentary reform. And yet he was not simply an advocate of popular politics. He stressed that the statesmen responsible for bringing about these changes must be versed in aristocratic manners, for he considered elegance, fine sentiments and

[13] Ibid., 342–343.
[14] [Thomas Babington Macaulay], "Lord Nugent's *Memorials of Hampden*," *Edinburgh Review*, 54 (December, 1831): 505–511, 518–519, 545–549.

politeness remedies against fanaticism. The possession of aristocratic manners had been the special strength of Milton and Hampden; the absence of such refinement had been the weakness of the Puritans and, during his own age, was one of the failings of the philosophical radicals as well. "Metaphysical and political science," he wrote, referring to the Benthamites, "engage their whole attention. Philosophical pride has done for them what spiritual pride did for the Puritans in a former age; it has generated in them an aversion for the fine arts, for elegant literature, and for the sentiments of chivalry. It has made them arrogant, intolerant, and impatient of all superiority."[15] As the Whigs attempted to define their position in relation to the radicalism of the Benthamites, Macaulay's conception of the English past provided them with at least one possible framework. The philosophical radicals, with their narrow vision and lack of reverence for the past, were the modern-day counterpart to the Puritans; like their seventeenth-century predecessors, they were prone to enthusiasm. The Whigs, on the other hand, combined what was best in both the Parliamentary and royalist parties – a love of freedom tempered by moderation.

In making the case that British politics could be opened to non-Anglicans without endangering political stability, the Whigs challenged the monopoly which the Established Church had on political power and confronted the doctrine of the Anglican constitution. Robert Southey, one of the Anglican constitution's most uncompromising defenders in the 1820s, had laid out the doctrine's underlying principles: "religion," he wrote in his *Colloquies on Society*, "is the basis upon which civil government rests." It was from religion that "power derives its authority" and "laws their efficacy." But even more important was Southey's conviction that Anglican Christianity provided the best means to ensure that the people obeyed the government and laws which religion sanctioned. In this respect the doctrine extended into the early nineteenth century the Elizabethan injunction that no state would rest secure unless it was religiously uniform. The union of Church and state would guarantee that those who were brought up in the Anglican faith would remain loyal to the constitution of which the Church was an

---

15 [Thomas Babington Macaulay], "The Present Administration," *Edinburgh Review*, 46 (June, 1827): 260–261.

integral part. For Southey, the religious instruction of the people was one of the state's primary duties precisely because it would improve the moral well-being of the nation as well as encourage obedience to its institutions. Religious dissent, on the other hand, was seditious and morally culpable because it undermined the foundations of obedience and deprived the people of spiritual guidance.[16]

Liberal Anglicans, as Brent has shown, typically responded to High Church Tories like Southey by arguing that Catholics and Protestant Dissenters could exist freely and equally alongside the Established Church without threatening the cohesion of society because as Christians they all adhered to the same basic truths. The points of doctrine, discipline and worship that separated the various Christian denominations were regarded by these liberals as inessential accretions to a common faith which need not stand in the way of social harmony. Macaulay could at times argue this way. In his essay on Burghley, for example, he praised the nondogmatic Christianity of the English people, which during the Reformation had enabled them to accept Catholicism under Mary and then Protestantism under Elizabeth, and he lamented the fact that Elizabeth had not constructed a comprehensive and tolerant religious settlement on that basis.[17] But for his more theoretical statements he chose a secular line of attack. In his essay on Southey, he undermined the Anglican constitution by denying that Christianity sanctioned the exercise of authority in any but the most general way. The real justification for government, he asserted, was the need that people had for the protection of their lives and property. It was not a common religion that ensured social cohesion and loyalty to government, but the requirement of all citizens for security. In his defense of Jewish emancipation, he developed the point further. Because power was derived from property, not religion, the constitution actually granted Jews power when it permitted them to own property. To deny Jews a seat in Parliament was merely to withhold the trappings of what had

---

16 Robert Southey, *Sir Thomas More: Or, Colloquies on the Progress and Prospects of Society*, second edition (London: John Murray, 1831), 1: 349–350. For some of the doctrine's variants, see G. F. A. Best, "The Protestant Constitution and Its Supporters, 1800–1829," *Transactions of the Royal Historical Society*, fifth series, 8 (1958): 105–127.

17 Macaulay, "Nare's *Memoirs of Lord Burghley*," 285–293. For the liberal Anglican position, see Brent, *Liberal Anglican Politics*, 60–61.

already been granted in substance. The effect of Macaulay's polemic was thus to separate politics and religion. Since religious preferences had little bearing on one's capacity for politics, Macaulay saw no reason why a Dissenter, Jewish or otherwise, should not take as great an interest in securing property or make as good a chancellor of the exchequer as an Anglican.[18]

Macaulay then challenged the paternalism on which the Anglican constitution was predicated. Why should the state, he asked rhetorically, be allowed to interfere with the private lives of its subjects and provide them with religious instruction when it was no more likely to arrive at religious truth than they were? Indeed, Macaulay discerned compelling reasons for removing the state altogether from the realm of private belief. Governments, he argued, were wholly inadequate for dealing with religious questions because they relied on force, not reason, in what were actually matters of opinion. History taught that whenever the state interfered with religion, persecution was the likely result. In his essay on Hallam, he emphasized that the Elizabethan preoccupation with uniformity had led to the persecution of the Catholics and Puritans. The Reformation, he argued, was a political act aimed at freeing England from the Papacy and increasing the power of the monarchy. Arising from such origins, the Established Church had become the servant of the state and the opponent of liberty. The Anglican faith was inherently tolerant, acknowledging that salvation could be achieved outside its communion, but once corrupted by politics it began to persecute.[19]

Finally, Macaulay refuted the political assumptions on which the Anglican constitution stood. The history of the Stuarts demonstrated that state interference with religion would neither guarantee political stability nor bring about the moral improvement of the nation. The disputes of the seventeenth century showed clearly that the interests of religion and politics were best served when the two remained separate. Laud's attempt to coerce the

---

[18] [Thomas Babington Macaulay], "Southey's *Colloquies on Society*," *Edinburgh Review*, 50 (January, 1830): 547–548, and "Civil Disabilities of the Jews," *Edinburgh Review*, 52 (January, 1831): 363–367. For the background to Jewish emancipation see Ursula Henriques, "The Jewish Emancipation Controversy in Nineteenth-Century Britain," *Past and Present*, 40 (1968): 126–146, and *Religious Toleration in England, 1787–1833* (Toronto: University of Toronto Press, 1961), 175–205.

[19] Macaulay, "Southey's *Colloquies on Society*," 548–552, "Hallam's *Constitutional History*," 100–110.

Puritans into conformity had turned his victims into rebels who eventually destroyed the monarchy and the Church which had persecuted them. After their victory, the Puritans were obsessed with the need for moral guidance, but their efforts to impose an austere faith merely made a mockery of religion and led to the licentiousness of the Cavaliers following the Restoration.[20] Macaulay went on to suggest that the Established Church had survived during the early nineteenth century precisely because it had refrained from meddling with private consciences, and that a resumption of the policies of Laud, rather than protecting the Church, would incite a rebellion as severe as that of the Puritans. The best defense of Christianity against the inroads of unbelief, he continued, would be to let it stand alone, without the encumbrance of government support, to compete in a free market of ideas: "The real security of Christianity," he wrote, "is to be found in its benevolent morality, in its exquisite adaptation to the human heart, in the facility with which its scheme accommodates itself to the capacity of every human intellect . . . To such a system it can bring no addition of dignity or of strength, that it is part and parcel of the common law . . . The whole history of the Christian religion shows, that she is in far greater danger of being corrupted by the alliance of power, than of being crushed by its opposition."[21]

The position that Macaulay was developing in these essays, written in the years before he assumed his post in India, represented a popular Whiggism that called for a broadening of the political nation to include members of the middle class, regardless of religious affiliation. Looking back on British affairs from India, Macaulay summed up his position in a long article on Sir James Mackintosh. Written late in 1834, the essay presented a spirited defense of the Whigs and their accomplishments at the Revolution, setting out the principles on which the party had acted in 1688. Though it marked a change in Macaulay's rhetorical strategy – he now praised the Revolution whereas he had disparaged it earlier – his ideological position was essentially the same. The Whiggism that emerged from its pages was reforming and popular, based on the premise that political power should be exercised for the public

[20] Macaulay, "Southey's *Colloquies on Society*," 552–553, "Hallam's *Constitutional History*," 110–112, 152–154.
[21] Macaulay, "Southey's *Colloquies on Society*," 553–555.

good, and, in religious matters, thoroughly latitudinarian. The Revolution, coming after the Long Parliament and the exclusion crisis, was the third act in a great popular drama that would culminate in the constitutional revolution of 1828, 1829 and 1832. With his defense of Mackintosh, Macaulay took one of the Whigs' greatest liabilities – their ambivalence toward the French Revolution – and used it to vindicate a tradition of moderate Whiggism that stretched from Charles James Fox, through Mackintosh, to younger Whigs like Macaulay himself. It was a tradition that saw the French Revolution, "in spite of all its crimes and follies," as a "great blessing to mankind," but that also valued order and legitimate authority. The ability to combine the radical's love of liberty with the Tory's love of order, Macaulay claimed, was the Whigs' special strength and qualification for office.[22]

On his return to England, Macaulay threw his full support behind Melbourne's ministry. As he told Lansdowne in December 1838: "I feel that at this juncture no friend of toleration and of temperate liberty is justified in withholding his support from the ministers . . . I would therefore make some sacrifice of ease, leisure, and money, in order to serve the government in the house of Commons."[23] He represented Edinburgh from 1839 until his defeat in the general election of 1847, and then again from 1852 until he retired from the House in 1856, and he served for several years as Minister at War under Melbourne and as Paymaster General under Russell. Religious issues continued to dominate British politics during this period and Macaulay, representing a city with a large and vocal Dissenting population, could not escape the controversies over the Maynooth grant, patronage in the Scottish Kirk, Tractarianism and Papal aggression. Meanwhile, within a year of his return home, he had set to work on his *History of England*, and from then on he gave the book as much time as his other commitments would allow. His first two volumes were published in 1848, the second two in 1855, and a final volume appeared posthumously in 1861. Not surprisingly, religious discussions figured prominently in them all.

---

22 [Thomas Babington Macaulay], "Sir James Mackintosh's *History of the Revolution*," *Edinburgh Review*, 61 (July, 1835): 273–278, 283–322.
23 Macaulay to Lord Lansdowne (19 December 1838), *Letters*, 3: 266.

II

Macaulay's personal religion will always remain an enigma. Born into one of England's great Evangelical families, he seems to have outgrown the faith in which he was raised just as he deviated from his father's Tory politics. Although there is little evidence in either his journals or letters of an active Christian life, which has led some commentators to suggest religious indifference, there is also little evidence of a hostility to Christianity. Indeed, Macaulay seems to have retained a lasting respect for Christianity as a moral system capable of appealing to the human spirit. As he wrote in his essay on Southey, the strength of Christianity was its "benevolent morality," its "exquisite adaptation to the human heart," its ability to accommodate the "human intellect."[24] What discouraged Macaulay about the Christian faith was not its moral essence, but rather the doctrinal absurdities that had grown up around it. In his review of Ranke's *History of the Popes*, he derided the discipline of theology. Compared to the natural sciences, theology was an inherently ambiguous enterprise because it dealt with matters beyond the reach of human reason. Despite centuries of effort, the world's theologians, from Socrates to Paley, had still not arrived at a definitive answer to any of their questions.[25] But we must be careful not to mistake Macaulay's impatience with theological speculation for an aversion to Christianity itself, and we must not place him among religion's enemies. Though he applauded the *philosophes* for their love of justice, seeing within it a Christian morality, he also scolded them for attacking Christianity "with a rancour and an unfairness disgraceful to men who called them-selves philosophers."[26]

As Macaulay grappled in the 1840s and 1850s with the practical problems of Church and state, he adopted a latitudinarian approach that was consistent with his nondogmatic appreciation of the Christian faith. Acknowledging that Britain was religiously plural, he believed that denominational differences could be overcome if people, who otherwise agreed on the basic truths of

---

[24] Macaulay, "Southey's *Colloquies on Society*," 555.
[25] [Thomas Babington Macaulay], "Ranke's *History of the Popes* – Revolutions of the Papacy," *Edinburgh Review*, 72 (October, 1840): 229–232.
[26] Ibid., 253-254.

Christianity, would only accept the greatest diversity on those inessential matters that divided them. Certainly, for one who distrusted dogmatic assertions, convinced that more often than not they were mixed with error, disagreements on such intangibles as the Eucharist or baptism were never sufficient grounds for depriving men of their political rights. Politics for Macaulay was a practical affair in which doctrinal disputes had no place. In what was perhaps a close approximation to his own position, Macaulay once praised Francis Bacon for being tolerant and pragmatic at a time when Europe was convulsed with pointless and often destructive theological controversy: "He was, we are convinced, a sincere believer in the divine authority of the Christian revelation . . . He loved to consider that religion as the bond of charity; the curb of evil passions; the consolation of the wretched; the support of the timid; the hope of the dying. But controversies on speculative points of theology seem to have engaged scarcely any portion of his attention . . . While the world was resounding with the noise of a disputatious philosophy, and a disputatious theology, the Baconian school . . . preserved a calm neutrality, – half scornful, half benevolent, and, content with adding to the sum of practical good, left the war of words to those who liked it."[27]

Macaulay's concern with encouraging an undogmatic approach to religious politics found expression in his *History*, where he celebrated the Revolution as an important, though incomplete, triumph of latitudinarian principles. He traced to the 1680s the clear demarcation between the High Church party, anxious to preserve the exclusive rights and privileges of a narrowly defined Anglican Establishment, and the Low Church, or latitudinarian party, ready to tolerate Dissent and to broaden the doctrines and practices of the Establishment so as to include as many Protestants as possible. Leading the latitudinarians was William III, the hero of Macaulay's *History*, and in his portrayal of William, Macaulay made his own liberal sentiments clear. William was a Calvinist, but unlike other adherents of that faith, he was neither intolerant nor dogmatic. He abhorred all persecution, and was flexible concerning forms of church government and worship. He accepted Episcopacy and the Anglican ritual as perfectly legitimate, but did not consider them in any way essential to Christianity. Other kinds of

27 [Thomas Babington Macaulay], "Lord Bacon," *Edinburgh Review*, 65 (July, 1837): 87.

ecclesiastical government and worship, the Presbyterian and
Calvinist for instance, he found just as valid, perhaps even
preferable. Because William was able to envision a religiously
plural society, in which a variety of Protestants, sharing a common
Christianity, organized and practiced their faiths in different ways,
he was well suited to arrange a compromise between Anglicanism
and Dissent.[28] His legacy was the religious settlement of 1689, in
which the English Dissenters were granted toleration and the
Presbyterian Kirk was established in Scotland.

In contrast to his admiration for William's pragmatic liberalism,
Macaulay deplored the bigotry of James II. He rejected outright
those interpretations that presented James as a misunderstood
advocate of toleration. The enthusiasm with which he persecuted
the Presbyterians of Scotland, if nothing else, served to refute such
claims on his behalf. Macaulay criticized James precisely because
he tried to advance one religious sect by persecuting all others.
Only a genuinely tolerant policy, pursued within the bounds of
the constitution, could have won for England's Catholic minority
complete civil and religious liberty. James, however, resorted to
persecution, turning first against the Puritans and then against the
Church of England, only to lose his crown and set back the Catholic
cause. Indeed, one of Macaulay's most serious accusations was that
James, the most influential Catholic of his age, had the means to
eliminate the English prejudice against Catholicism, but failed
to do so. Had James governed morally and legally, Macaulay
suggested, had he demonstrated that Catholicism was compatible
with the constitution, then the antipathy which much of the nation
felt toward the Catholics would have abated considerably and
emancipation might have come much earlier than it did.[29]

In his own approach to contemporary religious problems,
Macaulay was as undogmatic and as practical as either Bacon or
William. "Expediency" was the word he used most often when
addressing questions of Church and state. As he explained to Adam
Black: "I do not agree with the High Churchmen in thinking that
the state is always bound to teach religious faith to the people. I do
not agree with the Voluntaries in thinking that it is always wrong in
a state to support a religious establishment. I think the question a

[28] Macaulay, *Works*, 2: 327–328, 345, 399–400, 4: 15–16.
[29] Ibid., 1: 518–525, 2: 162–167.

question of expediency, to be decided on a comparison of good and evil effects."[30] In his critique of Gladstone's *State in Its Relations with the Church*, a High Anglican defense of the Establishment, as well as in his Parliamentary speeches, Macaulay extended the principles he had set down earlier in his article on Southey. While on a theoretical level he may have considered the coupling of government and religion pernicious, in practice he was presented with circumstances, arising from the nation's past, that must be treated pragmatically. In essence Macaulay's arguments were utilitarian. Churches were institutions set up to provide the people with religious instruction, and whatever relationship they took to the state, it should be the one best suited to carry out this purpose. Under certain circumstances, where denominational diversity was found alongside general affluence, the voluntary system might make sense. But in a country such as Ireland, where the vast majority of the people adhered to a single faith and were too poor to procure religious instruction on their own, the state was justified in endowing the Catholic priesthood. The specific doctrine sponsored by the government must be acceptable to the majority of the nation, for only then would the Church find a receptive audience for its teaching. Reasoning such as this, based on considerations of expediency rather than doctrine, led Macaulay to defend the Established Churches in England and Scotland because they effectively met the spiritual needs of their communities, and to condemn the Protestant Church of Ireland because it represented the faith of only a minority. Though he often defended religious establishments, Macaulay was equally sympathetic to the needs of Dissenters. Whenever the state chose to support a specific religion, he cautioned, it must not forget that its primary responsibility was secular, to protect the lives and property of its subjects. It must never persecute, nor should it make use of civil disabilities in order to enforce conformity. These considerations led Macaulay to conclude that Dissenters should always enjoy the same rights and privileges as members of the Establishment.[31]

All through his career Macaulay advocated a politics of compromise that he found particularly appropriate to religious

---

[30] Macaulay to Adam Black (20 November 1840), *Letters*, 3: 346.
[31] [Thomas Babington Macaulay], "Church and State," *Edinburgh Review*, 69 (April, 1839): 273–280. See also his Speech on the Church of Ireland (23 April 1845), *Works*, 12: 139–153.

controversy. He believed that such laudable principles as absolute free trade or religious liberty must be brought into line with reality, modified and diluted by existing circumstances, if they were to be implemented with any degree of success. Reform was a gradual process made up of partial and imperfect measures. Legislation of any kind, despite what may be its abstract perfection, would achieve little good if it proved unacceptable to the majority of the nation. As early as 1832, he explained to a member of the Leeds Political Union that the successful politician must define his goals "not according to his views of what might in itself be desirable, but according to his views of what might be practicable."[32] Years later, as member of Parliament for Edinburgh, he confronted the intransigence of his electors on the Corn Laws. As an advocate of free trade, he opposed all tariffs on imported grain, but believing in the early 1840s that the total abolition of the Corn Laws was at the moment unobtainable, he was content to support partial measures. Unfortunately, this position drew censure from the Edinburgh Anti-Corn Law Association, which stood for complete abolition and nothing less. Stressing the need for compromise, Macaulay explained his views: ultimate goals, no matter how admirable, must be subordinate to "practical prudence." The politician who "wish[ed] to effect practical good must often be content to obtain it by instalments, to purchase support by concessions, and to mitigate evils which he would gladly destroy."[33]

It was the intransigence of religious controversy, however, that tried Macaulay's patience most of all. Hoping to demonstrate the usefulness of compromise, he offered in his *History* the Toleration Bill of 1689 as an example of ecclesiastical legislation worthy of emulation. The bill was certainly imperfect in theory, acknowledging that persecution was still the rule and toleration only the exception, and it was also inconsistent, granting toleration to the Quaker, for instance, on grounds which it denied to the Independent. And yet the bill possessed one great advantage: it "removed a vast mass of evil without shocking a vast mass of prejudice." The contradictions, compromises and partial measures which it contained, Macaulay argued, were necessary to ensure its

[32] Macaulay to John Smithson (11 August 1832), *Letters*, 2: 178.
[33] Macaulay to John Howison (1 May 1844), ibid., 4: 185–186.

acceptance by the nation. The Toleration Bill passed both houses of Parliament with ease, whereas the Comprehension Bill, a far more perfect piece of "legislative workmanship" when viewed abstractly, failed because it was not "adapted to the wants, the feelings, and the prejudices of the existing generation."[34]

Macaulay's latitudinarianism did not go unnoticed and not surprisingly it provoked the more zealous among his audience. Evangelicals of all denominations accused him of religious indifference. The *Christian Observer*, for instance, which Macaulay's father had once edited, complained of Macaulay's lack of religious "earnestness" – "no one mode of faith or discipline," the reviewer noted, "except as it is supposed to bear upon the civil interests of the community, appears to have much preference in his eyes" – and then went on to lament that Macaulay was no longer the partisan of "scriptural religion" that his father had been. The Evangelical and Congregationalist editor of the *British Quarterly Review*, Robert Vaughan, similarly remarked that the cause of true religion had suffered because of Macaulay's "practical scepticism". Even the Catholic *Rambler* was struck by Macaulay's apparent indifference, his refusal to judge on theological questions and his complacent belief that "*all* religions are good, if a man be sincere and benevolent, and say his prayers (in some shape or other)."[35] But the kind of sectarian partisanship represented by these reviewers was precisely the affliction that Macaulay wanted to see eliminated from Victorian politics. Indeed, one purpose of his *History* was to promote a model of political conduct that would encourage moderation by reducing religious controversy. So long as sectarian passions inflamed the nation, prudent and moderate politics would remain unobtainable since Parliamentary government was, for Macaulay, an imperfect process, requiring from its participants a willingness to compromise that was rarely found among religious controversialists. The latitudinarian approach, which set out to remove the disabilities against Catholics and Protestant Dissenters, aimed at tempering sectarian politics by alleviating the inequities on which they prospered. Macaulay further criticized

34 Macaulay, *Works*, 3: 374–383.
35 "Review of Macaulay's *History of England*," *Christian Observer* (January, 1850): 61, 64–65. [Robert Vaughan], Postscript to "The Art of History – Macaulay," *British Quarterly Review*, 23 (April, 1856): 324–325. "Macaulay's *History of England*," *Rambler*, 3 (February, 1849): 421.

religious parties because their vision was myopic, focusing on the interests of one denomination while ignoring what was best for the nation as a whole. Indeed, it was their unreasonable tendency to sacrifice large goods for small gains that annoyed Macaulay most of all.

III

The repeal of the Test and Corporation Acts in 1828 and the extension of the franchise in 1832 gave Dissent an official voice in British politics for the first time since the Interregnum. As a result of these constitutional changes, Dissenters would play a prominent role in early Victorian politics, and to win their support would become a problem that would occupy the Whigs in the years to come. In the 1830s, Melbourne's government appealed successfully to Dissenters by sponsoring a significant body of legislation, including granting a charter to the London University, breaking the Establishment's hold on the registration of births, deaths and marriages, and permitting Nonconforming clergymen to preside over marriages. But this was as far as the Whigs would go, and their reluctance to press for more extensive reforms eventually cost them the wholehearted support of many Dissenters. Their failure to abolish Church rates in 1837 and to pass an acceptable program for national, nonsectarian education in 1839 discouraged many Nonconformists, turning them into advocates of voluntaryism and disestablishment. In the 1840s and 1850s, the Dissenters threatened to become political adversaries whenever the Whigs displayed too great a fondness for the Establishment or began to contemplate the endowment of Catholicism in Ireland, a policy which many Nonconformists thought violated the voluntary principle.[36]

Macaulay, no less than his party, found it difficult to please the Dissenters. As member of Parliament for Edinburgh, he was dependent on the city's Nonconformist electorate. On one level, he was genuinely sympathetic to their needs. He believed that the state should regard Churchmen and Dissenters as equals, and he

---

[36] For the role of Dissent in early Victorian politics, see: Norman Gash, *Reaction and Reconstruction in English Politics, 1832–1852* (Oxford: Clarendon Press, 1965). G. I. T. Machin, *Politics and the Churches in Great Britain, 1832 to 1868* (Oxford: Clarendon Press, 1977). Richard Brent, *Liberal Anglican Politics*.

supported everything the Whigs had done for the Dissenters since the repeal of the Test and Corporation Acts. He saw no reason why Dissenters should pay taxes to finance an Established Church which they chose not to attend, he supported the creation of a nonsectarian system of state-funded education and he argued in Parliament for the abolition of religious tests in the Scottish universities. He thought that positions such as school inspectors and prison chaplains should be open to Dissenters as well as to Churchmen, and that the Scottish Church should relinquish its monopoly on printing the Bible.[37]

And yet Macaulay never won the Dissenters' complete approval. His pragmatic approach to practical problems and his readiness to accept partial measures led some of Edinburgh's Dissenters to accuse him and his party of equivocation. Voluntaries took exception to his defense of the Established Churches in England and Scotland, and especially to his willingness to endow the Catholic clergy in Ireland. Macaulay replied that the Dissenters' demands were too inflexible. He grew impatient with their reluctance to compromise with the Establishment on insignificant matters in order to win its support for more important reforms such as a national system of education. The Scottish Dissenters, he complained, were prepared to sacrifice the public good for "some trifling matters of punctilio," and he criticized the narrowness of their vision, their tendency to regard all issues "merely as Dissenters" and not as "citizens."[38] By 1843, Macaulay's stand on religious questions was at such odds with the opinions of his electors that he considered Edinburgh, "for the present, lost. The demands of the liberals, heated as they are by religious fanaticism, are such as I will not comply with. I will not vote for the abolition of the Churches now established in this island; and I will support any well-digested plan for establishing the Catholic Church in Ireland."[39] When Macaulay finally lost his seat for Edinburgh in 1847, he attributed the defeat

37  Macaulay to Adam Black (20 November 1840), to Duncan McLaren (5 December 1840), to Duncan McLaren (11 December 1840), to Andrew Rutherfurd (16 July 1845), to Duncan McLaren (11 April 1853), to Dr. John Lee (16 July 1853), to Adam Black (? January 1854), to Adam Black (20 January 1854), to Frances Macaulay (24 September 1859), *Letters*, 3: 346, 350–352, 355–358, 4: 262, 5: 325, 341, 377, 379, 6: 238–239. Macaulay, Speech on Theological Tests in the Scottish Universities (9 July 1845), *Works*, 12: 163–183.
38  Macaulay to Duncan McLaren (15 June, 5 and 11 December 1840), *Letters*, 3: 327, 350–352, 355–358.
39  Macaulay to Sir James Gibson Craig (24 November 1843), ibid., 4: 161.

in part to the displeasure he had caused among "Dissenters, Voluntaries, Free Churchmen."[40]

Macaulay's ambivalence toward the Dissenters no doubt colored his assessment of the Puritans in his *History*. On the one hand, he dismissed the Puritans as religious enthusiasts, noting sardonically the varieties of their fanaticism:

they mistook their own vindictive feelings for emotions of piety, encouraged in themselves by reading and meditation a disposition to brood over their wrongs, and, when they had worked themselves up into hating their enemies, imagined that they were only hating the enemies of heaven . . . The extreme Puritan was at once known from other men by his gait, his garb, his lank hair, the sour solemnity of his face, the upturned white of his eyes, and nasal twang with which he spoke, and above all, by his peculiar dialect.[41]

After their victory, the Puritans became dangerous radicals and their zeal turned oppressive: "They proved," Macaulay concluded, " . . . as intolerant and as meddling as ever Laud had been."[42] And yet Macaulay was equally aware of the Puritans' more attractive features, particularly their achievements in the cause of liberty. By pointing out how their fanaticism had developed as a reaction to the persecution they had suffered at the hands of the Church, he lessened the severity of that criticism. In the struggle against the Stuarts, he noted, it was the Puritans who provided the Parliamentary opposition with much of its strength. The image of Cromwell that emerged from Macaulay's *History* was as laudatory as the eulogy he had presented many years earlier in his essay on Milton. Cromwell's achievements were prodigious: he built a formidable army which defeated the Royalists and brought glory to England, he tried to arrange a compromise between Charles and the Parliament, and after the king's execution he restored as much of England's traditional constitution as circumstances would permit. In the end, Macaulay tried to free Cromwell from the charges of hypocrisy, fanaticism and republicanism that had routinely been leveled at him by the opponents of radicalism and Dissent.[43]

---

[40] Macaulay to Mrs. Charles Trevelyan (30 July 1847), ibid., 4: 341.
[41] Macaulay, *Works*, 1: 84–86.
[42] Ibid., 1: 122–123, 124–126, 133–135, 138, 168–172.
[43] Ibid., 1: 63, 84, 108, 123–124, 126–129, 130–133, 138–146.

In British political rhetoric, Puritanism was an evocative term. Connoting political extremism, cultural superficiality and hypocrisy, it was frequently applied to those Dissenters or radicals whose activities placed them outside the nation's traditional institutions. During the French Revolution, for example, Edmund Burke had attempted to discredit Dissenters like the Unitarian Richard Price by linking them with the radicalism of seventeenth-century Puritanism, and John Wilson Croker used the same rhetorical strategy to disparage reformers at the time of the first Reform Bill. By the mid-Victorian years, Matthew Arnold would accuse Nonconformists of Puritanism in order to highlight what he took to be their cultural provincialism. Macaulay himself was not above using the term pejoratively, as when he tried to revile the followers of Jeremy Bentham by characterizing them as modern-day Puritans. Given the close association in contemporary rhetoric between Puritanism and Dissent, it is hardly surprising that Macaulay's ambivalence toward the Puritans in his *History* elicited a double-sided response from Nonconformist readers. On the one hand, they welcomed his favorable interpretation of Cromwell. "Full justice is done by Mr. Macaulay to the personal character of Cromwell," declared the Nonconformist *Eclectic Review*, "nor are we disposed to take much exception to the view given of his adminis-tration . . . England had never witnessed such a combination of legislative wisdom with administrative vigour."[44] But above all, Dissenters objected to Macaulay's description of the Puritans as fanatics. Walter Bagehot, for instance, writing in the Unitarian *National Review*, claimed that Macaulay was simply unable to comprehend the "passionate eras" of the past. "The whole course of his personal fortunes, the entire scope of his historical narrative, show an utter want of sympathy with the Puritan disposition." For a more complete appreciation of Puritan "passion," Bagehot directed his readers to Thomas Carlyle, whose biography of Cromwell displayed an "instinctive sympathy" toward its subject: "No one will now ever overlook, that in the greater, in the original Puritans – in Cromwell, for example – the whole basis of the character was a passionate, deep, rich, religious organisation."[45]

But regardless of Macaulay's ambivalence toward Puritanism,

44 "Macaulay's *History of England*," *Eclectic Review*, 25, new series (January, 1849): 8–9.
45 [Walter Bagehot], "Mr. Macaulay," *National Review*, 2 (April, 1856): 364, 368, 370.

the lasting contribution of his *History* was to make the case for admitting Dissenters into the political nation. However fanatical they may have been during the Civil War, their conduct at the Revolution, when they united with Churchmen to defend the constitution, showed that they had become responsible citizens deserving the full benefits of English citizenship. Hoping to enlist the Dissenters in his attack on the Church, James had used the dispensing power, a prerogative considered incompatible with constitutional government, to grant them toleration. It was in their interest as Dissenters to accept this toleration, even though they would acknowledge in the process that the king possessed absolute powers. As Macaulay pointed out, James had every reason to expect the Dissenters to acquiesce in his use of the dispensing power, despite the dangers it posed to good government, since in the past the constitution, with its alliance of Church and state, had never protected them from persecution. And yet, at this crisis, the most influential Dissenters chose to act not simply as Dissenters, but as citizens, rallying behind the Church and resisting the king. "At this conjuncture," Macaulay reflected, "the Protestant Dissenters of London won for themselves a title to the lasting gratitude of their country . . . The time had come when it was necessary to make a choice; and the Nonconformists of the City, with a noble spirit, arrayed themselves side by side with the members of the Church in defence of the fundamental laws of the realm."[46]

Macaulay's account of the Revolution, then, served as an argument for granting Nonconformists full membership in the political community and as an illustration of the responsibilities that such citizenship entailed. One of Macaulay's principal complaints about the Dissenters had been that their denominational interests often blinded them to their obligations as citizens. At the Revolution, however, they had for once acted in a way that was not narrowly sectarian. Responsible conduct, Macaulay was arguing, demanded from the Dissenters a willingness to compromise with others, and above all with the Anglican Church, that they rarely exhibited. In support of his case, Macaulay pointed to the example of the Presbyterian Richard Baxter, who was among Dissenters what the latitudinarians were among Churchmen: "He

[46] Macaulay, *Works*, 2: 367–399, 508–509, 517–521.

heartily concurred in the Restoration, and was sincerely desirous to bring about an union between Episcopalians and Presbyterians. For, with a liberality rare in his time, he considered questions of ecclesiastical polity as of small account when compared with the great principles of Christianity, and had never, even when prelacy was most odious to the ruling powers, joined in the outcry against Bishops . . . His political opinions, in spite of the oppression which he and his brethren had suffered, were moderate."[47] It was precisely this kind of moderation that he found so lamentably absent among the Scottish Dissenters and that his *History* aimed to encourage.

IV

Ireland was the other great area of religious conflict that Macaulay and the Whigs had to contend with in the 1830s and 1840s. An Irish minority in the Commons after 1833 and the growing strength of O'Connell's movement for the repeal of the union ensured that the problem would receive immediate attention. Determined to preserve the union at all costs, the Whigs hoped to win the confidence of the Irish by redressing at least some of their grievances and, in particular, by reforming the Protestant Church of Ireland. They were prepared to reduce the size of the Irish Establishment, and the more liberal among them were ready to appropriate its surplus revenue for purposes benefiting the entire nation. They were willing to commute the tithe and they seriously considered endowing the Catholic clergy. For many Tories, however, concessions to Catholicism were unacceptable attacks on the Irish Establishment. Convinced that a common Protestant Church was the principal bond uniting England and Ireland, the Tories were afraid that concessions to Catholicism would represent the first steps toward disestablishment and the eventual rupture of the union. A strong conservative and Protestant opposition in the Lords ensured that the Whigs would only succeed partially in their efforts at Irish Church reform. They reduced the Establishment in 1833, commuted the tithe in 1838 and supported Peel's grant to the Catholic seminary at Maynooth in 1845. But to appropriate

---

[47] Ibid., 1: 513.

Irish Church revenue or endow the Catholic clergy remained impossible.[48]

Macaulay emerged from the Parliamentary debates of the early 1830s a staunch upholder of the union. Repeal, he argued, would not solve Ireland's problems since most of these had originated before the union itself. During the debates on the Coercion Bill in 1833, he recommended that force be used in Ireland to maintain the union, and he urged the suspension of habeas corpus and trial by jury in order to put an end to the disturbances caused by the tithe war and the movement for repeal. But Macaulay was not simply a spokesman for English supremacy. Like other Whigs, he advocated reform as the only way to create a durable relationship between the two nations. In 1833, he endorsed the Whigs' Irish Church Temporalities Bill, which called for a significant reduction in the number of bishoprics and active parishes. He considered the revenue of the Irish Church to be "public property" and believed that "a considerable portion of the church property ought . . . to be applied to public services . . . "[49]

After returning to English politics in 1839, Macaulay continued to promote measures aimed at removing the inequalities that marred the religious settlement in Ireland. His position was consistent with his latitudinarian principles and remarkably farsighted. At least once he hinted privately that he was prepared to disestablish the Church of Ireland. "Let us once get rid of those [Corn] laws and of the Irish Church," he wrote to his sister in 1839, "and I shall begin to think of being a Conservative."[50] But most of the time he advocated using the property of the Irish Establishment to endow the Catholic priesthood, though he knew that for the moment this too was impractical. As he explained to Macvey Napier in 1843:

---

[48] For the Whig response to the Irish problem, see: A. D. Kriegel, "The Irish Policy of Lord Grey's Government," *English Historical Review*, 86 (1971): 22–45. Mary D. Condon, "The Irish Church and the Reform Ministries," *Journal of British Studies*, 3 (1964): 120–142. Donald Harman Akenson, *The Church of Ireland: Ecclesiastical Reform and Revolution, 1800–1885* (New Haven: Yale University Press, 1971), 146–194. Brent, *Liberal Anglican Politics*, 65–103. Machin, *Politics and the Churches*. Angus Macintyre, *The Liberator: Daniel O'Connell and the Irish Party, 1830–1847* (London: Hamish Hamilton, 1965).

[49] Macaulay, Speech on Repeal of the Union with Ireland (16 February 1833), *Works*, 11: 519–521, 523–526, Speech on the Disturbances (Ireland) Bill (28 February 1833) and Speech on Church Reform, Ireland (1 April 1833), *Speeches by the Rt. Hon. Thomas Babington Macaulay, M.P.* (New York: Redfield, 1853), 1: 217–218, 239. Macaulay to Joseph Lees (15 March 1832), *Letters*, 2: 116.

[50] Macaulay to Frances Macaulay (29 January 1839), *Letters*, 3: 275.

My own view is this. I do not on principle object to the paying of the Irish Catholic priests. I regret that such a step was not taken in 1829. I would even now gladly support any well digested plan which might be likely to succeed. But I fear that the difficulties are insurmountable.

And he continued:

I . . . would transfer a large part of the Irish Church revenues from the Protestants to the Catholics. For such a measure I should think it my duty to vote, though I were certain that my vote would cost me my seat in parliament.[51]

Speaking in Parliament on the condition of Ireland in 1843, he pronounced the Irish Church indefensible since it had failed in its main purpose of providing the people with religious instruction, and he recommended that it be reduced further to reflect the actual size of Ireland's Protestant community.[52] He voted for the Maynooth grant in 1845, and spoke in favor of an amendment that would provide funding for the seminary out of the surplus revenue of the Establishment. He condemned the Irish Church as a "most absurd" institution because it served only a small portion of the population and yet received the exclusive support of the state. Addressing the Tories' fears that any alteration in the Irish Establishment would threaten the union, Macaulay suggested that the Church's unpopularity, in fact, posed the greatest obstacle to a peaceful settlement in Ireland. The best way to safeguard the union would be to respect the religious preferences of the Irish people.[53]

In his *History*, Macaulay approached the Irish problem in a manner consistent with his other pronouncements. He provided his readers with an interpretation of the Anglo-Irish past designed in part to reconcile the two nations, moderate the religious conflict and strengthen the union. But no matter how genuinely Macaulay may have intended his *History* to mediate between religious and national parties, it was little calculated to appeal to an Irish or Catholic audience since it looked at the seventeenth-century origins of the Irish problem from a perspective that was unabashedly Protestant and English. A condescending belief in the

[51] Macaulay to Macvey Napier (25 November 1843), ibid., 4: 162.
[52] Macaulay, Speech on the State of Ireland (7 July 1843), *Speeches*, 2: 168–169.
[53] Macaulay, Speech on the Church of Ireland (23 April 1845), *Works*, 12: 139, 142, 154–157.

superiority of Protestantism colored everything he wrote about the Anglo-Irish past. Equating Protestantism with progress, he made Catholicism synonymous with material, political and intellectual backwardness. "From the time when the barbarians overran the Western Empire," he asserted, "to the time of the revival of letters, the influence of the Church of Rome had been generally favorable to science, to civilization, and to good government. But, during the last three centuries, to stunt the growth of the human mind has been her chief object. Throughout Christendom, whatever advance has been made in knowledge, in freedom, in wealth, and in the arts of life, has been made in spite of her, and has everywhere been in inverse proportion to her power."[54]

Catholics, as we might expect, considered these observations offensive. John Henry Newman, for one, felt called upon to answer the charge that Catholicism promoted backwardness.[55] C. W. Russell, the Irish Catholic co-editor of the *Dublin Review*, grew increasingly indignant at Macaulay's often "gratuitous" anti-Catholicism and at his unfair treatment of such prominent Catholics as James II and Mary of Modena. Russell, it seems, had expected something different. Aware of Macaulay's reputation as an outspoken advocate of Irish reform, he had looked forward to a history that would show greater "liberality" toward the Irish and Catholics. Instead, he was given a narrative permeated with Protestant "bigotry."[56] The Catholic *Rambler* also grew disillusioned with Macaulay's work. Reviewing his first volume, it deemed Macaulay more "impartial" on religious matters than most Protestant historians even though his discussion of Catholicism was distorted by "misconception, error, and irreligious ideas." But as subsequent volumes appeared, the *Rambler* became more and more critical of their "anti-Catholic *animus*," accusing Macaulay of

[54] Ibid., 1: 49–50.

[55] John Henry Newman, *Certain Difficulties Felt by Anglicans in Catholic Teaching Considered*, new impression (London: Longmans, Green and Co., 1918), 229–260. Although Newman never mentioned Macaulay in this lecture, Macaulay was certain that he was its intended target: "Read among other things Newman's lectures just published . . . One lecture is evidently directed against me, though not by name; and I am quite willing that the public should judge between us." Journal (12 October [1850]).

[56] [C. W. Russell], "Macaulay's *History of England*," *Dublin Review*, 26 (June, 1849): 393–394, 396–400, 404–433, and "Macaulay's *History of England*," *Dublin Review*, 40 (March, 1856): 158–168.

misrepresenting facts and choosing his authorities selectively in order to malign Catholics such as James II, Louis XIV and the Jesuits.[57]

Macaulay's *History* was also informed by an Anglo-Saxon ethnocentrism that drew conceptually on the developmental approach to society found in the writings of the Scottish conjectural historians. Beneath the religious conflict in Ireland, Macaulay saw a much deeper antagonism between "races," between the Anglo-Saxon English who had conquered and the Celtic Irish who had succumbed. These two races, he asserted, were at "widely different stages of civilization," a difference in development that he attributed to racial characteristics, religion and the accidents of history. Implicit in his analysis was the conviction that the seventeenth-century Celts shared more in common with primitive societies than they did with their more advanced Anglo-Saxon contemporaries. To contrast the English colonizers with the Irish colonized, Macaulay frequently made use of Victorian anthropological stereotyping, referring to the Irish as "savage" or "aboriginal," and giving them habits such as laziness, slovenliness, drunkenness or polygamy often associated with other conquered peoples of the empire.[58] This developmental approach provided Macaulay with one possible way of conceptualizing the Irish problem. Before a lasting reconciliation between the two nations could take place, the Irish must achieve the same level of civilization as the English. As always, England provided the standard against which Ireland was to be judged: "There could not be equality," Macaulay claimed, "between men who lived in houses, and men who lived in sties, between men who were fed on bread and men who were fed on potatoes, between men who spoke the noble tongue of great philosophers and poets, and men who, with perverted pride, boasted that they could not writhe their mouths into chattering such a jargon as that in

---

57 "Macaulay's *History of England*," *Rambler*, 3 (February, 1849): 422, 425, and 3 (March, 1849): 523. "Macaulay's *History of England*," *Rambler*, 17 (February, 1856): 149–155, and 17 (March, 1856): 208–212.

58 Macaulay, *Works*, 2: 289, 291. For the developmental views of the Scottish historians, see J. W. Burrow, *Evolution and Society: A Study in Victorian Social Theory* (Cambridge: Cambridge University Press, 1966), 10–16, and for their influence on Macaulay, see Burrow, *Liberal Descent*, 41. For other examples of how the Victorians stereotyped the Irish in this way, see L. Perry Curtis, Jr., *Apes and Angels: The Irishman in Victorian Caricature* (Washington: Smithsonian Institution Press, 1971).

which the Advancement of Learning and the Paradise Lost were written."[59]

Macaulay, however, believed in the union, and at least one purpose of his *History* was to present an interpretation of the Anglo-Irish past that would help reconcile the two nations. Despite his deep-seated religious and ethnic prejudices, he saw no reason why in the long run England and Ireland could not be brought together for their mutual benefit. In formulating such an interpretation, however, Macaulay had to confront the anti-Catholicism that had provided so much of the impetus behind the events of 1688. Spokesmen for the Establishment had typically represented the Revolution as the triumph of Protestantism over Catholicism in both England and Ireland. Indeed, members of the Protestant Ascendancy regarded William as a hero precisely because his victory over James had finally ensured their supremacy, and the lesson they drew from the Revolution was that Protestant interests required the subjugation of Irish Catholicism. In the political rhetoric of the Anglo-Irish, William was presented as a defender of the faith, and the Revolution was used to sanction a century and a half of Protestant dominion. As one perceptive spokesman for the Ascendancy remarked, referring specifically to Macaulay: "The advocate and admirer of the Whig William of England, is under the necessity of being the advocate and admirer of the Orange William of Ireland."[60]

But Macaulay never intended to apologize for the Ascendancy, and in his *History* he reversed this Protestant rhetoric by demonstrating that intolerance toward Catholics was not intrinsic to the Whiggism of the Revolution. In 1688, he argued, the Whigs pursued anti-Catholic policies because the king gave them no alternative. So long as James persisted in using Catholic appointees to subvert the constitution, the Whigs had no option but to restrict all political, ecclesiastical and military offices to Protestants. This apparent anti-Catholicism, Macaulay implied, was not essential to Whiggism, which was for the most part latitudinarian, but was rather the unfortunate product of circumstances unique to the 1680s.[61] Macaulay then went on to justify the anti-Catholicism of

[59] Macaulay, *Works*, 2: 296–297.
[60] "Macaulay's *History of England*," *Dublin University Magazine*, 47 (February, 1856): 152.
[61] Macaulay, *Works*, 2: 403–409.

the Revolutionary settlement in Ireland. It was necessary, he claimed, because James, whose common religion with the Irish and common nationality with the English should have made him an ideal mediator, had failed to arrange a compromise between the contending parties. Had he guaranteed the English settlers the possession of their lands, compensated the Irish for their losses, governed justly without favoring one religion over the other, and enlisted the Catholic hierarchy in the cause of peace, then relations between the two nations might have improved. But instead, James did the opposite. He attempted to reverse the existing property arrangements, reassert Irish supremacy, promote Catholicism exclusively and use an Irish army to subvert the English constitution. It was these myopic policies, Macaulay argued, not the anti-Catholicism of the Whigs, that brought ruin to Ireland.[62]

The lessons of the Revolution finally taught that England and Ireland could be united much as England and Scotland had been brought together after the union of 1707. Macaulay found the Scottish parallel particularly germane since in the case of Scotland a religious conflict similar to the one dividing England and Ireland had been overcome. For much of the seventeenth century, he pointed out, the Stuarts had tried to impose Episcopacy on the reluctant Scottish Presbyterians, and the consequences of this intolerance had been nearly a hundred years of animosity. Following the Revolution, however, the Whigs had abandoned this policy. Realizing that harmony between the kingdoms could only be achieved if the Scots were allowed to worship in their own way, the Whigs established Presbyterianism as the state religion of Scotland, which brought the ecclesiastical conflict to an end and laid the groundwork for political unification. The union of 1707, Macaulay wrote, "has been a blessing because, in constituting one State, it left two Churches . . . Had there been an amalgamation of the hierarchies, there never would have been an amalgamation of the nations."[63] For Macaulay, the resolution of the Scottish problem was the crowning achievement of William's latitudinarian principles. His undogmatic approach to ecclesiastical questions and his ties to both Presbyterianism and Episcopacy had enabled him to negotiate between the two religious parties. "He was the King of a prelatical kingdom," Macaulay explained: "He was the Prime

[62] Ibid., 2: 287, 294–298, 5: 118–124.     [63] Ibid., 4: 9–13.

Minister of a presbyterian republic . . . His conscience was neutral. For it was his deliberate opinion that no form of ecclesiastical polity was of divine institution . . . Which form of [church] government should be adopted was in his judgment a question of mere expediency."[64] The lesson for Ireland was obvious. Before England and Ireland could be joined peacefully and beneficially, the policy of maintaining a Protestant Establishment in Ireland enjoying exclusive rights and privileges must come to an end, and Catholicism must receive at least a measure of state recognition.


v


The breakdown of the Anglican constitution between 1828 and 1832 raised the question of whether the state should retain the authority to regulate the spiritual and temporal affairs of the Church for the benefit of the nation. So long as the Anglican Establishment had enjoyed a virtual monopoly on political power, the Erastian relationship between Church and state had rarely troubled the clergy. But once the repeal of the Test and Corporation Acts, Catholic emancipation and the Reform Act had broken that monopoly, High Anglicans grew alarmed since the Church now seemed to be at the mercy of a Parliament in which Catholics or Dissenters might play a significant role. Reacting to these reforms, High Anglicans began to challenge the Erastianism of the constitution, demanding that the Church should acquire a spiritual jurisdiction independent of the state, and pronouncing under Tractarian influence the divine nature of its Episcopal government and the inviolability of its apostolic succession. These ecclesiastics continued to regard the union of Church and state as necessary but, challenged by the growth of liberalism after 1832, they argued that only a greater autonomy in spiritual matters would protect the Church from the religious indifference of the politicians.[65]

Macaulay, whose position on the relationship between Church and state was thoroughly Erastian, opposed the aspirations of the High Anglican party. Between 1830 and 1850, as Whigs and High

---

[64] Ibid., 4: 15.
[65] Machin, *Politics and the Churches*, 26–27, 75–91. E. A. Varley, *The Last of the Prince Bishops: William Van Mildert and the High Church Movement of the Early Nineteenth Century* (Cambridge: Cambridge University Press, 1992). Perry Butler, *Gladstone: Church, State, and Tractarianism: A Study of His Religious Ideas and Attitudes* (Oxford: Clarendon Press, 1982).

Churchmen clashed frequently over clerical appointments, Macaulay consistently gave his support to the liberal candidates. He sympathized with Thirlwall, for instance, who in 1834 had been deprived of his assistant tutorship at Trinity College for backing a measure which would have made it possible for Dissenters to receive degrees at Cambridge. "When you see Thirlwall," Macaulay wrote from India, "tell him that I congratulate him from my soul on having suffered in so good a cause: and that I would rather have been treated as he has been treated on such an account than have the Mastership of Trinity. There would be some chance for the Church, if we had more Churchmen of the same breed – worthy successors of Leighton and Tillotson."[66] The most celebrated disputes, however, were over the Hampden and Gorham cases. High Churchmen objected to the appointment of the liberal Anglican Hampden to the Regius Professorship of Divinity at Oxford in 1836, complaining that it was an unwarranted intrusion by the state into the spiritual affairs of the Church. They considered Hampden an unsuitable candidate, finding his views on doctrine heterodox and his advocacy of admitting Dissenters to Oxford a dangerous threat to the Anglican integrity of the university. Macaulay, however, applauded the appointment and censured those who were harassing Hampden, calling them the "genuine successors, in everything but wit and eloquence of South and Atterbury."[67] Years later, in 1850, Macaulay again revealed his Erastian tendencies when he praised the Privy Council for overruling the ecclesiastical courts and upholding the presentation of Gorham to the living at Brampford Speke. In contrast to High Churchmen, who denounced the government for meddling in Church business, Macaulay termed the Council's judgment "excellent."[68]

Macaulay's Erastianism became most apparent, however, in his stand on the patronage controversy in Scotland. At issue was whether lay patrons or local congregations should have the final decision in clerical appointments. In 1834, the General Assembly of the Kirk, supporting the rights of the congregation, passed a measure enabling parishioners to reject ministers appointed by lay

[66] Macaulay to Thomas Flower Ellis (15 December 1834), *Letters*, 3: 112.
[67] Macaulay to Lord Mahon (31 December 1836), ibid., 3: 206.
[68] Macaulay to Thomas Flower Ellis (9 March 1850), ibid., 5: 99.

patrons. The Court of Session, however, the ultimate civil court in Scotland, took the opposite side and in 1838 declared against the measure, thereby initiating a conflict between the ecclesiastical jurisdiction of the General Assembly and the civil authority of the state. Spokesmen for the anti-patronage party in the Assembly, like High Churchmen in England, soon began proclaiming the independence of the Kirk.[69] Macaulay was drawn into the controversy as a member of Parliament for Edinburgh. Though inclined to support the rights of the congregation on the grounds of utility, he objected to the High Church pretensions of the anti-patronage party. As he explained to Adam Black: "[if] the legislature can make the church more useful to the country, the legislature is bound to do so. And on these grounds I am favorable to a settlement of the non-intrusion [patronage] question on the basis of a popular veto. But to the high pretensions put forth by a portion of the church, I am decidedly opposed. I think that the veto or some similar measure may be a desirable measure, but I deny the claim to independence which the Established Church sets up against the state."[70] Reasserting his position even more forcefully, he underscored its essential Erastianism: "While the State and the Church are connected, the State must control the Church. It ought indeed to exercise its powers in such a way as to make the Church in the highest degree useful to the people. But it must control. And I will never put the State under the feet of that Church which it feeds out of the common funds of the empire."[71]

In his *History*, Macaulay endeavored to undermine the High Anglican rhetoric of his contemporaries by asserting that High Church principles, having entered Anglican thinking only in the seventeenth century, represented a pernicious departure from the precedents established at the Reformation. Examining the sixteenth-century origins of the Anglican Church, Macaulay confidently affirmed that the English reformers were Erastians who conceived of the monarch as the temporal and spiritual head of the Church:

---

69  For the background to this controversy, see G. I. T. Machin, "The Disruption and British Politics," *Scottish Historical Review*, 51 (1972): 20–51, and *Politics and the Churches*, 118–147.

70  Macaulay to Adam Black (20 November 1840), *Letters*, 3: 346.

71  Macaulay to Duncan McLaren (30 January 1841), ibid., 3: 364–365.

The King was to be the Pope of his kingdom, the vicar of God, the expositor of Catholic verity, the channel of sacramental graces. He arrogated to himself the right of deciding dogmatically what was orthodox doctrine and what was heresy, of drawing up and imposing confessions of faith, and of giving religious instruction to his people. He proclaimed that all jurisdiction, spiritual as well as temporal, was derived from him alone, and that it was in his power to confer episcopal authority, and to take it away.[72]

Macaulay further insisted, contrary to the claims of High Church-men and Tractarians, that the founders of the Church had never regarded Episcopacy as a divine institution, but chose to preserve it because at the time it was expedient to do so.[73] High Church principles, then, were not intrinsic to Anglicanism, but were actually a seventeenth-century deviation from precedent that reached their epitome under Laud. Churchmen, relaxing their hatred of Roman Catholicism and directing it against the Puritans, began under the Stuarts to defend Episcopacy as a divine insti-tution and denounce dissenting alternatives as illegitimate. Practices previously associated with Roman Catholicism entered the Anglican ritual, while Anglican theology, retreating from its original Calvinism, became increasingly Arminian.[74] After the Restoration, High Church principles remained dominant, finding expression in the penal laws against Dissenters and in the Establishment's advocacy of passive obedience and non-resistance, doctrines Macaulay considered incompatible with good govern-ment.[75]

What worried High Churchmen most about the Erastian relationship between Church and state was the possibility that the government might, as a result of Catholic emancipation, choose to weaken the Protestantism of the Establishment. These fears seemed confirmed in 1833, when the Whigs began tampering with the temporalities of the Irish Church. As evidence of how serious the present danger was, spokesmen for the Establishment pointed to the disaster that had nearly destroyed the Church in 1688, when James had used the royal supremacy in order to subvert its Protestantism. John Wilson Croker, writing in the *Quarterly Review* amid the crisis over the Irish Church, used a number of simplistic

[72] Macaulay, *Works*, 1: 57–58, 60–61.     [73] Ibid., 1: 55, 78–80.
[74] Ibid., 1: 78–84, 92–93.     [75] Ibid., 1: 73–76, 78–84, 168, 184–188.

analogies to denounce the Whigs: the repeal of the Test and Corporation Acts, Catholic emancipation, the Parliamentary Reform Act and the attempt to open Oxford and Cambridge to non-Anglicans all found seventeenth-century parallels. Like James's toleration of Dissenters, his efforts to promote Catholics, his changes in the Corporations and his attempt to appoint Catholics to positions in the universities, they were all intended to "overthrow the Church."[76] Macaulay answered these High Church accusations by pointing out that the constitutional changes brought about by the Revolution had made it impossible for a monarch to make alterations in the national faith that were not accepted by Parliament as beneficial. Not only was the line of succession now restricted to Protestants, but "the power of the House of Commons in the state had become so decidedly preponderant that no sovereign, whatever might have been his opinion or his inclinations, could have imitated the example of James."[77]

Macaulay reserved some of his harshest words for the High Churchmanship of the Oxford Movement. Like other Whigs, he considered the Tractarians a Roman Catholic sect within the Anglican Church.[78] As Newman's conversion to Rome in 1845 and the publication of Tract XC – which Macaulay termed "the quintessence of Jesuitism"[79] – made the Oxford Movement's Catholic tendencies all the more apparent, Macaulay's distaste for both Catholicism and the Tractarians became compounded. "Odd," he noted in his journal, at the height of the crisis over Papal aggression, "that I begin to feel the same disgust at the Anglo Catholic & Roman Catholic cants which people after the Restoration felt for the Puritan cant. Their saints' days begin to affect me as the Puritan Sabbath affected drunken Barnaby."[80] Macaulay had

---

76  [John Wilson Croker], "Revolutions of 1688 and 1831," *Quarterly Review*, 51 (June, 1834): 499–505.

77  Macaulay, *Works*, 2: 239–240, 248–250, 405, 409.

78  For the Whigs' views on the Tractarians, see [Henry Rogers], "Puseyism, or the Oxford Tractarian School," *Edinburgh Review*, 77 (April, 1843): 501–562. Macaulay found the article "excellent," which suggests that it may be a fair representation of his own opinions on the Oxford Movement. Macaulay to Charles Bird Smith (3 July 1843), *Letters*, 4: 128–129.

79  Macaulay, Journal (28 October [1857]).

80  Macaulay, Journal (30 October [1850]). For the so-called Papal aggression, see: J. B. Conacher, "The Politics of the 'Papal Aggression Crisis', 1850–1851," *Canadian Catholic Historical Association Report* (1959), 13–27. Machin, *Politics and the Churches*, 210–228. For the tendency of other Whigs, notably Lord John Russell, to see Tractarianism and Papal

always felt an aversion to any form of clerical domination, whether by the Catholic priesthood, traditional High Churchmen or adherents to the Oxford Movement. The spread of Tractarian practices in the Anglican Church beginning in the late 1840s, combined with the Pope's decision in 1850 to restore the Catholic hierarchy in England, seemed to him unmistakable evidence of a clerical resurgence.

In his *History*, Macaulay used his discussion of the Nonjurors to dismiss the Oxford Movement. There had always been an affinity between the Tractarians and those Nonjuring Churchmen who had refused to take the oath of allegiance to William and Mary on the grounds that resistance to James had violated the doctrine of passive obedience. In a sermon preached in 1837 on the anniversary of the Glorious Revolution, the Tractarian E. B. Pusey had established the connection between the two parties. Conjuring up the moribund notions of passive obedience and non-resistance, Pusey had denounced the Revolution as a national sin and rehabilitated the churchmanship of the Nonjurors.[81] Like the Tractarians, the Nonjurors had believed in the real efficacy of the sacraments and were vehemently anti-Erastian. When ordered by William to relinquish their livings, they had defied the king, arguing that the civil authority could not take from them what had been sanctioned by ordination. For Macaulay, the Nonjurors, and by analogy their modern counterparts, were little more than fanatics. Their justification for the inviolability of the apostolic succession was specious. Their dedication to the principles of non-resistance and passive obedience was absurd because it rested on an arbitrary interpretation of the Scriptures and because it led to the unreasonable conclusion that allegiance was due to a deposed tyrant rather than to a virtuous ruler in actual possession of power. At best the Nonjurors were a marginal movement among the clergy, at worst they were schismatics who threatened to divide the Church by establishing a rival hierarchy.[82]

Macaulay's antipathy toward the Nonjurors, with its implied

aggression as two prongs of the same attack on English Protestantism, see G. I. T. Machin, "Lord John Russell and the Prelude to the Ecclesiastical Titles Bill," *Journal of Ecclesiastical History*, 25 (1974): 278–284.

[81] [Herman Merivale], "Dr Pusey's *Sermon on the Fifth of November*," *Edinburgh Review*, 66 (January, 1838): 396–398, 409–411.

[82] Macaulay, *Works*, 3: 393–397, 4: 205–214, 230–231, 5: 41–45.

criticism of the Tractarians, was only to be expected in a work that championed the latitudinarianism of the Revolution's religious settlement. Macaulay's approach to the issues of Church and state had been shaped by his experiences as a practical politician grappling with the controversies of the 1830s and 1840s, as well as by his scholar's knowledge of the sectarian strife of the seventeenth century. He was aware that circumstances, rooted in the nation's past, always placed limits on the options available to politicians. Tracing the sectarian controversies of his own day back to the seventeenth-century crises that had left England religiously plural, he was able to appreciate the extent of these circumstances. The Anglican Church, history showed, despite its obvious failings, was intimately connected with the growth of the English nation and could not be eliminated without removing at great cost a vital element of the national character. But history also taught that England contained Dissenters who had made meaningful contributions to the nation's past, both during the Civil War and at the Revolution, that Scotland was Presbyterian, and that Ireland, for good or for ill, would remain Catholic. For Macaulay, the religious settlement of 1689, the culmination of William's latitudinarian policies, had demonstrated how political stability could be achieved in the face of such diversity. Applied to the problems of the Victorian age, it demanded a liberal Establishment in which the clerical pretensions of the High Churchmen and Tractarians had no place.

The attitudes informing Macaulay's approach to sectarian politics – pragmatism, toleration for Dissent, scorn for the Protestant Church of Ireland, acceptance of the majority Establishments in England and Scotland, dislike of High Churchmen and Tractarians – were characteristic of mid-Victorian Whiggism. In the decades following Macaulay's death in 1859, religious controversy continued to play an important role in British politics as the transition from the confessional to the secular state was an uneasy one. Liberalism, as it was redefined in the 1860s and 1870s, continued to address questions of Church and state, and Macaulay's *History*, given its immense readership, helped in this process by imparting an older Whiggism to the new Gladstonian era.

# CHAPTER 3

# Puritanism and the ideology of Dissent

The rise of Protestant Dissent as a political force and effective challenge to the supremacy of the Anglican Establishment was one of the most important developments of the Victorian age. The repeal of the Test and Corporation Acts in 1828 and the Reform Act of 1832, by removing the formal barriers against the participation of Dissenters in national politics and by transferring Parliamentary representation to areas where Nonconformity was strong, gave Dissenters a larger role in shaping English affairs than they had enjoyed before, except perhaps during the mid-seventeenth century under the Commonwealth. The Municipal Corporation Act of 1835 increased further the influence of Dissent by breaking down the Anglican exclusiveness of local government. By 1833, Nonconformists had formulated the principal demands that would inform their politics for the next fifty years. Seeking parity with the Establishment, they insisted on exemption from Church rates, the right to conduct marriages and burials according to their own ceremonies, the civil registration of births, marriages and deaths, the removal of religious tests at Oxford and Cambridge, and the granting of a charter to the nondenominational London University. Throughout the nineteenth century, Dissenters found supporters for their cause among Whigs and Liberals, although the alliance was never an easy one. During the 1830s, Melbourne's governments attempted to meet the Dissenters' demands while at the same time maintaining the ascendancy of the Anglican Church. In 1836, London University received its charter, the civil registration of births, marriages and deaths was established and Dissenting ministers obtained the right to preside over marriages. But the inability of the Whigs to deal successfully with the vexing problems of education and Church rates discouraged many Nonconformists, some of whom, becoming increasingly militant, adopted the voluntary principle and began to agitate for disestablishment.[1]

As Dissenters began to question the prominence of the Anglican Establishment, they looked back to the seventeenth century for inspiration and direction. It was hardly surprising that they should have based an ideology of Dissent on the Stuart past, for it was during the seventeenth century that the Puritans emerged as a powerful force, confronted the Church of Archbishop Laud and the monarchy of Charles I, triumphed briefly under the Commonwealth and Protectorate, only to be excluded at the Restoration, giving rise to modern Dissent. As the disabilities restricting the activities of non-Anglicans were gradually removed in the nineteenth century, Dissenters began to foresee a time when they might exercise the same degree of influence on contemporary society as their predecessors had in the mid-seventeenth century. The Puritan past would provide Dissenters with a set of traditions, heroes and principles that would give their cause both legitimacy and direction. In answer to their detractors, Dissenters could now look to the past and insist that they were confronting the Anglican Establishment in order to advance the movement for civil and religious liberty which had begun when the Puritans in Parliament first challenged the presumptions of the Stuarts.

I

In the decades after Waterloo it was the descendants of the eighteenth-century Rational Dissenters who first took a scholarly interest in the radical politics and religion of the Commonwealth and Protectorate. A product of the English Enlightenment, Rational Dissent had taken hold chiefly among the Presbyterians and, to a much lesser extent, the Independents. Believing in the self-sufficiency of the Scriptures and the individual's right to free inquiry, these Dissenters from the Anglican Establishment rejected the authority of church creeds and looked to reason as the guarantor of religious truth. This conviction eventually brought

---

[1] For the role of Dissent in British politics during the first half of the nineteenth century, see: Norman Gash, *Reaction and Reconstruction in English Politics, 1832–1852* (Oxford: Clarendon Press, 1965). Richard Brent, *Liberal Anglican Politics: Whiggery, Religion, and Reform, 1830–1841* (Oxford: Clarendon Press, 1987). G. I. T. Machin, *Politics and the Churches in Great Britain, 1832 to 1868* (Oxford: Clarendon Press, 1977).

the doctrine of the Trinity into question and led the Rational Dissenters increasingly toward heterodoxy. Since it entailed an approach to theological questions rather than a specific body of dogma, Rational Dissent generated a variety of doctrinal positions, including the Arianism of Richard Price, the Socinianism of Joseph Priestley, and even the atheism of William Godwin.[2] The existence of the Test and Corporation Acts, which made it difficult for Dissenters to participate in politics, and the Blasphemy Act, which banned the expression of non-Trinitarian ideas, ensured that Rational Dissenters would oppose the Establishment and embrace radical politics. They led the movement for the repeal of the Test Acts, backed efforts to reform the franchise, and sympathized with the American colonies in their bid for independence. The outbreak of the French Revolution, which they welcomed, exacerbated their differences with the Establishment as Burke and others drew an explicit parallel between atheism, radicalism and non-Trinitarian forms of Dissent.[3]

In the years before the French Revolution, not all Rational Dissenters were prepared to endorse the radicalism of the Interregnum. Intent on gaining support for their campaign against the Test Acts, they sought to establish the respectability of their cause by dissociating it from the politics of the Commonwealth and the religion of the Independents, which they believed lacked rationality. Instead, their efforts to define their political position historically tended to focus on the far less controversial Glorious Revolution. In his *Lectures on History*, published in 1788, Joseph Priestley described the Interregnum as a period of "absolute anarchy and confusion," observing that the "enthusiasm" of the Independents was an "enemy to all power." Rather than tracing England's political prosperity to the Commonwealth, he attributed it in good

---

[2] For the development of Rational Dissent, see: C. Gordon Bolam, Jeremy Goring, H. L. Short and Roger Thomas, *The English Presbyterians: From Elizabethan Puritanism to Modern Unitarianism* (Boston: Beacon Press, 1968), 113–235. Michael R. Watts, *The Dissenters: From the Reformation to the French Revolution* (Oxford: Clarendon Press, 1978), 464–490.

[3] For the politics of the Rational Dissenters, see: Richard W. Davis, *Dissent in Politics, 1780–1830: The Political Life of William Smith, M.P.* (London: Epworth Press, 1971), 22–27, 44–52, 62–76, 92–104. Isaac Kramnick, "Religion and Radicalism: English Political Theory in the Age of Revolution," *Political Theory*, 5 (1977): 505–534. Anthony Lincoln, *Some Political and Social Ideas of English Dissent 1763–1800* (New York: Octagon Books, 1971), 4–65. J. E. Cookson, *The Friends of Peace: Anti-war Liberalism in England, 1793–1815* (Cambridge: Cambridge University Press, 1982).

Whig fashion to the Revolution of 1688 which finally put an end to the struggle between king and Parliament.[4] Andrew Kippis, preaching in 1788 on the anniversary of the Glorious Revolution, similarly praised William for delivering England from the twin evils of Popery and absolutism. Whereas the Revolution, "one of the most illustrious and happy events recorded in history," had ushered in "the most delightful period" in the nation's past, the Commonwealth had achieved nothing that was "solid, effectual, and lasting."[5] Addressing the charge that the violence of the Puritans toward the Established Church demonstrated the danger of empowering contemporary Dissent, the historian William Belsham exonerated the moderate Presbyterians by pinning the blame for the excesses of the Commonwealth on the Independents under Cromwell: "This was the man," he wrote, "who, at the head of an army of Enthusiasts and Fanatics, passionately devoted to their leader, effected the subversion of the Constitution."[6]

By the 1820s, however, the Interregnum began to attract a number of historians. The French Revolution had excited radical activity in England and hardened the oppositional tendencies among Dissenters as the government repression in the 1790s fell hardest on them. When Burke in his *Reflections* captured the Revolution of 1688 for the Establishment, asserting its essential conservatism and denying its suitability as a precedent for reform, Dissenters turned to the Commonwealth, though the severity of the repression and the unpopularity of radical causes ensured that no major scholarly appreciation of England's republican past would be likely to appear. With the end of the wars against France and the revival of the reform movement, however, interest in the Commonwealth awakened. The years after Waterloo saw a renewed curiosity about Oliver Cromwell – a reflection, perhaps, of England's need for a national hero to equal Bonaparte[7] – and in

4  Joseph Priestley, *Lectures on History, and General Policy; to which is Prefixed, An Essay on a Course of Liberal Education for Civil and Active Life* (Birmingham: J. Johnson, 1788), 262, 263, 446.
5  Andrew Kippis, *A Sermon Preached at the Old Jewry, on the Fourth of November, 1788, before the Society for Commemorating the Glorious Revolution* (London: G. G. J. and J. Robinson, 1788), 4–10, 26, 31, 32–39.
6  William Belsham, "Observations on the Test Laws," *Essays, Philosophical, Historical, and Literary* (London: C. Dilly, 1789–1791), 2: 568–574.
7  Oliver Cromwell, *Memoirs of the Protector, Oliver Cromwell, and of His Sons, Richard and Henry*, second edition (London: Longman, Hurst, Rees, Orme, and Brown, 1821). Thomas Cromwell, *Oliver Cromwell and His Times*, second edition (London: Sherwood, Neely and

1822, George Brodie, a radical Whig about whom we know little, published a *History of the British Empire* which was noteworthy for its refutation of Hume's defense of the Stuarts and its well-intentioned appreciation of the Commonwealth and Protectorate.[8]

The most extensive defense of the republic to appear at this time, however, was William Godwin's *History of the Commonwealth*, published between 1824 and 1828. Born into a family of Independents and educated in the Dissenting academies, Godwin remained attached to the Rational Dissenting tradition of Richard Price and Joseph Priestley long after he had become a nonbeliever.[9] The conviction, so essential to Dissent, that the free exercise of one's private judgment was both a right and a duty informed his own thinking about religion and politics. An advocate of intellectual freedom, Godwin abhorred religious tests and favored those republican forms of government which encouraged people to act as independent, rational agents. His political "creed," he explained in 1819, was simple: "I am in principle a Republican, but in practice a Whig."[10] His speculations were progressive. He was known as a friend to the French Revolution and the appearance in 1793 of his *Political Justice* made him for a time one of the principal theorists of English radicalism. But in practice he was more cautious. He opposed revolutionary change for England, advocating instead gradual improvement through the free exchange of ideas. His *History of the Commonwealth*, with its defense of the republican ideal, was a significant contribution toward this end. Assessing the prospects for England in the early nineteenth century, however, Godwin was not overly optimistic. The nation was not yet ready for republican government and consequently all that a "liberal-minded and enlightened man" could do, he told a correspondent in 1820, was to support the Whigs in their efforts to achieve moderate reform.[11]

Jones, 1822). [Robert Southey], "Life of Cromwell," *Quarterly Review*, 25 (July, 1821): 273–347.

8  George Brodie, *A History of the British Empire from the Accession of Charles I to the Restoration* (Edinburgh: Bell and Bradfute, 1822).

9  For Godwin's debt to Rational Dissent, see: M. Fitzpatrick, "William Godwin and the Rational Dissenters," *Price-Priestley Newsletter*, 3 (1979): 4–28. William Stafford, "Dissenting Religion Translated into Politics: Godwin's *Political Justice*," *History of Political Thought*, 1 (1980): 279–299. Peter H. Marshall, *William Godwin* (New Haven: Yale University Press, 1984). Mark Philp, *Godwin's Political Justice* (London: Duckworth, 1986).

10  Godwin to Lady Caroline Lamb (25 February 1819), C. Kegan Paul, *William Godwin: Friends and Contemporaries* (London: Henry S. King and Co., 1876), 2: 266.

11  Godwin to H. B. Rosser (7 and 27 March 1820), ibid., 2: 263, 265.

The purpose behind Godwin's history was to rehabilitate his country's republican tradition by writing an account of the Commonwealth which would judge the period fairly – something he felt had never adequately been done before, though he thanked his "friend" George Brodie for "many valuable hints."[12] Godwin readily admitted that the republic had failed in England, and in fact, like Millar and Brodie, he believed that it could hardly have done otherwise. The nation was not prepared for a republican government in the mid-seventeenth century and perhaps, he reflected, it never would be. And yet, the Commonwealth's failure by itself hardly constituted sufficient grounds for dismissing the experiment altogether: there may be "men," he noted, "worthy of our admiration, whose cause has not prospered." Godwin's history also set out to vindicate England's Dissenting tradition. For as Godwin understood it, republicanism was the political expression of seventeenth-century Independency and by demonstrating what was admirable and constructive in one tradition, his book showed what was laudable in the other.[13] As England in the 1820s debated the merits of admitting Dissenters to full political equality and reforming Parliament, a work of history such as Godwin's, which stressed the legitimacy of England's Puritan and republican past, took on political significance.

In his treatment of the Long Parliament, Godwin challenged directly Hume's complaint that the Commons' preoccupation with the forms of religious worship corrupted their cause by tainting it with fanaticism. The leaders of this Parliament, Godwin pointed out, were striving to establish a republic in England and to do so successfully required reshaping the moral character of the nation, transforming values of subservience into those of independence. Religion was necessary for morality, and without morality there could be "no real liberty, and no good political government."[14] This concern with changing the moral climate of the age lay behind the Puritans' preoccupation with the details of religious life. In his discussion of their desire to ban stage plays, Godwin made clear his conception of Puritanism as a moral force:

---

[12] William Godwin, *History of the Commonwealth of England, from its Commencement, to the Restoration of Charles the Second* (London: Henry Colburn, 1824–1828), 1: v–vii, x–xi.
[13] Ibid., 1: 1–6.    [14] Ibid., 1: 41–42, 46.

It was their aim [he wrote] to new mould the character of the people of England. The nation had hitherto subsisted under a king; they were desirous to change the government into a republic. Nothing can be more unlike than the different frames of public mind demanded under these two forms of government ... The republicans in the Long Parliament were called upon to endeavour to substitute, for the manners of a court ... , a severe, a manly, and an independent mode of feeling.

To encourage this reform of the English character, it was necessary to prohibit the staging of plays written with the approbation of kings and permeated with the "doctrines of non-resistance and passive obedience."[15] It was equally necessary for the Puritans to eliminate from religious worship any symbol or practice, such as the altar and vestments, consecrated candles and incense, which seemed associated with the principles of monarchy, and to substitute in their place new ones aimed at instilling the values of independence which they so cherished. "Great changes," Godwin noted, "cannot take place in the minds of generations of men, without a corresponding change in their external symbols." The leaders of the Long Parliament wished to bring about such a change, "they designed to introduce a more simple and a severer tone of religious profession, and a more manly spirit in the ordinary conduct of life." They may have failed in the end, but still, he wrote in answer to Hume, "we ought ... to do justice to the steadiness and sagacity with which their intentions were prosecuted."[16]

Godwin's partiality for the Independents became most apparent in his account of the conflicts that arose within the Puritan movement during the course of the Civil War. The Independents, he argued, were the ones who fought against the monarchy of Charles and the Church of Laud in order to achieve for England a greater degree of political and religious liberty. Where the Presbyterians, by the end of the Civil War, sought a mixed monarchy with restrictions on the power of the king, the Independents desired a republic; and where the Presbyterians and Episcopalians insisted on a rigid conformity to their respective conceptions of the Church, the Independents desired a broad, "generous spirit of toleration," demanding for themselves "no other liberty ... than [they were] willing to yield to all others."[17] Like most Dissenters, Godwin valued immensely religious toleration and freedom of thought, and

---

[15] Ibid., 1: 77, 78, 79.   [16] Ibid., 1: 85.   [17] Ibid., 1: 335–337, 344, 354–357.

his history demonstrated the debt that England owed to the Independents for the growth of these liberties. They were the first to understand the benefits of toleration and intellectual freedom. Had the Presbyterians been victorious, Godwin asserted, they would have established an intolerant and persecuting Church. If Britain in the early nineteenth century enjoyed a large sphere of liberty, then it was due in large part to the efforts of the Independents. If reformers were now striving to widen this sphere, then they were furthering the process that the Independents had begun more than a century and a half earlier.

In his history, Godwin suggested the advantages that a republic would bring to the nation. More than any other form of government, it would enable its members to achieve their highest potential. Under a republic, people became autonomous and rational agents, thinking for themselves and acting as they thought best. Man, Godwin believed, would never be all that he could "so long as he is not penetrated with the sentiment of independence, so long as he looks up with a self-denying and a humble spirit to any other creature of the same figure and dimensions as himself."[18] Where a monarchy rewarded submission, a republic, with its emphasis on political and intellectual liberty, encouraged this very independence. The citizens of a republic acknowledged no superiors other than those whose talents were objectively greater. Rank and prestige were based not on patronage, but on merit alone. Under a republic, Godwin remarked, "every citizen should know himself the equal of every other citizen, and feel convinced that the highest elevation in the state, was open to every one, whose virtues and talents might qualify him to fill it."[19] Although independent, the virtuous citizen renounced personal ambition, if he felt it at all, in order to serve the commonwealth, whether in Parliament, the army or any other capacity. Opposed to ambition, republican virtue consisted in the willingness to sacrifice personal gain for the public good.[20] The soldiers of the republican army, Godwin observed, "were not ordinary individuals. They were citizens, who had left their usual occupations . . . to fight for liberty. They exercised their understandings; each man was a thinking and reflecting being; they valued their independence."[21] In all of these remarks, Godwin's

---

[18] Ibid., 4: 18.   [19] Ibid., 4: 259.
[20] Ibid., 2: 496–497, 499, 3: 488.   [21] Ibid., 2: 294.

rhetoric lay solidly within the tradition of English republicanism that stretched back to the Commonwealth itself.

If liberty was the ideal of the Independents, it was imperfectly put into practice. The statesmen of the Commonwealth, Godwin acknowledged, actually limited freedom of expression, substituted high courts of justice for trials by jury in cases of political import, and – here was the most serious charge against them – steadfastly refused to make the Commonwealth truly republican by dismissing the Rump Parliament and convening a popular assembly elected by the nation as a whole. Under the Commonwealth, political power remained in the hands of the few. In defense of the Independents, Godwin pointed out that their regime was opposed by the majority of Englishmen. The goal of the Commonwealthmen was to confer on England the benefits of a republic, but no matter how noble their vision, it was not shared by the multitude. Had they surrendered their power to a representative assembly in which their enemies would have predominated, then everything they had accomplished would have been undone. Not until the nation had come to accept the republic on the strength of its virtues could the leaders of the Commonwealth relinquish their exclusive hold on the state.[22]

According to Godwin, no one understood better than Cromwell how precarious the republic actually was. Mixing personal ambition with sound reasoning, Cromwell recognized that given the conservative bent of most of his countrymen, England would remain politically unstable until the nation's traditional constitution of king, Lords and Commons was in some measure restored. To make himself king, Cromwell used the army to disperse the republic.[23] A love of power, Godwin lamented, was his great weakness and the cause of his apostasy. As a citizen of a republic, Cromwell was flawed. Where other leaders of the Commonwealth such as Hampden or Vane were truly virtuous, acting with disinterest and always ready to sacrifice personal gain for the good of the community, Cromwell adulterated virtue with its opposite.[24] For the ambition of one man, the Commonwealth was sacrificed, its ideals violated and the ground made ready for what was now almost

[22] Ibid., 2: 500–504, 547–550, 3: 108–123, 187–193, 298–300, 341–348, 467–471.
[23] Ibid., 3: 301–304, 434–438.
[24] Ibid., 1: 101–102, 121–122, 2: 200–202, 3: 218–219.

inevitable – the restoration of the Stuarts. Here was Cromwell's one lasting accomplishment: "He deprived the whole nation," Godwin wrote, " . . . of the desire and the hope to achieve great things. He taught his countrymen to be incredulous to the name of public liberty. He prepared the way for all the profligacy, the inhumanity, the persecutions, and the infamy of the reign of Charles the Second."[25] In truth, Godwin argued, Cromwell's reign conferred few benefits on England. He was a statesman of immense capabilities, his intentions may have been laudable in part – first to become king, but then to grant the nation "a free and a full parliament, the equal and genuine representative of the people of England"[26] – but in the end he was defeated by the same obstacle as were the Commonwealthmen. His usurpation was unpopular and to maintain power in the face of such opposition he was forced to resort to violent means. After dismissing the Long Parliament, his government became notoriously arbitrary.[27]

And yet Godwin saw more in Cromwell than a self-serving usurper who trampled on the virtuous republic solely to promote his own ambition. He was an Independent, sincere in his religious beliefs, concerned with improving the moral character of the nation. Because of these "qualities," Godwin noted, " . . . we should be almost disposed to place him in the number of the few excellent princes that have swayed a sceptre, were it not for the gross and unauthorised manner in which he climbed to this eminence."[28] As this observation suggests, there was an ambivalence in Godwin's appraisal of Cromwell that, perhaps, can be explained by his own loyalties. As a republican, Godwin could not countenance the fact that Cromwell's usurpation had put an end to the republic and destroyed the benefits which in time that government might have given to England. But as a Dissenter, Godwin was equally drawn to Cromwell as the greatest historical figure whom the Dissenters had ever produced. That Cromwell had his faults and committed his crimes, Godwin's narrative made abundantly clear; but he was also a better ruler than any of the Stuarts, either before or after him.[29] A Dissenting king, Godwin's history seemed to say, could do as well, if not better for England than one who conformed. Godwin ended his book with the speculation that given ten more years, Cromwell's

[25] Ibid., 3: 304, 472–473.     [26] Ibid., 3: 435.
[27] Ibid., 4: 580–586, 597–605.     [28] Ibid., 4: 587–596.     [29] Ibid., 4: 409.

administration would have become increasingly popular, more legal and less arbitrary.[30]

By defending what many claimed were the origins of the reform movement, Godwin's *History of the Commonwealth* represented an important contribution to the political debate of the 1820s and early 1830s. Where Establishment polemicists had denied the Dissenters and republicans a constructive role in the nation's past, claiming that they had always existed outside England's fundamental institutions in Church and state, Godwin demonstrated to the contrary the legitimacy of the Dissenting and republican heritage by showing what was admirable in the aspirations not only of the Commonwealthmen, but of Cromwell as well. In some respects Godwin's rhetorical strategy resembled that which Macaulay would use in his essay on Milton, shifting the focus of the historical debate from the Glorious Revolution to the Civil War in order to encourage a more vigorous approach to popular reform. But Godwin went much further than Macaulay, for the republicanism that animated Godwin's history was alien to the young Whig. The Commonwealth which Godwin vindicated, Macaulay dismissed as a "Venetian oligarchy," and Cromwell's usurpation, which Godwin viewed with distress, Macaulay regarded as a necessary restoration of order.[31] Indicating its pertinence to contemporary debate, reviewers judged the book along predictable party lines. While the Dissenting *Eclectic* and radical *Westminster* reviews welcomed Godwin's book, the Tory and High Church *British Critic* found it "a jejune, commonplace narrative . . . , embodying all the errors, prejudices, and intemperance . . . of the revolutionary school."[32]

Even after the repeal of the Test and Corporation Acts and the passing of Parliamentary reform, the history of the Interregnum continued to figure in contemporary debate as middle-class and Dissenting radicals pressed for an extension of the gains made in 1828 and 1832. The early historical works of John Forster attest to the enduring importance of the Puritan past for Dissent in the decade after the Reform Act. Between 1836 and 1839, Forster

---

[30] Ibid., 4: 341–343, 605–608.
[31] [Thomas Babington Macaulay], "Milton," *Edinburgh Review*, 42 (August, 1825): 335.
[32] "Godwin's *History of the Commonwealth of England,*" *Eclectic Review*, 22, new series (September, 1824): 193–205. "Godwin's *History of the Commonwealth of England,*" *Westminster Review*, 8 (October, 1827): 328–351. "Godwin's *History of the Commonwealth of England,*" *British Critic*, 3, third series (October, 1826): 77.

published biographies of Eliot and Strafford, Pym and Hampden, Vane and Marten, and Cromwell. Commissioned originally by Dionysius Lardner for *Lardner's Cabinet Cyclopaedia* and republished in 1840 as Forster's *Statesmen of the Commonwealth*, these studies represented the most significant attempt to reevaluate the successes and failures of the Commonwealth and its leaders since Godwin's history, written a decade earlier. Raised a Unitarian, Forster, like Godwin, was rooted intellectually in Rational Dissent. He attended Cambridge briefly, but then chose to study law in London, perhaps because as a Dissenter he was barred from taking a degree at the university. By 1832, he had started to move in London's literary circles, developing the ties that would provide the basis for his own literary career. He was on good terms with Leigh Hunt, Charles Lamb, Edward Bulwer and the actor William Macready. Robert Browning helped him write his biography of Strafford, and later he cultivated friendships with Charles Dickens, Walter Savage Landor and Thomas Carlyle. As a man of letters, Forster's achievements were diverse: he was a historian of Stuart England, a biographer of Swift, Defoe and Goldsmith, the author of the official lives of Landor and Dickens. A respected literary and drama critic, he also edited at one time or another the *Examiner*, Edward Moxon's short-lived *Reflector*, and the *Foreign Quarterly Review*.[33]

Forster belonged to the tradition of liberal politics and rational religion that stretched back to Richard Price and Joseph Priestley. He remained a practicing Unitarian into the 1840s, if not longer, attending services at the chapel of the Benthamite and Unitarian minister W. J. Fox.[34] When in 1833 Forster became drama critic for the *Examiner*, that radical periodical was backing wholeheartedly the demands of the Dissenters, going so far as to advocate the separation of Church and state. Also indicative of Forster's political position was one of his first ventures into journalism – a series of articles on "Our Early Patriots" which he contributed in 1831 to the *Englishman's Magazine*, a radical monthly calling for Parliamentary reform, the abolition of slavery, freedom of conscience, free trade and the general improvement of social conditions. In these essays on Pym, Eliot and Vane, which anticipated in many ways his later

[33] James A. Davies, *John Forster: A Literary Life* (Leicester: Leicester University Press, 1983).
[34] Ibid., 75, 91.

*Statesmen of the Commonwealth*, Forster portrayed Parliament's contest with the Stuarts as a popular and patriotic struggle to restore the constitution to its "original free principles." Published after the Whigs had introduced their first Reform Bill in March, 1831, Forster conceived of these biographical studies as contributions to the reform effort, pointing out the similarities between the crisis of the mid-seventeenth century and that of his own age. In both cases, he argued, the issue at stake was the same – the survival of Parliamentary government. The reformers of the 1830s were thus continuing a process initiated almost two centuries earlier by that "sacred band of patriots," of whom Eliot, Pym and Vane were the most illustrious representatives.[35] For a young John Forster who was embarking on a literary career in London, Unitarian Dissent, liberal politics and engaged journalism were three of his central concerns.

The *Statesmen of the Commonwealth* was Forster's first major book, written when he was still in his mid-twenties and informed by the same liberal sentiments as his earlier articles for the *Englishman's Magazine*. As S. R. Gardiner remarked, Forster was "the last of those writers who carried into historical investigation the spirit which animated the Reformers who rose to power upon the ruins of the Tory party in 1830, and who dealt with Tory principles in history as Lord John Russell dealt with them in politics."[36] When Forster republished his *Statesmen* in 1840, he prefaced it with a "Treatise on the Popular Progress in English History" that chronicled the growing political importance of the "people" from the granting of Magna Carta through the reign of Queen Elizabeth, a process which entailed creating a limited monarchy, developing the rights and privileges of Parliament and increasing the importance of popular liberties and representation. Forster clearly considered this "popular progress" to be the fundamental dynamic in English history and by emphasizing its centrality to the past, his *Statesmen* provided in effect a historical justification for the reform movement

---

[35] For the political views of the *Englishman's Magazine*, see "Our Principles," and "The Country and Its Prospects," *Englishman's Magazine*, 1 (April, 1831): 1–4, 4–8. For Forster's contributions, see "Our Early Patriots," "John Pym," "Sir John Eliot," *Englishman's Magazine*, 1 (April–August, 1831): 351–356, 499–512, 623–637, and "Sir Henry Vane's Scheme of Parliamentary Reform," *Englishman's Magazine*, 2 (September, 1831): 1–13. For the attribution of these articles, see Davies, *John Forster*, 10.

[36] Samuel Rawson Gardiner, "Mr. John Forster: Obituary," *Academy*, 9 (5 February 1876): 122.

of the early nineteenth century – what Magna Carta had begun, the reformers of the 1830s had come near to completing.[37]

In his *Statesmen*, Forster portrayed his subjects as the leaders of a great "patriotic" cause, aimed at securing for England a more "popular" form of government, and culminating in the founding of the Commonwealth. Like Godwin, on whose history he drew considerably, Forster believed that the Commonwealthmen had never received the recognition they deserved, and he conceived of his *Statesmen* in part as an attempt to remedy this situation. The leaders of the Commonwealth, he proclaimed confidently, quoting Warburton, the eighteenth-century Bishop of Gloucester, were the "GREATEST GENIUSES FOR GOVERNMENT THE WORLD EVER SAW."[38] Above all, they were moderates who had rejected monarchy and become republicans only as a last resort. Here was a crucial distinction between Godwin's radical interpretation and Forster's more conservative view: where Godwin had presented the Commonwealthmen as thoroughgoing republicans and had used his history to vindicate the republican ideal, Forster saw their republicanism as incidental, as no more than a means to a more moderately liberal end. What they wanted, he maintained, "was popular and good government, embracing extensive represen-tation, security for person and property, freedom of thought, freedom of the press, and entire liberty of conscience. It was only because they could not find these under a monarchy that they became republicans; but under a monarchy they would have been happy with these."[39] For the most part, Forster considered the Commonwealth to have been a success. The most serious charge against its leaders was that they had refused to dissolve the Long Parliament and place the republic on a truly popular base. But as Forster pointed out, they were moving steadily in this direction at the very moment when Cromwell and the army turned them out.[40] As it emerged from Forster's account, the Commonwealth was the first significant attempt to achieve popular reform in England and although Cromwell undid its immediate accomplishments, it set a precedent which would not be forgotten.

---

[37] John Forster, *The Statesmen of the Commonwealth of England; with a Treatise on the Popular Progress in English History*, ed. J. O. Choules (New York: Harper and Brothers, 1846), vii–xxviii.
[38] Ibid., 532.    [39] Ibid., 491.    [40] Ibid., 515.

Although his interpretation of the seventeenth century concentrated largely on secular issues, Forster was not oblivious to the importance of religion. Aware that religious motives played an important part in the lives of his subjects, he was most concerned with freeing them from the accusation of fanaticism. He generally avoided the term "Puritan," which carried connotations of irresponsible enthusiasm, preferring instead to describe his statesmen when appropriate as "Nonconformists." Forster's approach to religion came out most clearly in his biography of the younger Vane, where he argued that Vane's Puritanism was above ridicule. He admitted that Vane was zealous, but added that his zeal was restrained by "knowledge" and "charity." Vane's visionary fanaticism was in truth nothing less than a clear-headed far-sightedness. "He was called a fanatic," Forster explained, "because he was the most strenuous advocate that religious liberty ever possessed. He was called a wild, unintelligible visionary, because through life he never ceased to urge, with all the strength of his passions and the subtlety of his intellect, a UNIVERSAL TOLERATION of sects and opinions." Toleration became the essence of Puritanism at its best, and Vane became the progenitor of a line of tolerant thinking that stretched through Milton and Locke to Charles James Fox and Lord Holland.[41]

Henry Vane was the hero of Forster's *Statesmen*. He was the culmination of that movement for popular reform that originated with Eliot, Hampden and Pym, and he best represented the values of the Commonwealth. "He sought to achieve for the English people, *for us, his posterity*, the blessings of a government responsible to the governed, the basis of which was to be security for person and property, and perfect and uncontrollable freedom in all matters appertaining to the conscience and intellect. Failing of this object in that day under a monarchical form, he struck for a republic."[42] And in Oliver Cromwell, Forster found Vane's nemesis. Where Vane was sincere in his faith, Cromwell often acted the hypocrite, using religion to promote his own ends. Where Vane struggled selflessly for the good of the people, Cromwell desired above all to realize his own ambition. And where Vane was a politician of "genius" and "virtue," Cromwell was a flawed character, suffering from a "WANT OF TRUTH."[43] During most of the decisive crises

---

[41] Ibid., 274, 277.   [42] Ibid., 302. Forster's italics.   [43] Ibid., 266–267, 315, 454.

in the history of the Commonwealth, Vane and Cromwell stood as opposites. Vane disapproved of Pride's Purge because he considered it an act of illegal violence, and he objected to the king's execution on the grounds that it was impolitic. Cromwell, meanwhile, was a force behind both events, seeing them as preliminary steps in his own quest for power. At the very moment when Cromwell and the army turned against the Commonwealth, Vane was in the process of designing a scheme of electoral reform that anticipated in many ways the Reform Act of 1832 and that would have made the Commonwealth a truly popular republic.[44] Assessing the immediate effects of Cromwell's usurpation, Forster echoed the judgment of William Godwin: "Whatever . . . had been thought sacred, [Cromwell] made profane." The Commonwealth, and everything it stood for, had been tried and "found wanting." The cause of liberal reform had come to an end.[45]

II

From the American Revolution through the passing of the Reform Act, Rational Dissent provided much of the impetus behind middle-class radicalism. In their attempt to discover a usable past, Dissenters like Godwin and Forster focused on the Interregnum, and in particular on the Commonwealth, a period they thought exemplified the Independent's belief in free religious inquiry and the republican's ideal of political liberty. But with the spread of evangelical Dissent in the early nineteenth century, leadership of the Dissenting cause passed from the heirs of Price and Priestley to those denominations that had felt the impact of evangelicalism. Though politically more conservative than the Rational Dissenters, the Congregationalists and Baptists were no less strident in their campaign against the Anglican Establishment. An important spokesman for evangelical Nonconformity, and one who used the past in order to define a role for Dissent in the present, was Robert Vaughan, a Congregationalist minister, professor of modern history at the London University and editor of the *British Quarterly Review*. A prolific historian, Vaughan published in the 1830s and 1840s two studies of Wycliffe and his age, three works on the seventeenth century as well as numerous other articles, pamphlets,

44  Ibid., 305–306, 309–310, 314–317, 443, 476–477.        45  Ibid., 522.

addresses and books on a wide range of theological, political and historical subjects.[46]

Like most Dissenters, Vaughan was a liberal in politics. He believed in progress and welcomed the emergence of modern commercial society, the "age of great cities," which he found vastly superior to the feudal order that had preceded it. Where feudalism had been characterized by military aristocracies and established churches, commercial society was noted for its free and peaceful economic activity, civil and religious liberty, representative government and democratic churches. Because of its popular tendencies and its emphasis on the individual's right to private judgment, Vaughan considered Congregationalism, and Dissent in general, conducive to progress and wholly compatible with modernity.[47] He lamented the intolerance that the Anglican Establishment continued to display toward Dissenters, and looked forward to a time when religious discrimination would cease and all Christian denominations would coexist peacefully. In daily politics, Vaughan for the most part supported the Whigs. He applauded the efforts they had made toward Catholic emancipation, Parliamentary reform and the repeal of the Test and Corporation Acts. He approved of the abolition of slavery and the Municipal Corporation Act of 1835. An advocate of free trade, he considered it the only remedy for the economic distress that plagued England in the 1840s and the only way to ensure harmony between nations. And yet his support for the Whigs was not without reservations. He considered them conservatives, strongly attached to the nation's traditional institutions and in particular to the Anglican Church, who were thus unwilling to meet all the Dissenters' demands. "Even in the case of Lord John Russell," Vaughan observed in 1845, "the ecclesiastical is placed before the civil, and the sympathies of his Lordship with an established priesthood, are manifestly stronger than his sympathies with general freedom. Civil liberty is good, but the civil establishment of religion is a greater good."[48]

[46] *Dictionary of National Biography*, s.v. "Vaughan, Robert (1795–1868)."
[47] Robert Vaughan, *Congregationalism: Or, the Polity of Independent Churches, Viewed in Relation to the State and Tendencies of Modern Society*, second edition (London: Jackson and Walford, 1842), 5–37, and *The Age of Great Cities: Or, Modern Society Viewed in Its Relation to Intelligence, Morals, and Religion* (London: Jackson and Walford, 1843).
[48] Robert Vaughan, "Lord John Russell," *Essays on History, Philosophy, and Theology* (London: Jackson and Walford, 1849), 1: 59–62, 79.

As a Congregationalist, Vaughan believed that every body of Christians had the right to worship, admit members, impose discipline, choose officers and manage its affairs independent of any authority but that of God. Accordingly, he found the idea of a state-endowed religious establishment untenable. Not only was the alliance of Church and state contrary to Scripture, which endorsed the voluntary principle, but it also tended to corrupt Christianity since the civil magistrate as a rule was not competent to decide religious questions and since the Church, backed by the power of the state, had a tendency to persecute those who dissented from it. But in the current contest between Church and chapel, Vaughan took a more moderate position. He recognized the legitimate grounds on which the Church of England stood: its version of Christianity may not have been the purest, but it enjoyed the support of a majority of English men and women, its history was intimately connected with the progress of the English nation, and it was integral to many national institutions. Acknowledging, then, that England was religiously plural and that a case could be made for the Establishment and Dissent, he called on both Church and chapel to accommodate one another. Dissenters, he urged, should refrain from demanding immediate disestablishment and should concentrate instead on building up the strength of their own denominations, while Churchmen – and here he was most emphatic – should moderate their pretensions, accept the legitimacy of Dissent and grant it a complete toleration.[49]

With his first study of the seventeenth century, Vaughan set out to establish the legitimacy of Dissent by an appeal to its past. His *Memorials of the Stuart Dynasty*, published in 1831, offered a distinctly Nonconformist interpretation of its subject. It emphasized the centrality of religious controversy to the contest between king and Parliament and stressed the contribution that the "puritans and their descendants" had made to the progress of political and religious liberty in England.[50] His *Protectorate of Oliver Cromwell*, an edition of the Pell papers published in 1838, and his *England under*

---

[49] Robert Vaughan, *Thoughts on the Past and Present State of Religious Parties in England* (London: Jackson and Walford, 1838), xvi–xviii, 7–8, *Congregationalism*, 1–4, 92–116, 126–146, 171–174, "Church and State," *Essays*, 2: 176–221.

[50] Robert Vaughan, *Memorials of the Stuart Dynasty, Including the Constitutional and Ecclesiastical History of England, from the Decease of Elizabeth to the Abdication of James II* (London: Holdsworth and Ball, 1831), 1: iii–iv.

*the House of Stuart*, which appeared in 1840 under the auspices of the Society for the Diffusion of Useful Knowledge, developed the interpretation further.

Puritanism for Vaughan began as a movement within the Elizabethan Church, involving those loyal but extreme Protestants who wanted to rid the established faith of certain practices which they considered relics of Roman Catholicism. Unfortunately, the Church at this time was intent on uniformity and unwilling to countenance dissent. It persecuted the Puritan clergy, deprived them of their livings and transformed them into a formidable opposition. The alliance between Church and state, an undesirable if unavoidable consequence of the English Reformation, ensured that what began as a purely religious movement soon became political. Churchman and king supported one another and turned against their mutual antagonist. Laud preached the doctrines of divine right and passive obedience while Charles in return supported Laud's Arminian theology and Roman ritual.[51] For Vaughan, it was the Puritans in Parliament who opposed the arbitrary measures of the court, and he made plain the debt that England owed them for the preservation of its liberties. "It is the confession of their enemies," he wrote,

> that to this people we "owe the whole freedom of our constitution" . . . The principles which made them Protestants made them Puritans, teaching them to regard oppression as an evil to be resisted, whether practiced by popes, by princes, or by a Protestant clergy. Animated by these principles, and persecuted by the crown and the court clergy, the Puritans not only became connected with every popular movement, but gave to every such movement the peculiar energy of religious motives. The interests of religion and of civil freedom were seen to be every where interwoven, so that to forsake either would be to give an ascendancy to the enemies of both.[52]

Vaughan's account of this contest emphasized the excellence of the Puritan clergy, their popularity, loyalty and willingness to compromise. They remained Calvinists, the preference of the nation, at a time when the court was Arminian, and they stayed

[51] Ibid., 1: 39–43, 51–60, 110–112, 129–148, 275–296, 331–336, 346–347, 425–444, 469–476, 481–508. Robert Vaughan, *The History of England under the House of Stuart, Including the Commonwealth* (London: Baldwin and Cradock, 1840), 1: 26, 33–46, 109–131, 243–246, 268–271, 273–288.

[52] Vaughan, *England under the House of Stuart*, 1: 45.

within the Church until the intolerance of the court made accommodation impossible.[53]

As a Dissenter, Vaughan was particularly concerned with the problem of religious liberty, and as a historian of Stuart England, he was painfully aware that creating a tolerant society was one area where Anglican Churchmen and a good many Puritans had failed. Vaughan readily acknowledged that many of the early Puritans were just as committed to the principle of religious uniformity as the Churchmen. Their initial disagreement with the Church was not over toleration but over which practices the Establishment should enforce, and the Puritans were outspoken in their hatred of the Roman Catholics, often upbraiding the court for its lax enforcement of the penal laws.[54] But among one group of Puritans, the Independents, ideas of toleration did emerge. Believing that all churches were voluntary associations, organized solely for the purposes of religion, the Independents called for the separation of religion and politics. Here for Vaughan was the origin of all modern ideas of toleration. The very idea of religious uniformity he considered incompatible with Protestantism, which was founded on two principles – the sufficiency of the Bible and the individual's right to private judgment. When the Anglican Establishment or the Puritans demanded uniformity, they were actually adopting the Papal practice of infallibility and denying the individual the right to decide on matters of faith by a personal appeal to Scripture. What made religious diversity particularly troublesome in the seventeenth century was the close alliance of Church and state which, confusing the spiritual and the temporal, equated dissent from the Church with disloyalty to the state. The Independents pointed the way out of this dilemma when they argued that the separation of Church and state would enable religious differences to coexist with political loyalty. Their ideas first gained popularity among the soldiers of the Parliamentary army, found a patron in Oliver Cromwell, and then, after the Restoration, provided the foundation for modern Nonconformity.[55]

The political position that Vaughan took in his works of history

---

[53] Vaughan, *Memorials of the Stuart Dynasty*, 1: 61–71, 147–148, 336, 345–346, *England under the House of Stuart*, 1: 35.
[54] Vaughan, *Memorials of the Stuart Dynasty*, 1: 41–43, 65–66.
[55] Ibid., 1: 39–42, 297–304, 327. Vaughan, *England under the House of Stuart*, 1: 124–131.

was a moderate one, consistent with his Whig sympathies. He applauded the Long Parliament for its tendency to preserve rather than innovate, he remained relatively unimpressed with the radical politics of the Commonwealth – he was no republican – and he saved his praise for Cromwell. In his *Protectorate of Oliver Cromwell*, as in his other seventeenth-century studies, he presented one of the most favorable portraits of the Puritan statesman to appear at this time. He accepted the usual criticisms of his subject – Cromwell did dissemble in order to promote his own ambition – but Vaughan went on to insist that there was more to Cromwell's behavior than mere hypocrisy. Cromwell was above all a pragmatist, shaping events for the public good, and this practical approach to politics explained many of his apparent inconsistencies. After the Civil War, three hostile parties contended for supremacy and the victory of any one of them would have ended in tyranny. The royalists would have restored the Stuarts, the Presbyterians planned to impose a religious settlement as intolerant as Laud's, and the republicans subjected the nation to an oligarchy. Cromwell at first attempted to arrange a compromise between these parties and when this policy failed, he sided with the army, consenting to the king's execution in order to safeguard what the war had achieved. Realizing at last that only a mixed monarchy would restore stability while preserving freedom, Cromwell dismissed the Rump Parliament and proceeded to reestablish as much of England's traditional constitution as circumstances would allow. Like Macaulay, Vaughan was impressed with Cromwell's efforts to balance liberty and order. Although he acknowledged that the Protectorate was far from perfect – to govern in the face of such opposition was difficult and Cromwell was forced at times to resort to arbitrary measures – Vaughan stressed that Cromwell brought greatness to England. His rule was just and humane, and he granted a large degree of religious toleration.[56] Cromwell, Vaughan wrote, "secured to the country comparative order and tranquillity; encouraged learning, agriculture, and commerce; and so far augmented her general resources and naval power, as to confer

[56] Robert Vaughan, *The Protectorate of Oliver Cromwell, and the State of Europe during the Early Part of the Reign of Louis XIV* (London: Henry Colburn, 1839), 1: lxiii–xcviii, cxiv–cxx, *England under the House of Stuart*, 2: 498–499, 500–505, 521–522, 533–536, 541–542, 545–548, *Memorials of the Stuarts*, 2: 202–204, 238–239, 244–245, 254–255, 261–265.

upon England a name and influence in the affairs of Europe, which
she had not attained under the sway of any sovereign in the long
line of her princes."[57]

An unadulterated Protestantism, political liberalism, a commitment to toleration – here were the important characteristics of
Puritanism as it developed in the course of the seventeenth century.
Given the centrality of the rivalry between Church and Dissent to
the politics of the early nineteenth century, Vaughan's interpretation of the Puritan past carried an ideological significance. Just as
the Puritans had defended England's Protestant faith against the
Romanizing innovations of Archbishop Laud, so the evangelical
Dissenters were preserving a vital Protestantism in the face of
the "heartless formalism" of the Church and the Romanizing
tendencies of the Tractarians. Evangelicalism, Vaughan once
remarked, was a "revival of the piety of the elder puritans, and of
the still older protestant reformers."[58] And just as the Puritans had
protected England's traditional liberties against the tyranny of the
Stuarts and attempted to found a just, free and tolerant commonwealth under the leadership of Oliver Cromwell, so contemporary
Dissenters should continue to pursue similar liberal ends. Like
others, Vaughan was often alarmed at the virulence of the
sectarian strife that plagued England in the 1830s and 1840s, and in
the interest of national unity he called for moderation.[59] Although
he addressed this plea to both Churchmen and Dissenters, his
historical studies made it clear that more often than not the
Establishment, because of its unwillingness to compromise, was
responsible for inciting this hostility between Christians. In the
seventeenth century, Francis Bacon had suggested that harmony
might have been maintained so long as the Church demanded
obedience to only the essentials of Christian doctrine, while
allowing the greatest diversity on the inessentials pertaining to
worship and discipline. This had been the position of the more
moderate Puritans, and Vaughan speculated that much of the
century's religious conflict might have been avoided if only
the Establishment had accepted this liberal principle.[60] Though it

[57] Vaughan, *Protectorate of Oliver Cromwell*, 1: ciii.
[58] Vaughan, "Lord John Russell," *Essays*, 1: 53, 57, "Oxford and Evangelical Churchmen,"
*Essays*, 1: 108–110.
[59] See, for example, Vaughan, *Congregationalism*, 105–116.
[60] Vaughan, *England under the House of Stuart*, 1: 119–120, *Memorials of the Stuarts*, 1: 71–72.

referred to an earlier age, Vaughan's speculation was no less germane to his own troubled time.

The appearance in the late 1830s of Vaughan's *Protectorate of Oliver Cromwell* and Forster's *Statesmen of the Commonwealth* was indicative of a changing emphasis in English thinking about the Stuart past. Where earlier writers from Edmund Burke to Henry Hallam had seen the Interregnum as largely destructive and had looked instead to the Glorious Revolution for the establishment of the nation's liberties, these Dissenting historians, building on the work of William Godwin, were now stressing the importance of the Puritan past, the Commonwealth and Protectorate, in the shaping of modern England. Defenders of the Establishment had often tried to discredit Dissent by associating it with seventeenth-century Puritanism. The Dissenters, they charged, had always existed in opposition to the nation's institutions, were prone to enthusiasm and when given the opportunity to influence affairs, had demonstrated their subversive tendencies by overturning the monarchy, Church and Lords. Historians like Forster and Vaughan, despite the differences in their interpretations, answered this accusation. They freed the Puritans from the charge of fanaticism, located the origin of toleration among the Independents, and demonstrated that the leaders of the Parliament were political moderates wholly acceptable to early Victorian liberalism. Whether turning to Vane and the Commonwealth or Cromwell and the Protectorate they emphasized that Dissent and liberty – especially liberty of conscience – went hand in hand. Within this historical context, the Dissenters' assault on the Anglican Establishment ceased to be an act of disloyalty, becoming instead a necessary step in the pursuit of those liberties that had made England, in the past and in the present, a great and unique nation.

This preoccupation with the Puritan past was part of a larger effort by Dissenters to justify their nonconformity. Absent from their argument was any mention of the millenarianism of the Puritans. Though millenarian aspirations may have been common in the first half of the seventeenth century, affecting almost all segments of society, subsequent defenders of the Establishment had come to see the Puritans' conviction that they were God's instrument for creating His kingdom on earth as a defining characteristic of their fanaticism. Well before the nineteenth century, however, Dissenters had started to distance themselves from this Puritan millenarianism, replacing it with a secular conception of progress in which Dissent became synonymous with the attainment of civil and religious liberty.[61] As Dissenters in the 1820s and 1830s intensified their campaign against the Establishment, their interpretation of the Puritan past, in which the Commonwealth and Protectorate were seen as a liberal alternative to the Stuart Church and monarchy, gave them a framework in which to understand who they were and what it was they were trying to accomplish.

Cromwell's reputation provided the Dissenters with their most troublesome historiographical problem. For upholders of the Establishment, Cromwell represented everything that was most destructive in Puritanism and, by association, in Dissent. His fanaticism and hypocrisy, ambition and disregard for traditional institutions clearly required comment. And yet for Dissenters, the defense of Cromwell was no easy task. While he was without a doubt the greatest Dissenter English history had yet produced, he also seemed to have violated the very liberalism that the Dissenters claimed to embrace. According to conventional wisdom, it was Cromwell, after all, who had turned against the republic and erected a military despotism on its ruins. A defense of Cromwell thus threatened to become an apology for tyranny, an admission that Puritanism and liberty were hardly compatible. Vaughan and Forster confronted the complexities of Cromwell's career with different interpretive strategies, neither of which was wholly satisfying. Unwilling to endorse the radicalism of the Commonwealth, Vaughan argued that Cromwell's practical achievements in the cause of liberty and good government far surpassed the deplorable effects of his hypocrisy and ambition. Though Macaulay in his early essays had used a similar approach with great rhetorical success, it seemed an almost intentional misrepresentation of the more unpleasant aspects of Cromwell's rise to power. Forster, on the other hand, genuinely repelled by Cromwell's usurpation, abandoned the Protector to his detractors, and concentrated instead on making Vane and the Commonwealth conform to the expectations of early Victorian liberalism. Not until

---

[61] For the Dissenters' retreat from millenarianism in the years after the Restoration, see Russell E. Richey, "The Origins of British Radicalism: The Changing Rationale for Dissent," *Eighteenth-Century Studies*, 7 (1973–1974): 179–192.

Carlyle shifted attention from Cromwell's politics to his religion would Dissenters see a more attractive way out of their dilemma.

III

By far the most significant contribution to the early Victorian reappraisal of the Commonwealth and Protectorate was the publication in 1845 of Thomas Carlyle's edition of the *Letters and Speeches of Oliver Cromwell*. Steeped in Scottish Calvinism and Dissent, Carlyle felt an enduring fascination for the Puritan past. In 1838, he had agreed to write an article on Cromwell for John Stuart Mill's *London and Westminster Review* but never completed it because Mill's assistant, John Robertson, broke the agreement and wrote the article himself. Unwilling to give up the project altogether, Carlyle decided to continue on his own and set to work on the book that emerged seven years later as the *Letters and Speeches*.[62] The period of composition was difficult. At one time, Carlyle intended to produce a complete history of England from the death of Elizabeth through the Protectorate, but as the materials proved intractable, he abandoned the project in 1843 and concentrated on a biography of Cromwell instead. Some of the manuscripts for the history were used in the biography, the remainder were locked away until 1898, when they were published posthumously as the *Historical Sketches*. To make the work on Cromwell even more demanding, other projects impinged on Carlyle's time: he wrote *Chartism* in 1839, delivered the public lectures on *Heroes and Hero-Worship* in 1840, and wrote *Past and Present* in 1843.[63] The proximity in composition and the similarity in theme

---

62  Thomas Carlyle to John A. Carlyle (26 December 1838), *The Collected Letters of Thomas and Jane Welsh Carlyle*, Duke-Edinburgh edition (Durham, N.C.: Duke University Press, 1970–1987), 10: 250–251. Robertson's article, a review of Vaughan's *Protectorate* and Forster's *Statesmen*, appeared in 1839 and was another Dissenter's attempt to reassess Cromwell favorably. John Robertson, "Oliver Cromwell," *Westminster Review*, 33 (October, 1839): 181–256.

63  For a more complete account of the writing of Carlyle's Cromwell, see: James Anthony Froude, *Thomas Carlyle: A History of His Life in London, 1834–1881* (London: Longmans, Green and Co., 1884), 1: 149–364. C. H. Firth, introduction to Thomas Carlyle, *Letters and Speeches of Oliver Cromwell*, ed. S. C. Lomas (London: Methuen and Co., 1904), 1: xxi–xxxiii. For some recent appraisals of Carlyle as a historian, see: John D. Rosenberg, *Carlyle and the Burden of History* (Oxford: Clarendon Press, 1985). A. Dwight Culler, *The Victorian Mirror of History* (New Haven: Yale University Press, 1985), 39–73. Rosemary Jann, *The Art and Science of Victorian History* (Columbus, Ohio: Ohio State University Press, 1985), 33–65. For the controversy over the "Squire papers," a set of forgeries that Carlyle was

suggest that all these works, including *Cromwell*, were actually one creative effort. When the biography of Cromwell did finally appear in 1845. it was, much to its author's surprise, a great success. Even those most critical of the book admitted that Carlyle had seen better than anyone before him the importance of Puritanism as the key to both Cromwell and the seventeenth century. "It was an historical event," S. R. Gardiner observed many years later, "changing our whole conception of English history in its most heroic period."[64]

Carlyle once said that "a man's religion is the chief fact with regard to him,"[65] and nowhere was this observation more applicable than to Carlyle himself. Born in Scotland, he was raised within the Burgher Secession Church, a body of Dissenters among whom the Covenanting tradition remained strong. The Burghers had separated from the Scottish Church in the early eighteenth century in large part because they objected to the influence which the Church accorded to lay patrons in clerical appointments. The Church, as the Burghers saw it, had neglected its obligation to bring about that Calvinistic commonwealth in which Church and state worked together to spread God's word and enforce His laws. True religion, they believed, could only exist among Dissenters, where the right of the congregation to elect its ministers ensured doctrinal purity.[66] Raised within this tradition, the spirit of Dissent never left Carlyle, and it colored everything he wrote about contemporary as well as seventeenth-century England. He opposed the Established Churches in Scotland and England because they had long ago departed from true religion. He based the critique of Victorian society which he presented in *Past and Present* partly upon the observation that England, from the Restoration onward, had deviated from the ideal of the Godly community, and his remedy

persuaded to accept as genuine, see Clyde de L. Ryals, "Thomas Carlyle and the Squire Forgeries," *Victorian Studies*, 30 (1987): 495–518.

[64] Samuel Rawson Gardiner, "A New Book by Carlyle," *Daily News*, 28 November 1898, 7.

[65] Thomas Carlyle, *On Heroes, Hero-Worship, and the Heroic in History*, in the *Centenary Edition of the Works of Thomas Carlyle*, ed. H. D. Traill (London: Chapman and Hall, 1896–1899), 5: 2.

[66] For the Secession Church, see John M'Kerrow, *History of the Secession Church*, revised and enlarged edition (Edinburgh: A. Fullarton and Co., 1848), 1–82. For a discussion of the role of the "Godly commonwealth" in early nineteenth-century Scottish religious thinking, see Stewart J. Brown, *Thomas Chalmers and the Godly Commonwealth in Scotland* (Oxford: Oxford University Press, 1982), xv–xviii, 43–49, 70–72. See also Andrew L. Drummond and James Bulloch, *The Scottish Church, 1688–1843: The Age of the Moderates* (Edinburgh: Saint Andrew Press, 1973), 40–44.

for the nation's ills was to bring that ideal somehow back into practice. He praised Cromwell for defeating the false Establishment of Laud and Charles I, for tolerating the Sectaries, and for attempting to create in England a commonwealth based on Scriptural law.

Intending to enter the ministry, Carlyle attended the University of Edinburgh, but in the course of his studies lost his faith. The contradiction between the Evangelicalism of his youth and the moderate theology then prevalent at Edinburgh provoked a spiritual crisis that marked him for life. He turned to German philosophy and after a conversion experience regained a semblance of his faith, clothing it now in metaphysics. Carlyle portrayed this spiritual odyssey in his first major book, *Sartor Resartus*, written early in the 1830s. Though Carlyle's religious outlook at this time was certainly not Christian, it did retain many of the assumptions of his early Calvinism. As his disciple and biographer, James Anthony Froude, put it, Carlyle remained a "Calvinist without the theology."[67] Carlyle's thinking was always predestinarian. He believed there was a God in heaven, and that God's laws, or God's justice, reigned on earth. If men and women did not live according to these laws, then God would have his revenge, usually in some apocalyptic event, which would punish them for their errors and redirect their affairs. The history of mankind was predestined because it would, in one way or another, conform to these laws. Carlyle also believed in the elect, or as he termed it, in heroes. The hero was that person who believed in God and God's justice, who thus had insight into the divine, who understood his duties and had the strength to fulfill them, and who would succeed because he alone had God's sanction for what he did. The hero was of the elect, and his success was proof of his election. Ordinary men and women, Carlyle further argued, were for the most part ignorant of God's laws, and it was their duty to obey the elect, to worship the hero. Finally, Carlyle placed great stress on work, and showed nothing but contempt for idleness. Man's purpose on earth was to work, and work alone was noble and virtuous. Speaking in praise of his father, Carlyle wrote: "[he knew] that man was created to work – not to speculate, or feel, or dream. Accordingly he set his whole heart

---

[67] James Anthony Froude, *Thomas Carlyle: A History of the First Forty Years of His Life, 1795–1835* (New York: Charles Scribner's Sons, 1882), 2: 2.

thitherwards. He did work wisely and unweariedly."[68] This
emphasis on God's justice and predestination, on the heroic and
the elect, on obedience and duty, and above all on work, reflects the
Calvinism of Carlyle's childhood spent among the Dissenters in
the rural borderlands of Southern Scotland.[69] Carlyle valued
immensely this Calvinism, or "Puritanism," as he often termed it.
He wrote in his book on Cromwell that England's most valuable
possession was its Puritan heritage of the seventeenth century, and
he described this heritage as a "Scotch mist" coming down on
England "from the land of [John] Knox," hinting that England's
most valuable possession was, in fact, of Scottish origin.[70]

Carlyle's immersion in Calvinism and Dissent drew him – almost
inexorably it seems – to the Puritan past. As early as 1817, he was
reading deeply in English history and, like other Dissenters at
the time, was soon attracted to the Commonwealth. "Oliver
Cromwell's reign," he remarked to his brother in 1820, "is more
interesting than any other." Two years later he was contemplating
writing a book on the Civil War and Commonwealth that would use
"mental portraits" of such worthies as Milton, Cromwell, Laud, Fox
and Hyde in order to illustrate "some features of the national
character as it was then displayed." The project, however, was short
lived, perhaps because he had not yet developed a meaningful interpretation of the period. The subject, he said, had lost its "charm."[71]

Carlyle's interest in Puritanism revived a decade later when he
discovered by accident some books about John Knox and the

---

[68] Thomas Carlyle, *Reminiscences*, ed. James Anthony Froude (London: Longmans, Green and Co., 1881), 1: 10.

[69] For the development of Carlyle's religious thinking, see: Charles Frederick Harrold, *Carlyle and German Thought: 1819–1934*, Yale Studies in English, vol. 82 (New Haven: Yale University Press, 1934), and "The Nature of Carlyle's Calvinism," *Studies in Philology*, 33 (July, 1936): 475–486. G. B. Tennyson, *Sartor Called Resartus: The Genesis, Structure and Style of Thomas Carlyle's First Major Work* (Princeton: Princeton University Press, 1965). Peter Allan Dale, *The Victorian Critic and the Idea of History: Carlyle, Arnold, Pater* (Cambridge: Harvard University Press, 1977), 15–88. David J. DeLaura, "Carlyle and Arnold: The Religious Issue," in K. J. Fielding and Roger L. Tarr, eds., *Carlyle Past and Present: A Collection of New Essays* (New York: Barnes and Noble, 1976), 127–154.

[70] Thomas Carlyle, *Historical Sketches of Notable Persons and Events in the Reigns of James I and Charles I*, ed. Alexander Carlyle (London: Chapman and Hall, 1898), 15.

[71] Thomas Carlyle to Robert Mitchell (19 November 1817), to James Johnston (20 November 1817), to John A. Carlyle (29 March 1820), to Matthew Allen (19 May 1820), to James Johnston (8 April 1822), to Alexander Carlyle (27 April 1822), and to Jane Baillie Welsh (28 October 1822), *Collected Letters*, 1: 112–113, 115, 237, 252, 2: 84, 94, 189. Thomas Carlyle, *Two Note Books of Thomas Carlyle: From 23d March 1822 to 16th May 1832*, ed. Charles Eliot Norton (New York: The Grolier Club, 1898), 1–31.

Scottish Reformation. He had spent much of 1831 and 1832 in London, trying to interest publishers in *Sartor* and watching with alarm the progress of English politics during the crisis over Parliamentary reform. Like many others, he feared that England was heading toward revolution. Modernity, he worried, with its emphasis on industry and commerce, on mechanism and material-ism, had destroyed the fabric of traditional society and had removed the religious bonds which had once held that society together. With the old sources of authority gone and nothing adequate in their place, England appeared on the brink of anarchy.[72] Turning at this crisis to the Scottish Church during the Reformation, Carlyle concluded that in contrast to all other Protestant churches, it alone had been a "real Church."[73] In Scottish Calvinism of the sixteenth century, Carlyle saw the kind of authentic religion that England in the 1830s so desperately needed – a religion capable of impressing upon ordinary men and women the existence of a divine order and a sense of their mutual responsibilities. At a time of political unrest, a Puritan hero such as John Knox provided a welcome example of true leadership. "I find in Knox," Carlyle explained, "one of those unmanageable fellows who once for all have taken in hand to act and speak not respectably but honestly; and have no manner of notion that God's Truth should alter its attitude for man's pleasure, be the man who he may: a true Reformer, of the sort much wanted now and always, seldom rarer than now."[74]

This conception of Puritanism as a genuine religiosity and of the Puritan hero as an authentic leader capable of ensuring that human affairs conformed to God's plan would provide the basis for Carlyle's future reflections on the Puritan past. Alarmed by the course of liberal reform, Carlyle had found in Puritanism a reverence for authority and social order that he saw as a reassuring antidote to the social disintegration caused by the collapse of traditional belief. Receptive to the rhetoric of seventeenth-century Puritanism, he would adapt it to his own purposes, molding it into an idiosyncratic, but verbally powerful, critique of contemporary British institutions. It was this openness to the language and spirit of Puritanism that ultimately set Carlyle apart from other

[72] Thomas Carlyle to John A. Carlyle (13 November 1831), *Collected Letters*, 6: 52.
[73] Thomas Carlyle to John Stuart Mill (19 November 1832), ibid., 6: 260–261.
[74] Thomas Carlyle to John Stuart Mill (12 January 1833), ibid., 6: 303.

historians and enabled him to recapture the Puritans' own understanding of their accomplishments.

Carlyle's final and most prolonged engagement with Puritanism
began in the late 1830s. His fascination with the Scottish Reformation and the English Civil War would influence the lectures on
*Heroes and Hero-Worship* as well as *Past and Present*, and it would
receive its fullest expression in his edition of Cromwell's *Letters and
Speeches* in 1845. Beneath this preoccupation with the Puritan past
lay Carlyle's deepening fears about England's troubled condition as
the economic distress of the late 1830s and early 1840s turned into
one of the worst depressions of the century. What disturbed him
most was the apparent inability of England's leaders to deal
effectively with this impending crisis. The Reform Act of 1832 had
promised a time of improvement, but the emergence of Chartism
and the Anti-Corn Law agitation made it abundantly clear that the
Whigs and their Tory successors were unable to bring this about.
The failure of reform fed Carlyle's anger and in his writings he
attacked what he considered to be the errors of his age: the selfishness of politicians, the ineffectiveness of Parliamentary democracy,
the idleness of the aristocracy, the greed of the industrialists, the
inhumanity of classical economics, the spiritual barrenness of
Benthamite utilitarianism, and the atheism of the Anglican
Church, which he believed had lapsed into the worship of formulas
and was no longer able to see into the essence of things. With
*Chartism*, written in 1839, Carlyle began an assault on England's
contemporary institutions which he sustained into the 1850s with
the publication of the *Latter-Day Pamphlets*. His book on Cromwell
was part of this campaign.

When he delivered his lectures on *Heroes and Hero-Worship* in 1840,
Carlyle had much to say about Knox, the Puritan priest, and
Cromwell, the Puritan king. The hero for Carlyle was that rare
individual who understood God's laws, realized them on earth and
thereby imposed order on chaos. The nineteenth century was a time
of revolution and disorder precisely because it lacked heroes and
hero-worship. Developing his earlier thoughts on the Scottish
Reformation, Carlyle described Knox as an example of the hero as
priest and reformer in order to criticize implicitly the would-be
reformers of his own day. Neither radical nor Benthamite, Whig nor
Tory, as far as Carlyle was concerned, shared Knox's genuine
sense of the divine. Lecturing on Cromwell and placing him in the

category of the hero as king, Carlyle sketched much of the interpretation that he would express later in the *Letters and Speeches*. For Carlyle, Cromwell was a Christian hero, sincere in his faith and ambitious in a purely heroic way. Those historians, who viewed the seventeenth century solely in political terms and criticized Cromwell for deserting the republican cause in order to make himself king, had totally missed the point. The Civil War, Carlyle insisted, was actually a religious struggle of Puritan "Belief" against Laudian "Unbelief." Throughout his career, Cromwell labored to create that Puritan commonwealth of which Knox had dreamed, and never once did he desert this cause. Under his leadership and inspired by a true religiosity, England momentarily achieved greatness.[75]

In *Past and Present*, Carlyle presented a compelling critique of early industrial society. Attributing the problems of his age ultimately to the erosion of religious belief, he offered a spiritual solution. What England needed, he urged, adopting the language of the Puritan sermon, was a new reformation. The return of the Stuarts in 1660 had marked the defeat of Puritanism and had brought the English Reformation to an end. Atheism had triumphed, and to this fact Carlyle traced many of the nation's ills.[76] England needed in the nineteenth century a spiritual reawakening that would provide men and women with an understanding of their duties to one another and compel them to work for the good of the community. England required a new hero, someone who understood God's justice, who would teach the people those Calvinistic values which Carlyle cherished, and who would finish the work that he believed Cromwell had begun.

For Carlyle, Puritanism was the culmination, the most heroic phase of the English Reformation. The Puritans, with Cromwell as their leader, were true believers who attacked the false Church of Archbishop Laud, and the false kingship of Charles I. They brought a terrible justice to Ireland, and by creating a Godly commonwealth, they attempted to bring true government to England. Cromwell and the Puritans carried out in the seventeenth century that very assault on traditional, but empty institutions which Carlyle was urging in his own age. In Cromwell, Carlyle had found the model hero. Oliver Cromwell, he declared in *Past and Present*,

---

[75] Carlyle, *Works*, 5: 204–237.   [76] Ibid., 10: 166–169.

"remains to me by far the remarkablest Governor we have had here for the last five centuries or so . . . When you consider that Oliver believed in a God, the difference between Oliver's position and that of any subsequent Governor of this Country becomes . . . the more immeasurable!"[77] Carlyle put forth this image of Cromwell hoping, but not really believing, that it might inspire England in the nineteenth century to an even greater Puritanism. As he wrote to Ralph Waldo Emerson in 1842: "My heart is sick and sore in behalf of my own poor generation; nay, I feel withal as if the one hope of help for it consisted in the possibility of new Cromwells, and new Puritans: thus do the two centuries stand related to me, the seventeenth *worthless* except precisely in so far as it can be made the *nineteenth*; and yet let anybody *try* that enterprise!"[78]

The *Letters and Speeches of Oliver Cromwell* was by all counts an unusual work. Unable to master the materials of Cromwell's life and mold them into a balanced narrative, Carlyle abandoned the task of author for that of editor. Gathering together all Cromwell's known utterances and providing them with elucidations, he allowed the letters and speeches to furnish the book with its basic structure. The result was a biography lacking proportion. As an editor, Carlyle hardly compensated for the imperfections, digressions and omissions found in Cromwell's surviving statements. Despite this drawback, Cromwell's *Letters and Speeches* produced a powerful impression on its readers. In part, this was because Cromwell, through his own words, presented a more vivid and favorable portrait of himself than had any previous biographer. But above all, the book's effectiveness was due to Carlyle's vision of what the seventeenth century was about. As he imagined it, England during the Civil War was in the midst of a desperate struggle between Light and Darkness, God and the Devil, and Carlyle's prose, with its Biblical resonances, was admirably suited to convey such an image. At times, he seemed to deny that he was even writing conventional history. To the contrary, he was creating a *Cromwelliad*, an epic poem of the Civil War and Protectorate.[79]

Religion for Carlyle formed the essence of the seventeenth century. The most important transaction in Europe during this

[77] Ibid., 10: 222.
[78] Thomas Carlyle to Ralph Waldo Emerson (29 August 1842), *Collected Letters*, 15: 57.
[79] Carlyle, *Works*, 6: 5–6, 12–13.

period was the heroic "struggle of Protestantism against Catholicism," of true religion against false, and the Civil War in England, the "armed Appeal of Puritanism" against the "Ceremonialism" of Laud and Charles I, was one manifestation of this larger controversy.[80] Carlyle saw Puritanism as an intense religiosity. It consisted in a personal relationship between a man and his God, in which the individual was painfully aware that heaven and hell were real, that he had a soul to save, and that its salvation depended on his acting in accordance with God's laws. Within this relationship neither priests nor sacraments played an important role, which explained why Puritanism was founded primarily outside the Established Church, among the Independents and Sectaries. Because of its emphasis on conduct, Puritanism was also a powerful moral force. It was the principal impetus behind the Parliamentary party and a reforming influence in both Church and state. Opposed to Puritanism was the sham religion of the Anglicans and the Presbyterians. Because of its "Ceremonialism," its preoccupation with the outward forms of religion, the Anglican faith as practiced by Archbishop Laud had lost its insight into the divine and was no longer able to inspire true piety or moral conduct. In this failing it resembled Roman Catholicism. Also bound up in images were the Presbyterians of Scotland. Their Covenant was little more than a "formula" and their loyalty to the fraudulent Stuart kings reflected their inability to see beyond outward appearances.[81] Conceived in this manner, England's seventeenth century became an immense war of religion in which constitutional issues played absolutely no role. Do not, Carlyle admonished his readers, "imagine that it was Constitution, . . . Privilege of Parliament, Triennial or Annual Parliaments, or any modification of these . . . that mainly animated our Cromwells, Pyms, and Hampdens." They were "inspired by a Heavenly Purpose. To see God's own Law . . . made good in this world; . . . it was a thing worth living for and dying for!"[82]

Carlyle's greatest achievement was to see clearly that Cromwell had always been a sincerely religious man. He was the perfect Puritan, and the transforming episode in his life was the religious conversion he experienced sometime in 1623. Cromwell began as an honest gentleman farmer, prone to the melancholia and

---

[80] Ibid., 6: 39, 41.     [81] Ibid., 6: 64, 7: 169–171.     [82] Ibid., 6: 81–82.

hypochondria that came from contemplating "in thick darkness" the possibility of a meaningless world, whose despair was overcome once the "eternal ways and the celestial guiding-stars disclose[d] themselves." Cromwell's conversion as portrayed by Carlyle, his "clear recognition of Calvinistic Christianity" and his "deliverance from the jaws of Eternal Death," bore a striking resemblance to Teufelsdröckh's conversion in *Sartor Resartus*, and, to the extent that *Sartor* was autobiographical, to Carlyle's own conversion. In all three instances, the experience produced an acute awareness of the moral obligation to do right instead of wrong which became a call to work. After his conversion, Cromwell sensed that the "difference between Right and Wrong had filled all Time and all Space for man, and bodied itself forth into a Heaven and Hell for him," and it was this realization that made him a Puritan.[83] Because of their common religious background, Carlyle found Cromwell a sympathetic subject and although he emphasized their similarities probably to the point of distortion, his insight into Cromwell's religion enabled him to rehabilitate his character. Above all, it allowed him to refute the charge of hypocrisy. A Puritan such as Cromwell, who believed in the salvation of his soul, would·not risk damnation by prevaricating before his God.[84] Cromwell's words, Carlyle urged, must be taken for the truth. And having established his hero's basic honesty, Carlyle put an end to the accusation of ambition: for Cromwell stated repeatedly that personal gain had never been his object. He had worked first for the glory of God, then for the interests of the Godly in England, and finally for the rights and privileges of Parliament. Carlyle accepted these statements at face value and he urged his readers to do the same.

Cromwell attributed his success in all his endeavors to divine Providence. He viewed the favorable outcome of events as a sign of God's approval for the policies he had pursued and here Carlyle took him at his word. In the Civil War, Cromwell and the "Eternal Laws" were on one side, the enemies of God on the other, and the outcome of the struggle was foretold.[85] Carlyle attributed Cromwell's rise to Protector, not to his ambition, hypocrisy or opportunism, but to the working of God's will. After each of his military conquests, Cromwell explicitly denied that the triumph was his. "Give glory, all the glory, to God," he wrote following his

---

[83] Ibid., 6: 50–51.     [84] Ibid., 6: 80–81.     [85] Ibid., 6: 59, 68.

victory at Marston Moor, and he voiced similar thoughts after defeating the Royalists decisively as Naseby: "this is none other but the hand of God; and to Him alone belongs the glory."[86] The victories in the Civil War, Cromwell suggested, were Providential signs that God had called on the army to challenge the king, and Carlyle, writing in the same spirit, turned his execution into an act of divine retribution. No event in modern history was "graver" than when the army, marching on London, demanded the king's trial. It was a spectacle "earnest as very Death and Judgment." They had "decided to have Justice, these men; to see God's justice done, and His judgments executed on this Earth." The High Court, finding the king guilty and sentencing him to die, was "executing the judgments of Heaven above, and had not the fear of any man or thing on the Earth below."[87]

The beheading of Charles I, Carlyle argued, put an end to "Flunkyism" and "Cant," demonstrating that the fraudulent could no longer rule the genuine. Having fought the Civil War in order to pull down "Idolatrous Kingships," Cromwell and the army had now the daunting task of "setting-up Religious Commonwealths," of bringing God's law to bear on earth.[88] By emphasizing that Cromwell's motives were primarily religious, Carlyle avoided the problems of interpretation that arose from his alleged political apostasy. Cromwell should be judged not as a republican who turned against the republican cause, but as a sincere Puritan who worked consistently and heroically to make England a Puritan nation. He dismissed the Rump Parliament because its members were of insufficient caliber "to realise the high dream of those old Puritan hearts," and he convened the Little Parliament, hoping that a "Real Assembly of the Puritan Notables" would be able to create at last a Godly commonwealth. He dismissed his first Protectorate Parliament because it had done nothing to promote the Puritan interest, and he instituted the Major Generals in order to place power in the hands of the Godly.[89] Addressing his second Protectorate Parliament, Cromwell made plain his objectives: England, he said, needed a new reformation, a worthy ministry, a reform of the law, a profound change in manners, a victory over the "Profaneness, Disorder and Wickedness" formerly associated with

---

[86] Ibid., 6: 188, 215.  [87] Ibid., 6: 404–405, 408, 412.
[88] Ibid., 6: 414, 7: 2.  [89] Ibid., 8: 22–26, 38, 73–74, 78–80, 166–167, 201–203.

the Cavaliers, and toleration toward all those who practiced their religion quietly and peacefully since that was the true cause for which the Puritans had fought.[90] To judge Cromwell against modern standards and to condemn him for ruling unconstitutionally and often arbitrarily was thus to miss the point entirely. He was a Puritan striving to implement the will of God, not a usurper pursuing his own ambition.

The Puritans never finished building their Godly commonwealth and much of what they did manage to build was dismantled after the Restoration. With the death of Cromwell, Puritanism "fell into *Kinglessness*, what we call Anarchy," and "proved, by trial after trial, . . . that a Government of England by *it* was henceforth an impossibility."[91] The rapid collapse of the Puritan movement, which Carlyle did not deny, posed a serious problem for its eulogist: if Puritanism was truly of God, then why had Providence allowed it to fail so thoroughly? "My friend," Carlyle answered, "Puritanism was *not* the Complete Theory of this immense Universe; no, only a part thereof! To me it seems, in my hours of hope, as if the Destinies meant something grander with England than even Oliver Protector did!"[92] In the end, Carlyle fell back upon a cyclical view of history based on alternating periods of belief and unbelief and derived in part from his readings in the German Romantics and the French Saint Simonians.[93] Puritanism had flourished once in the seventeenth century, the Restoration had ushered in an age of anarchy and atheism, but they too would perish in the future when a new, even greater Puritanism would arise.

With the *Letters and Speeches of Oliver Cromwell*, Carlyle continued the attack against early Victorian liberalism that he had initiated earlier in *Chartism* and *Past and Present*. Compared to the considerable problems that plagued them in the 1830s and 1840s, the governments of Melbourne and Peel seemed inept, and their apparent inability to solve England's pressing social problems turned Carlyle into a critic of Parliamentary democracy. If such

[90] Ibid., 8: 290–291, 293, 296–298.     [91] Ibid., 9: 183.     [92] Ibid., 9: 184.

[93] For the debate surrounding Carlyle's general scheme of history, see: Harrold, *Carlyle and German Thought*, 66, 171–176. Hill Shine, *Carlyle and the Saint-Simonians: The Concept of Historical Periodicity* (Baltimore: The Johns Hopkins Press, 1941). René Wellek, "Carlyle and the Philosophy of History," *Confrontations: Studies in the Intellectual and Literary Relations between Germany, England, and the United States during the Nineteenth Century* (Princeton: Princeton University Press, 1965), 82–100. Culler, *Victorian Mirror of History*, 44–47, 50–73. Jann, *Art and Science of Victorian History*, 38–41.

governments were the best the electoral system could produce, then clearly England needed something else. Not surprisingly, Carlyle pointed to Cromwell as an example of the type of leadership he preferred. The Calvinistic doctrine of the elect, which permeated his political thinking, provided the premise for his critique. According to the Calvinist, the elect were entitled to govern because they alone were chosen by God and because they had verified their election by worldly success. To assume that the mass of the nation could do the work of God and select their true leaders was for Carlyle the great misconception underlying representative government. A nation of mediocrities, left to its own devices, would return Parliaments of mediocrity, totally unqualified for governing. In his account of the Civil War, Carlyle made his views on Parliamentary democracy clear: only Cromwell and the army, chosen on the field of battle, were capable of effective leadership. In contrast to the hesitation and pettiness of Parliament, Carlyle emphasized the decisiveness and wisdom of Cromwell.

Carlyle's assault on Parliamentary government amounted to an extended satire on the tendency of popular assemblies to mire in "Red-tape" and meaningless discussion. At no time was his contempt for representative institutions more evident than in his assessment of the Rump. Realizing that they could not sit forever, the members of this "Fag-end" of the Long Parliament had resolved to dismiss themselves, and yet, having decided on an act so simple as this, they found it a deed impossible to accomplish. All they could achieve, Carlyle wryly commented, was to debate and then agree to debate some more. Nor did their incompetence end here. Resolving at one point to attempt a reform of England's property laws, the Rump, disputing all the while, could not even define the term "incumbrance."

Incumbrance [Carlyle wrote sardonically]: yes, but what is "incumbrance"? . . . No mortal can tell. They sit debating it, painfully sifting it, "for three months"; three months by Booker's Almanac, and the Zodiac Horologe: March violets have become June roses; and still they debate what "incumbrance" is; – and indeed, I think could never fix it at all; and are perhaps debating it, if so doomed, in some twilight foggy section of Dante's Nether World, to all Eternity, at this hour!

Obviously the Rump was of insufficient caliber to govern England and bring God's laws to bear on earth. Obsessed with talking and unconcerned with acting, this Parliament had to go, and Cromwell, who understood its failings, dismissed it in one decisive act.[94]

In contrast to his scorn for representative institutions, Carlyle bestowed only praise on Cromwell and the army. One of his favorite conceits was to denounce Parliament as a "Talking Apparatus" while lauding the army as an "Acting Apparatus."[95] If England must have a Parliament, then it should resemble as closely as possible this "Army Parliament" of the seventeenth century. While the Rump was pointlessly disputing the meaning of "incumbrance," Cromwell was preserving the Commonwealth by acting decisively on the battlefield. The "destiny of this Commonwealth," Carlyle stressed, was decided not during the sessions at Westminster, but "in Oliver Cromwell's fightings." It was the prompting of the army that convinced Cromwell to dissolve the Rump, and at this moment, Carlyle wondered, what would have become of England if she "had not still her Army Parliament, rigorous devout Council of Officers, men in right life-and-death earnest, who have spent their blood in this Cause?" Finally, it was Cromwell, acting independently of Parliament, who began to build the Godly commonwealth, who created in England a genuine "Gospel Ministry," who reformed the Court of Chancery, and who established England's foreign relations.[96]

To see Cromwell as a critic of Parliamentary government was not without some justification. The Protector was not adept at managing his Parliaments and, as his speeches revealed, he addressed them at times in words which Carlyle himself might have written. When dismissing his first Protectorate Parliament, for instance, Cromwell pointed out that the arrival of peace had given this assembly a unique opportunity to implement God's will, to enact good laws, and in general to answer the grievances of the nation. But in fact, it had done nothing of the sort. "I do not know what you have been doing!" Cromwell declared in frustration: "I do not know whether you have been alive or dead . . . You have wholly elapsed your time, and done just nothing!" Within this final accusation lay the kernel of Carlyle's hostility toward representative government. When he delivered his opening speech to his second Protectorate Parliament, Cromwell began by expressing the same distrust for words and the same preference for deeds that

[94] Carlyle, *Works*, 8: 4–6, 17, 22.    [95] Ibid., 9: 179.    [96] Ibid., 8: 3–4, 22, 90–94.

Carlyle would later become famous for: "Rhetoricians, whom I do not pretend to [much concern with]; neither with them, nor with what they use to deal in: Words! Truly *our* business is to speak Things!" And then, having outlined the work which this assembly must do, Cromwell continued to emphasize the need to act: "Doubting, hesitating men, they are not fit for your work . . . Those that are called to this work, it will not depend [for them] upon formalities, nor notions, nor speeches! . . . Therefore I beseech you, do not dispute of unnecessary and unprofitable things which may divert you from carrying on so glorious a work as this is."[97] Living through troubled times, both Cromwell and his biographer shared a deep frustration with the apparent inability of Parliamentary government to comprehend the larger issues and act with determination. As Carlyle began to define his own political position, the speeches of Oliver Cromwell, delivered almost two centuries before, were certainly a fertile source of inspiration.

The one area where Carlyle believed that liberal policies were failing most drastically was Ireland. Ever since the writing of *Chartism*, the Irish problem had worried Carlyle, and his account of Irish affairs in his biography of Cromwell gave him an opportunity to reflect on one of its possible solutions. For Carlyle, the Irish problem was one of work – the Irish were capable of immense labor when managed honestly, there was an abundance of work to be done, and yet no one was doing it. Ireland was idle, and unemployment, starvation and beggary were the consequences. The difficulties of governing Ireland had plagued the English at least as far back as the seventeenth century, and in Cromwell's policies Carlyle found the only viable solution to the nation's problems. As a result of Cromwell's military victory, the Irish were brought under an "improved" aristocracy, and they were put to work, "ploughing, delving, hammering." Cromwell transformed them into a productive nation and, had his settlement survived, he would have made them Puritans as well.[98] Here for Carlyle was an effective solution to the Irish question, but unfortunately it was not allowed to run its course. The Restoration destroyed most of what Cromwell had accomplished, and Ireland was left to develop on its own, "not in the drabcoloured Puritan way."[99] As Carlyle understood it, the Irish problem of the 1840s was the inevitable

[97] Ibid., 8: 170–171, 181, 268, 305.        [98] Ibid., 7: 167.        [99] Ibid., 7: 168.

consequence of the Restoration, and the real injustice of the English in Ireland was that they had put an end to the process that Cromwell had begun. In order to be saved, Ireland must suffer in the nineteenth century a Cromwellian settlement more thorough than the last, and like before, this arrangement would not be implemented peacefully, or by philanthropy: Oliver Cromwell, Carlyle pointed out, "did not believe in the rose-water plan of Surgery; – which, in fact, is this Editor's case too!"[100]

IV

Despite its urgency, Carlyle's image of Cromwell as the great Christian hero hardly convinced all his readers. The religious divisions of the seventeenth century were still very much alive in the 1840s and not everyone was prepared to embrace Cromwell and the Puritans as wholeheartedly as Carlyle had. Writing in the Catholic *Dublin Review*, the Maynooth Professor George Crolly declared that nothing of value could be found in Carlyle's book, a judgment which was not unexpected since Carlyle had tried to vindicate what Crolly saw as the atrocities of Cromwell's Irish campaign. Carlyle's "two great volumes," Crolly wrote, were "an interminable sermon, written in the most approved cant of methodism," and their subject, Puritanism, was certainly not heroic: it was "a madness, an imposture, . . . a senseless fanaticism." Crolly's main complaint, however, was not that Carlyle had praised the Puritans, but that he longed for "the return of those times whose faith was the most abominable hypocrisy and the most diabolical bigotry."[101] Equally hostile was the review in the *Christian Remembrancer*, written by its High Church and Tractarian editor, J. B. Mozley. Tracing their own practices back to the Church of Archbishop Laud, the High Churchmen could not endure a book that abused both the Laudians and their nineteenth-century followers. Far from being a hero, Cromwell was little more than a successful hypocrite, dissembler, bigot and regicide, and Mozley's review formed one long litany of his sins. Nor in his opinion were the

---

[100] Ibid., 7: 51. See also Carlyle's essays on Irish subjects, published in 1848 and 1849 and reprinted in *Rescued Essays of Thomas Carlyle*, ed. Percy Newberry (London: The Leadenhall Press, 1892).

[101] [George Crolly], "The Great Irish Insurrection," *Dublin Review*, 21 (September, 1846): 66, 68, 69.

Puritans heroes. They had made religion ridiculous, and to glorify them was to reverse two centuries of received wisdom.[102] Writing in the conservative *Blackwood's Magazine*, William Henry Smith was willing to accept Carlyle's assessment of Cromwell as a sincere Puritan. If nothing else, his letters had established beyond doubt that Cromwell was not a hypocrite who merely used the language of Puritanism to promote his own ambition. But Smith could not agree with Carlyle that Puritanism was either admirable or the panacea for England's current ills. The Puritans lacked humanity, their religious enthusiasm blinded them to right and wrong, and their belief in Providence justified the most extreme acts of violence. A revival of Puritanism in the nineteenth century, Smith predicted, would result in a religious war that would benefit no one. "If church and dissent should take up arms," he wrote, "and . . . should blow out each other's brains with gunpowder, then Mr Carlyle would see his 'heroic ones' revive upon the earth."[103]

The Dissenters, however, were more receptive to Carlyle's work and for the most part welcomed his image of Cromwell as a Christian hero who did his best to establish a Godly commonwealth. Robert Vaughan expressed their position: Carlyle's biography was "on the whole, the most satisfactory in our language" because Carlyle alone had done "justice to the religion of Cromwell." Where other biographers had recognized in Cromwell the great soldier and statesman, Carlyle had seen the religious hero.[104] John Forster, writing almost two decades after he had published his *Statesmen of the Commonwealth*, now acknowledged that his earlier portrait of Cromwell had been woefully inadequate. By bringing together the *Letters and Speeches*, Carlyle had discredited not only the Tory interpretation of Cromwell as a dissembling, hypocritical regicide, but also Forster's own denunciation of Cromwell as a traitor to liberty. From Cromwell's words, Forster now explained, "there . . . broke forth the utterance of a true man, of a consistency of character perfect to an heroic degree." Carlyle had shown absolutely: "That *this* Cromwell was no hypocrite or actor of plays

---

102  [J. B. Mozley], "Carlyle's Cromwell," *Christian Remembrancer*, 11 (April, 1846): 258–261. For Mozley's account of Cromwell's rise to power, see 262–302.

103  [William Henry Smith], "Cromwell," *Blackwood's Edinburgh Magazine*, 61 (April, 1847): 394, 399–401.

104  [Robert Vaughan], "Cromwell's Letters," *British Quarterly Review*, 3 (February, 1846): 51, 60–61.

. . . , was no victim of ambition, was no seeker after sovereignty or temporal power. That he was a man whose every thought was with the Eternal, – a man of a great, robust, massive mind, and of an honest, stout, English heart." Surely, few historians have changed their minds as completely as Forster. Cromwell's purpose, he now emphasized, "was to serve the Lord." When the other republicans refused to go along with him, Cromwell "did well to strike them from his path."[105] Writing on Cromwell in the *Contemporary Review*, the Presbyterian essayist Peter Bayne similarly praised Carlyle's achievement: the *Letters and Speeches*, Bayne declared, was his "greatest book." Before Carlyle, Cromwell's "life was unintelligible." By identifying Puritanism as the single factor giving consistency and meaning to Cromwell's conduct, Carlyle had "raised him from the dead."[106]

But the Dissenters' approval was not without qualification. Vaughan, for one, lamented that Carlyle's perverse fear of seeming dull, of having nothing provocative to say, had made him disparage unnecessarily the efforts of previous historians. Before he even conceived his book, Vaughan asserted, the Dissenters Godwin and Forster – not to mention Vaughan himself – had set in motion a reappraisal of Cromwell that Carlyle, by stressing the importance of Cromwell's religion, was only completing.[107] By placing him in the company of these other historians, Vaughan implied that within Carlyle's work he heard the voice of evangelicalism and Dissent, even though Carlyle himself was unable, or unwilling, to acknowledge it. But more important, Carlyle had put Puritanism to a different use from most other Dissenters. Where they hoped to enlist the Puritan past in the cause of liberal reform, Carlyle had used it to indict the modern age of a spiritual barrenness and lack of order that were in part products of the very liberalism that Vaughan, Forster and others were trying to promote. When Carlyle told his readers to disregard the political dimension of the Civil War, he intentionally branded as unworthy much of what Dissent

---

[105] John Forster, "The Civil Wars and Oliver Cromwell," *Historical and Biographical Essays* (London: John Murray, 1858), 1: 279–284, 304–308, 311–317. See also John Forster, *The Debates on the Grand Remonstrance, November and December, 1641* (London: John Murray, 1860), 414, where the author admits that, in the wake of Carlyle's work, "the views I once held have suffered change in regard to the conduct and character of Cromwell."

[106] Peter Bayne, "Oliver Cromwell," *Contemporary Review*, 21 (February, 1873): 409–412.

[107] Vaughan, "Cromwell's Letters," 51–61.

had stood for.[108] Unconvinced by his admonishment, the Dissenters in turn criticized Carlyle for undervaluing liberty. Peter Bayne, for instance, pointed out that the great flaw in Carlyle's work was its hero-worship which, deteriorating all too easily into a celebration of tyranny, had led Carlyle to scorn unnecessarily the constitutional aspects of the struggle against the Stuarts.[109]

Robert Vaughan further lamented Carlyle's "one-sidedness." While he was admirably open and receptive to the past, he was blind to the present. Critical of the age in which he lived, he was unable to appreciate its virtues. Had he only opened his eyes, he would have seen in modern Dissent a contemporary Puritanism as vital, sincere and pious as its seventeenth-century predecessor. "In Great Britain," Vaughan pointed out, "there are, at this moment, some ten thousand pulpits in which the doctrines of our old puritanism, as to the substance of them, are constantly preached; before which multitudes listen . . . with a conviction not less sincere than that of the men whom we see storming the breach or crossing the battle-field at the bidding of Cromwell." That even greater Puritanism which Carlyle had sought to inspire, Vaughan declared, had in fact already arisen, and if the state were to abuse the liberties of present-day England as it had under the Stuarts, then these modern Puritans, these modern Dissenters, would come once again to their defense: "Place our civil constitution in abeyance, tax men without their consent, imprison them without law . . . ; silence the ten thousand men who preach Christ's holy gospel to these people, shut up their sanctuaries, summon them to your courts of Star Chamber and High Commission . . . – do all this, ye scorners of modern puritanism, *if you dare*, and then see if Marston Moor and Naseby Fight may not be in a fair way of coming back again!"[110]

In drawing this parallel between contemporary Dissent and seventeenth-century Puritanism, Vaughan captured the atmosphere in which Nonconformist politics would operate after the middle of the century. Taking their insights from Carlyle's work, Nonconformist biographers would portray Cromwell as the religious hero who was drawn into politics not because of worldly

---

[108] Carlyle, *Works*, 5: 208–211.

[109] Peter Bayne, *Lessons from My Masters: Carlyle, Tennyson and Ruskin* (New York: Harper and Brothers, 1879), 61–62, 65–68, and "The Younger Vane," *Contemporary Review*, 21 (March, 1873): 673–674.

[110] Vaughan, "Cromwell's Letters," 61–64. Vaughan's italics.

ambition, but because of his duty to God. Hoping to inspire a younger generation to increased political activity, they would present Cromwell as an example worthy of emulation, arguing that for Cromwell liberal politics were the outward expression of an inward piety. Carlyle's unique understanding of England's Puritan past, despite its reactionary tendencies, would provide these Dissenters with a means to infuse modern liberalism with that religious and moral earnestness which became characteristic of the "Nonconformist conscience." The Congregationalist minister and historian John Stoughton, for example, published as early as 1848 a series of short essays on *Spiritual Heroes*, designed, he said, to inspire "the youthful part of the community" with examples of Puritan martyrdom and Christian piety. The influence of Carlyle is apparent not only in the book's title, inconceivable before Carlyle had demonstrated that Puritanism could be "heroic," but in its author's acknowledgment that recent scholarship had vindicated the Puritans from "the unjust charges preferred by their enemies." The Scottish secession minister George Gilfillan similarly published in 1869 his own set of lectures on *Modern Christian Heroes*, in which Cromwell was presented as an individual of "excellent character" and "eminent piety" who "gave his country a model of excellence as a man and as a ruler." In his *English Puritanism*, a contribution to the bicentenary celebration of the Bartholomew Ejectment, Peter Bayne offered an appreciation of the Puritans that united Carlyle's understanding of their religiosity with a Dissenter's traditional concern for liberal policies. Their "special glory," Bayne maintained, was that they "combined all that is seen in them by Bentham with all that is seen in them by Carlyle."[111]

For the Dissenters, however, Cromwell was more than a source of political inspiration. The Cromwellian past, now illuminated by the *Letters and Speeches*, gave the Dissenters a means to legitimate their cause in the present. By establishing the basic honesty of Cromwell's intentions, Carlyle had helped to shift attention away from the vexing questions surrounding his rise to power and to

---

[111] John Stoughton, *Spiritual Heroes; Or, Sketches of the Puritans, Their Character and Times* (New York: M. W. Dodd, 1848), v–vii. George Gilfillan, *Modern Christian Heroes: A Gallery of Protesting and Reforming Men, Including Cromwell, Milton, the Puritans, Covenanters, First Seceders, Methodists* (London: Elliot Stock, 1869), 33, 80. Peter Bayne, *English Puritanism: Its Character and History*, prefixed to George Gould, ed., *Documents Relating to the Settlement of the Church of England by the Act of Uniformity of 1662* (London: W. Kent and Co., 1862), 59.

focus it instead on his achievements as Protector. Informed by Carlyle's work, Dissenters formulated an interpretation of the English past that attributed the greatness of Victorian England to the groundwork laid by Cromwell and the Puritans in the seventeenth century. This interpretation, which gained prominence as Dissent acquired political influence after the middle of the century, served to demonstrate that the Dissenters, far from playing the largely destructive role assigned to them by their adversaries, had in fact contributed constructively to the making of modern England. As Peter Bayne observed in 1862: "There is a general feeling that the hundred years during which the Puritan agitation was at its height are the most memorable in the history of England. The part played by England in modern civilization was then determined. The benefits, political, social, religious, which she has enjoyed, were then secured ... The essential aspects of our national character, in the widest sweep of their diversity and the profoundest conditions of their agreement, were then displayed. All this, we say, is matter of general assent."[112]

In his final narrative of the seventeenth century, the closing volume of his *Revolutions in English History*, Robert Vaughan gave substance to this interpretation. Building on his earlier work, he argued that Cromwell's rise to power was spontaneous and almost inevitable given his talent, and that the irregularities of his rule were necessary due to the extensive opposition to it. Cromwell's Protectorate was the best option available at the time since the triumph of any of his opponents – either the royalists, Presbyterians or republicans – would have imposed one form of tyranny or another. "No English sovereign," Vaughan concluded, "has governed England more constitutionally, none so liberally, as Cromwell would have governed it, had the men of his generation been more men of his own order. In his mind we see the England, not merely of his own day, but of a day still to come."[113] Cromwell and the Puritans, Vaughan pointed out, accomplished much that was lasting. Under the Commonwealth and Protectorate, England asserted itself on the continent, its army rivaling the soldiers of France and Spain, its navy surpassing that of the United Provinces.

---

112 Bayne, *English Puritanism*, 1.
113 Robert Vaughan, *Revolutions in English History* (London: Longman, Green, Longman, Roberts, and Green, 1863), 3: 392–396.

The Navigation Act prepared the foundation for England's commercial supremacy by wresting the carrying trade from the Dutch, while the empire in the West Indies began with the capture of Jamaica. The triumph of the Puritans gave great encouragement to manufacturing and trade since they were drawn primarily from the classes engaged in those pursuits. The licentiousness of the Stuart court was replaced by the sobriety of the Puritans, establishing an impeccable standard of domestic virtue. English literature reached new heights in Milton, science with the discoveries of Harvey and Boyle. Neither hypocrites nor fanatics, the Puritans were sincere in their piety. They were the first to understand the value of religious toleration and the first to implement it so far as the safety of the state would permit.[114]

The Cromwell who emerged from Vaughan's history was truly a national hero. Though a Puritan, a Dissenter, his policies were neither narrowly sectarian nor selfishly ambitious. Rather, they were intended to promote the greatness of the English nation. This image of Cromwell, which would endure with minor variations throughout the remainder of the Victorian period, was the epitome of almost half a century of Nonconformist scholarship. It combined the Dissenters' traditional view of the Puritans as defenders of political and religious liberty, expressed in the early works of Godwin, Forster and Vaughan, along with Carlyle's conviction that Cromwell's Puritanism was sincere, his intentions virtuous, and his accomplishments heroic. Once Carlyle had shown how Cromwell – previously controversial and troublesome because of his alleged ambition, hypocrisy and apostasy – could be vindicated, the Dissenters were able to concentrate in one colossal figure from the past all that they stood for. The story of Cromwell's progress from Puritan gentleman to Lord Protector gave them an inspiring example of political conduct as well as a powerful affirmation of the constructive role that Dissent had played, and would continue to play, in the making of modern England.

114  Ibid., 3: 397–427.

# CHAPTER 4

# Samuel Rawson Gardiner and the search for national consensus

In an essay on Macaulay, Lytton Strachey once identified those "qualities" that he thought essential for the successful historian: "a capacity for absorbing facts, a capacity for stating them, and a point of view. The two latter," Strachey went on, "are connected, but not necessarily inseparable. The late Professor Samuel Gardiner, for instance, could absorb facts, and he could state them; but he had no point of view; and the result is that his book on the most exciting period of English history resembles nothing so much as a very large heap of sawdust."[1]

When he aimed his sarcasm at Samuel Rawson Gardiner, Strachey was ridiculing one of the most important English historians of the nineteenth century, and the body of work that he reduced to "sawdust" was in fact the most sustained effort by any Victorian to come to grips with the complexities of the Stuart past. From the mid-1850s, when he came to London, having just taken his degree at Oxford, until his debilitating stroke in 1901, Gardiner worked diligently to compile a narrative history of England from the accession of James I to the Restoration of the Stuarts. Although this story had been told before, Gardiner sensed that it had not been told with candor, and to guarantee his own accuracy he based his account on a thorough reading of the evidence. Experience had taught him "that no quotations are sufficient to save an honest inquirer from the trouble of looking into the original documents."[2] This extended use of manuscript sources, which enabled him to portray the past in greater detail than before, distinguished his

---

[1] Lytton Strachey, *Portraits in Miniature and Other Essays* (London: Chatto and Windus, 1931), 169–170.

[2] Samuel Rawson Gardiner, *History of England from the Accession of James I to the Disgrace of Chief-Justice Coke, 1603–1616* (London: Hurst and Blackett, 1863), 1: vii.

histories from all others. Gardiner searched for source material not only in the principal British repositories, but he scoured the archives on the continent as well. Ransacking the libraries at Simancas, Venice, Brussels and Paris, he unearthed ambassadors' reports and other state papers to see what they would reveal about England's domestic and foreign affairs.[3] The results of this research he presented in three major works: his *History of England*,[4] *Great Civil War* and *Commonwealth and Protectorate*. These works of narrative history, totaling eighteen volumes in the cabinet edition, were undoubtedly Gardiner's masterpiece. But they were not the full extent of his achievement. He was an author of textbooks, an editor of documents and a contributor to the *Dictionary of National Biography*, the *Encyclopaedia Britannica* and many of the major Victorian periodicals.[5] He was director of the Camden Society for almost thirty years and editor of the *English Historical Review* for ten. He was among the first generation of professional historians and a prolific man of letters.

Strachey's dislike of the Victorians prevented him from seeing that Gardiner's *History of England* did, in fact, have a point of view.[6] Formed in the 1860s and 1870s, as the rivalry between Church and Dissent was reaching a new intensity, Gardiner's interpretation of the Stuart past was intended to moderate sectarian strife by approaching the most divisive period in English history with detachment and fairness. Gardiner's famed impartiality – his willingness to lay out the factual record without apparently taking sides – had, then, a specific political purpose. It was a Liberal response to one of the most troublesome issues of the age. Like other Liberals, Gardiner believed that a modern democracy

---

[3] Samuel Rawson Gardiner, *Prince Charles and the Spanish Marriage: 1617–1623* (London: Hurst and Blackett, 1869), 1: vi–xi.

[4] Samuel Rawson Gardiner, *History of England from the Accession of James I to the Outbreak of the Civil War, 1603–1642* (London: Longmans, Green and Co., 1883–1884). This ten-volume work is a slightly revised compilation of five earlier works: *History of England from the Accession of James I to the Disgrace of Chief-Justice Coke, 1603–1616* (1863), *Prince Charles and the Spanish Marriage: 1617–1623* (1869), *History of England under the Duke of Buckingham and Charles I* (1875), *The Personal Government of Charles I* (1877), and *The Fall of the Monarchy of Charles I* (1882).

[5] For an almost complete bibliography of Gardiner's published writings, see W. A. Shaw, *A Bibliography of the Historical Works of Dr. Creighton, Late Bishop of London, Dr. Stubbs, Late Bishop of Oxford, Dr. S. R. Gardiner, and the Late Lord Acton* (London: Royal Historical Society, 1903).

[6] This chapter will deal primarily with Gardiner's *History of England*, which contains his mature thinking on the origins of the Civil War. His work on the war itself, the Commonwealth and the Protectorate will be considered in the next chapter.

functioned best when the nation was more or less undivided. The unrestrained conflict between Anglicanism and Dissent, therefore, threatened to make national politics impossible. Gardiner hoped to remove the historical source of this rivalry by presenting an image of the past which would demonstrate that modern England was neither Anglican nor Puritan, but rather an amalgam of these two antagonistic traditions. To the extent that he was successful, he offered the Victorians a comprehensive interpretation of the seventeenth century that was broad enough to contain the nation's Puritan as well as its Anglican past.

I

Unlike many of the eminent Victorians whose biographies are documented in great detail, Samuel Rawson Gardiner's life remains relatively obscure. Except for a few particulars, we simply know very little about him. We do know, however, that for a significant portion of his life he was an Irvingite. The story of his religious affiliations merits telling, not only because it has never been told before, but because it sheds light on his work as a historian. The fact that Gardiner had ties to both Anglicanism and Dissent may help to explain his decision to write a history that attempted to promote understanding between England's conforming and nonconforming traditions. As an Irvingite, Gardiner had felt what it meant to be a Dissenter. He knew from personal experience the religious compromises and professional sacrifices that Dissenters were called upon to make in order to prosper in an Anglican society. But Gardiner's affinities extended beyond Irvingite Dissent. For the evidence suggests that during the final thirty years of his life, the time when he wrote most of his major works, he was in fact a communicant in the Established Church.

Rawson Boddam Gardiner, the historian's father, was born in 1788 at Whitchurch in Oxfordshire.[7] He could claim descent from both Oliver Cromwell and Henry Ireton, and a desire to learn about these ancestors accounts in part for his son's future interest in

[7] According to his death certificate, available at the General Register Office, London, R. B. Gardiner was 75 years old when he died in 1863. His will, available at the Principal Probate Registry, London, states that he came originally from the parish of Whitchurch, Oxfordshire.

the history of the Civil War.[8] Rawson Gardiner was employed, presumably in the 1820s, in the East Indian civil service,[9] and later in the decade, perhaps after securing his fortune, he married Margaret Baring Gould and fathered two sons: Samuel Rawson, born in 1829 at Ropley in Hampshire,[10] and Charles Baring, born in 1833.[11] Sometime in the early 1830s, Rawson Gardiner became involved with the Irvingites, a millenarian sect gathered around Edward Irving, Henry Drummond and John Bate Cardale, and this encounter was of great importance for the future of the Gardiner family, for Irvingism became their central concern for many years.

The career of Edward Irving stands as one of the most curious examples of evangelical religion in early nineteenth-century Britain. A clergyman of the Church of Scotland and an assistant for several years to the famous Dr. Thomas Chalmers of Glasgow, Irving was called to London in 1822, where he began to minister to the city's Scottish community. His dynamic and combative style of preaching immediately caused a sensation and at one time or another Lords Aberdeen and Liverpool, Sir James Mackintosh, Zachary Macaulay, Samuel Taylor Coleridge and William Hazlitt were all drawn to hear him. But as Irving's notoriety grew, his teachings became increasingly extravagant and eventually lapsed into heresy. By 1826, he had become immersed in the study of prophecy, and basing his reasoning on a reading of Daniel and Revelation, he predicted that the Second Advent would occur around 1868. Several years later, he moved deeper into heterodoxy as he began to preach the human nature of Christ. The doctrine of the Atonement, he argued, only made sense if Christ, while on earth, had assumed man's fallible nature and been capable of sin. Such views were deemed heretical by the General Assembly of the Church of Scotland and ultimately they cost Irving his living. But the most notable of his excesses occurred after 1831, when members of his congregation began speaking in tongues, a phenomenon which he interpreted as the legitimate operation of the Holy Ghost

---

[8] Samuel Rawson Gardiner, *The Fall of the Monarchy of Charles I, 1637–1649* (London: Longmans, Green and Co., 1882), 1: vi.

[9] The certificate for S. R. Gardiner's second marriage, in 1882, available at the General Register Office, London, lists his father's occupation as "East Indian Civil Service."

[10] *Dictionary of National Biography*, s.v. "Gardiner, Samuel Rawson (1829–1902)."

[11] A Biographical Index of Those Associated with the Lord's Work. Compiled by Seraphim Newman-Norton. Papers of the Catholic Apostolic Church, Record Group No. 55. Yale Divinity Library, Archives and Manuscripts. Series II, box 10, folder 68.

on human souls. Taken as a whole, Irving's religion had an attractive immediacy: the gift of tongues indicated that remarkable times were at hand, Scriptural prophecy revealed the proximity of the Millennium, while his views on Christ's human nature suggested that the Savior would appear not as a phantasm, but as a living human being. To the Church of Scotland, however, these notions appeared at best disruptive, at worst unorthodox, and in 1833 the Presbytery of Annan, charging Irving with heresy, withdrew his ordination. Forced out of the Church of his choice, Irving continued to preach before an independent congregation in London until his death in 1834.[12]

The Irvingite, or Catholic Apostolic Church as it became known, was founded on the teachings of Edward Irving, but due to his untimely death Irving himself played only a minor role in its development. For the most part, the Church evolved under the direction of two Englishmen: Henry Drummond, the scion of a wealthy banking family, and John Bate Cardale, a London solicitor. Both Drummond and Cardale were deeply concerned with prophecy and other religious manifestations such as the gift of tongues, and they were drawn to Irving on account of his similar interests. The organization which took shape under their guidance was based on the belief that Christ's Second Coming was imminent and that a new Church, governed by twelve Apostles and characterized by prophecy, miracles and other forms of divine intervention, should be established to await His arrival. To create such a Church was the task to which Drummond, Cardale and their followers applied themselves. Cardale was "called" in 1832 as the first restored Apostle, Drummond was "called" in 1833 as the second, and the remaining ten Apostles were all appointed by 1835. While the Apostles were certainly the most important officers in the new Church, they were not the only ones. Each individual congregation

---

[12] On Edward Irving, see: Mrs. Oliphant, *The Life of Edward Irving, Minister of the National Scotch Church, London* (London: Hurst and Blackett, 1862). Thomas Carlyle, *Reminiscences*, ed. James Anthony Froude (London: Longmans, Green and Co., 1882), 1: 70–338. Edward Miller, *The History and Doctrines of Irvingism, or of the So-Called Catholic and Apostolic Church* (London: C. Kegan Paul and Co., 1878), 1: 1–106. Andrew Landale Drummond, *Edward Irving and His Circle, Including Some Consideration of the "Tongues" Movement in the Light of Modern Psychology* (London: James Clarke and Co., 1937). Plato E. Shaw, *The Catholic Apostolic Church, Sometimes Called Irvingite: A Historical Study* (Morningside Heights, New York: King's Crown Press, 1946), 7–59. Columba Graham Flegg, *"Gathered Under Apostles": A Study of the Catholic Apostolic Church* (Oxford: Clarendon Press, 1992), 46–63, 325–331.

was governed by a complete ministry comprised of an Angel (roughly equivalent to an Anglican bishop), six Elders and seven Deacons.[13] The Irvingites were never a large group. Their first chapel was built in 1832 on Drummond's Albury estate and shortly thereafter chapels were established in London, other parts of England and, curiously enough, in Canada, the United States and Germany. By 1835 there were approximately twenty-four Irvingite chapels throughout England and by 1851, according to the religious census of that year, this number had grown to thirty-two.[14]

Irvingism arose in England as a reaction to the incipient liberalism of the 1820s and 1830s. Profoundly conservative, Edward Irving saw the repeal of the Test and Corporation Acts, Catholic emancipation, the Reform Act and other liberal measures of the time as disturbing proof that all true authority in Church and state had broken down in the face of growing democracy.[15] Dismayed by what he considered the atheism and anarchy of his age, he rejected the idea of a democratic Church and hoped to restore to that institution the authority, uniformity and obedience which had prevailed in the sixteenth and early seventeenth centuries.[16] Believing that modern theology had removed the life from Christianity, he hoped to revitalize it by urging a literal interpretation of the Scriptures. With this goal in mind, he insisted that the sacraments were real and not symbolic, that Christ had assumed man's fallen nature, that the Second Coming was imminent, and that the Holy Ghost made itself known, in the present as in the past, through prophecy, tongues, healings and miracles. When called upon to defend these ideas, Irving referred not only to the Bible, but to the original sixteenth-century Standards of the Scottish Church.[17]

In some respects, Irvingism resembled the Oxford Movement

[13] For the history and doctrines of the Irvingites, see: Miller, *The History and Doctrines of Irvingism*. Shaw, *The Catholic Apostolic Church*. Flegg, *"Gathered Under Apostles"*.
[14] Annals: The Lord's Work in the Nineteenth and Twentieth Centuries. Compiled from Various Sources by H. B. Copinger. Papers of the Catholic Apostolic Church, Record Group No. 55. Yale Divinity Library, Archives and Manuscripts. Series II, box 9, folder 64, pages 28, 55, 92.
[15] Oliphant, *Life of Irving*, 1: 258, 260, 262, 269–270, 283, 316–318, 341, 347, 376–384. For his followers' similar fears, see their "Great Testimony . . . " (1837), reprinted in Miller, *The History and Doctrines of Irvingism*, 1: 347–360.
[16] Oliphant, *Life of Irving*, 1: 286, 376–384.
[17] *The Collected Writings of Edward Irving*, ed. G. Carlyle (London: Alexander Strahan, 1866), 1: 600–610, 615–618.

since both arose in response to the intellectual and political liberalism of the early nineteenth century and since both hoped to infuse new life into Christianity by drawing on an earlier sacramentalism. The Irvingite clergy began in the 1840s to wear vestments of greater complexity as they presided over an increasingly elaborate ritual. The alb, girdle, stole, chasuble, cope and surplice were introduced in 1842, while the rochet and mozzetta were added several years later. Consecrated oil entered the service in 1846, lights and incense in 1852.[18] These developments occurred almost exactly as the first signs of ritualism were appearing in the Anglican Church, suggesting a similar impulse behind both Irvingism and the Oxford Movement. Indeed, one may have borrowed from the other. The Irvingites acknowledged that the aims of the Tractarians were similar to their own, but complained that in the long run the Oxford Movement had been too radical and had weakened the Church which it had set out to strengthen.[19]

Rawson Boddam Gardiner became involved with Irvingism almost from its inception. In 1834 he was ordained an Elder in the Church at Southampton, just one month after it had been organized, in 1836 he was made an Evangelist to the Nations, and in 1837 he was consecrated Angel of the Church in Everton and Lymington.[20] His two sons were likewise drawn to the movement, but whereas Charles Baring was firmly attached to the new faith, becoming Angel of Brighton in 1882,[21] Samuel Rawson's relationship to Irvingism was somewhat more ambivalent. He entered the Irvingite Church in 1851 and was ordained a Deacon Evangelist in 1852.[22] Deacons were elected by the members of their congregation and were ordained by an Apostle. They assisted with the sacraments, managed the financial affairs of the congregation, and performed pastoral duties. In addition to these responsibilities, a Deacon Evangelist was expected to encourage conversions. In 1853

---

[18] Annals, 77, 81, 96.
[19] Henry Drummond, *Substance of Lectures Delivered in the Churches* (London: Thomas Bosworth, 1847), 78.
[20] Annals, 43, 67, 70. Biographical index.
[21] Biographical Index.
[22] The Biographical Index compiled by Newman-Norton has no entry on Samuel Rawson Gardiner, presumably because he eventually left the Church. I obtained the dates for Gardiner's admission into the Irvingite Church, for his ordination as Deacon, and for his "lapsed" standing during an interview on 4 February 1983, with the Secretary to the Trustees of the Catholic Apostolic Church.

the Gardiner family moved to London from Southampton, where they had been living since the 1840s,[23] and in that same year the Irvingites built their great neo-Gothic church on a corner of Gordon Square. Sometime in 1854, Samuel Rawson was "blessed" there as a Deacon. Two years later, in 1856, he married Edward Irving's youngest daughter, Isabella,[24] and translated an Irvingite manual entitled *Christian Family Life*.[25] Written by the German H. W. J. Thiersch, the tract was devoted in large part to the responsibilities of marriage.[26]

If Gardiner seemed by the mid-1850s comfortably ensconced in the Irvingite faith, he was not to remain so for long. According to Sir Charles Firth, one of Gardiner's closest associates during his later years, he ceased to be a Deacon in 1866,[27] and the church registers declared him "lapsed" in 1872. There is no record of his reasons for quitting the sect, but in retrospect it seems hardly remarkable that he did so. The death of his father in 1863 followed by the failure of Irving's prophecy may have loosened the ties that bound Gardiner to the new religion. Because of its apocalyptic nature, Irvingism was most suited to, and would have had its greatest appeal in times of social and political unrest such as the 1820s and 1830s. Gardiner, however, joined the sect in the 1850s at the height of Victorian prosperity and stability, and it must have been difficult, if not in his case impossible, to maintain the apocalyptic vision. Gardiner's history, not surprisingly, was characterized by a confidence in the perfection of English institutions that seems

---

23  Post Office Directories for Southampton and London.
24  The marriage certificate is available at the General Register Office, London.
25  Nicholas Tyacke, "An Unnoticed Work by Samuel Rawson Gardiner," *Bulletin of the Institute of Historical Research*, 47 (November, 1974): 244–245.
26  One of Samuel Rawson Gardiner's cousins, the novelist Sabine Baring Gould, made the following observation on the Gardiner family's involvement with Irvingism: "My Aunt Margaret, born in 1803, was the beauty of the family, with the loveliest complexion imaginable. She had a disappointment in early life, and in pique accepted Rawson Bodham [sic] Gardiner, one of the ugliest men Nature ever turned out, and unamiable to boot. He took up with Irvingism, and was, I believe, promoted to be an angel. Certainly he was a libel on angelic beauty as dreamed of by painters and poets. She, gentle, sweet, and not having received any definite Church teaching complied with her husband's religious vagaries. She died in 1853. When on her death-bed, the Irvingites tried to perform a miracle and cure her. One of the soi-disant Apostles, Drummond, I believe, was summoned to her and in an authoritative tone bade her rise up and walk. The poor creature did rise from her bed, staggered round the room, sank on her bed again, and instantly expired." Sabine Baring Gould, *Early Reminiscences, 1834–1864* (London: John Lane, the Bodley Head, 1923), 110.
27  *DNB*, s.v. "Gardiner, Samuel Rawson."

hardly consonant with a belief that everything was soon to perish. As he began to study history, and in particular the history of England during the Civil War, he may have seen, if he did not know it already, that the rise and fall of millenarian religions was a periodic occurrence attributable to upheavals in the social order more than to divine providence. Furthermore, Irvingism was based on a literal interpretation of the Scriptures which was incompatible with the historical method. As Gardiner refined his technique and began to realize that documents must be "read in the spirit of the times in which they were drawn up,"[28] the inadequacy of a literal approach to the Bible must have become apparent. Indeed, the fifteen years or so which Gardiner spent in the Irvingite Church may have been a time of painful awakening as he came to recognize that the implications of his work and method as a historian were at odds with the religious beliefs of his family.

The most compelling motive, however, for Gardiner's decision to leave the Irvingites may well have been that his religious nonconformity was beginning to stand in the way of his career as a historian. In the late 1860s and early 1870s, teaching appointments at the major universities were still largely restricted to Anglicans and the fact that Gardiner left the Irvingites in order to resume his connection with the Established Church suggests that he may have done so for professional reasons. In 1871, he applied for the position of lecturer in modern history at King's College, London, and his letter of application, without mentioning his Irvingite past, stressed his newly acquired Anglican credentials: "I am 42 years of age," Gardiner declared, "and a member of the Church of England." Along with his other application materials, Gardiner enclosed a testimonial in which Arthur Richard Godson, the Anglican Vicar of All Saints, Gordon Square, attested that he had "known Mr. Gardiner for several years as a member of the Congregation of All Saints Church, and as a regular Communicant there."[29] Gardiner's bid for the job was successful and he held the position at King's for a number of years. Whether Gardiner left the Irvingites out of genuine conviction – and there is no evidence that he ever resumed

---

[28] Samuel Rawson Gardiner, *History of England from the Accession of James I to the Outbreak of the Civil War, 1603–1642*, new edition (London: Longmans, Green and Co., 1895), 2: 78.
[29] Samuel Rawson Gardiner to the Council of King's College (21 November 1871), Gardiner papers, King's College, University of London, KA/IC/G48.

his connection with them – or whether he did so simply to advance his career may well remain a mystery. But his move back into conformity with the Established Church made it possible for him to pursue opportunities which otherwise would have been closed to him.

Gardiner never mentioned, in either letters or diaries, what Irvingism meant to him, and it is impossible, therefore, to say with certainty what influence his religion might have had on his work as a historian. But there can be little doubt that such an influence did, in fact, exist. Gardiner conceived and began to research his history in the mid-1850s, at exactly the moment when he was most deeply involved with the Irvingites, but he wrote most of its volumes after he had resumed his connection with the Church of England. The complexities of his religious affiliations, it seems fair to say, would have provided him with a unique perspective on England's seventeenth-century past.

Gardiner certainly knew what it meant to be a Dissenter, and the obstacles he faced as a non-Anglican, particularly in education, possibly had the greatest effect on his thinking about religion, politics and toleration. He began to attend Winchester College in 1841, and six years later, in 1847, he matriculated at Christ Church, Oxford. Since admission to the university was restricted at this time to Anglicans, Gardiner must have felt sufficiently at ease in the Church of England to subscribe to its Thirty-Nine Articles, though it seems doubtful that he ever seriously intended a career in the Church. Little is known about his university years except that in 1851 he received his Bachelor of Arts degree in the school of *literae humaniores*, and that in 1850, while still an undergraduate, he was granted a studentship. The award carried with it a small stipend and did not require residence at the university. It could be held for life providing the student did not marry and providing he entered orders within a reasonable time, in some cases up to six or seven years. When Gardiner joined the Irvingites in 1851, making it clear that he would not become a clergyman in the Church of England, he removed his name from the books at Christ Church and the college withdrew the grant.[30] Since Gardiner never mentioned this

---

[30] *DNB*, s.v. "Gardiner, Samuel Rawson." E. G. W. Bill and J. F. A. Mason, *Christ Church and Reform, 1850–1867* (Oxford: Clarendon Press, 1970), 11–13, 17–20. Samuel Rawson Gardiner to William Anson (19 November 1884), Anson papers, All Souls College, Oxford.

act of religious discrimination, it is difficult to assess its impact on him. In a sense, his loss was small; the stipend was not large and the position brought with it little power either at Christ Church or elsewhere. And yet it can hardly be coincidental that shortly afterward he set to work on a history of England in which the growth of toleration was a principal theme. Gardiner's latitudinarian sentiments, expressed in everything he wrote, suggest that he knew the evils of intolerance at first hand.

And yet it would be misleading to regard Gardiner as a Nonconformist whose religious dissent led him to write a history of the Civil War from a distinctly Puritan point of view. In the first place, Irvingism was rather exceptional as a form of Dissent. Unlike many Dissenters, whose denominational origins lay in the religious struggles of the seventeenth century, the Irvingites traced their beginnings to certain political and intellectual developments unique to the early nineteenth century. Unlike a Baptist or a Congregationalist, an Irvingite, on the basis of his religion, would have felt no particular historical allegiance to either party in the Civil War. In the second place, Gardiner was not simply a Nonconformist since he had ties with the Church of England both before he joined the Irvingites and after he left the sect. Many of the Irvingites never considered themselves Dissenters at all, and some remained members of the Established Church. Gardiner's father, for one, was comfortable enough with Anglicanism to have sent his son to Winchester and Christ Church where he would have acquired an Anglican education. This suggests that until 1851, when Gardiner took his degree at Oxford and was forced by the inflexibility of the Establishment to choose between Anglicanism or Irvingism, neither he nor his father found the two faiths incompatible. Rather than viewing Gardiner as a Dissenting historian who wrote a Nonconformist history of the Civil War, we might just as easily regard him as an Anglican historian, frustrated and angered at the narrowness of the Establishment, who wrote a history of the seventeenth century designed to promote toleration for Dissenting sects and the widest possible comprehension within the Church.

Finally, Gardiner's impartiality, his ability to regard both Puritan and Churchman with equal sympathy, may have owed something to the peculiarities of his religious experience. By the time he became actively involved in Irvingism, its practices had become quite ritualistic. Gardiner's ability to appreciate the Laudian movement in the Stuart Church, which he termed an appeal to the senses, may have derived in part from his own exposure to ritual. Similarly, the millenarian aspects of Irvingism may have enabled Gardiner to respect the Puritans and to overcome the charge of fanaticism that was so often leveled against them. Because of his religion, then, Gardiner understood both sides in the struggle between Dissent and the Established Church and was able to evaluate both of them, in the past and the present, with a greater degree of dispassion.

II

Writing in 1885 to William Anson, Warden of All Souls College, Gardiner noted with amusement that a Conservative Committee had procured him a vote for the borough of Oxford in the coming election. It was "generous of them," he remarked, to have taken "so much care of a benighted Liberal."[31] The evidence concerning Gardiner's politics, scattered throughout his few extant letters, numerous short articles and reviews, is at best incomplete and impressionistic. But when gathered together, it presents a clear picture, providing substance to his description of himself as a "benighted Liberal." From the Midlothian campaign through the crises over Irish Home Rule, the expansion of empire and the Boer War, Gardiner took a position that was consistently Gladstonian. In retrospect, this is hardly surprising. Gladstone, after all, had represented Oxford during Gardiner's years at Christ Church and was largely responsible for drafting the bill that would abolish religious tests for undergraduates. Though the Oxford University Act would not affect Gardiner in any tangible way – he had already taken his bachelor's degree by the time it had passed and it did not alter the Anglican exclusiveness of fellowships – he would have welcomed it as the first step toward ending religious discrimination in the university.

The first general election on which Gardiner's position becomes clear was the contest in 1880 between Gladstone and Disraeli. The election was fought largely on foreign policy as Gladstone, beginning with the Bulgarian agitation in 1876 and continuing

---

[31] Samuel Rawson Gardiner to William Anson (9 October 1885), Anson papers, All Souls College, Oxford.

through the Midlothian campaigns of 1879 and 1880, hammered away relentlessly at Disraeli's misguided policy. It was immoral, Gladstone declared, dangerously aggressive, and threatened to disrupt the peace of Europe by unnecessarily antagonizing the continental powers while over-extending Britain's resources. Like Gladstone, Gardiner disliked foreign initiatives that were motivated not by a moral imperative, but by the desire to flatter national pride through the senseless acquisition of territory. The evidence for Gardiner's position is indirect and found in his contribution to the article on English history in the *Encyclopaedia Britannica*, where he described the elder Pitt's policy during the Seven Years War in evocative terms:

> The war seems to be a mere struggle for territory. There is no feeling in either Pitt or Frederick, such as there was in the men who contended half a century later against Napoleon, that they were fighting the battles of the civilized world. There is something repulsive as well in the enthusiastic nationality of Pitt . . . Pitt's sole object was to exalt England to a position in which she might fear no rival, and might scarcely look upon a second.

Gardiner's assessment of Pitt could very well have contained a veiled criticism of Disraeli:

> it was his love of war, not his skill in carrying it on, which was really in question. He would be satisfied with nothing short of the absolute ruin of France. He would have given England that dangerous position of supremacy which was gained for France by Lewis XIV in the 17th century, and by Napoleon in the 19th century. He would have made his country still more haughty and arrogant than it was, till other nations rose against it, as they have three times risen against France, rather than submit to the intolerable yoke. It was a happy thing for England that peace was signed.[32]

Whether Gardiner intended these observations, made in 1878 as Disraeli was threatening war with Russia in order to assert England's presence in the Near East, as a critique of Beaconsfield-ism may never be known. But it seems unlikely that someone who had chastised Pitt for his chauvinism and arrogance would have welcomed Disraeli's forward policy in the 1870s.

Gardiner's position on the rights of emerging nations reveals even more clearly the ground he shared with Gladstone at the time of Midlothian. Gardiner is, perhaps, best described as a liberal

---

[32] Samuel Rawson Gardiner, "England, History," *Encyclopaedia Britannica*, ninth edition, American reprint (Philadelphia: J. M. Stoddart and Co., 1875–1890), 8: 319.

nationalist who believed in the right of oppressed nations to
coalesce as states, even when statehood was achieved through
revolution. Like other Liberals, Gardiner preferred change when
it occurred gradually by means of a Burkean compromise with
tradition. But he acknowledged that in some circumstances, such as
those found in France in 1789, revolution was the only alternative
because "the historical method of gradual progress was impossible
where institutions had become so utterly bad."[33] In cases where
revolution was the expression of a burgeoning nationalism, as in the
Balkans at the time he was writing, Gardiner felt that Britain
should adopt an attitude of restraint which would allow emerging
nations to achieve their goals. To justify this position, Gardiner,
much like Gladstone, emphasized the liberal side of British foreign
policy which stretched from the younger Pitt through Canning,
Palmerston and Russell, and was predicated on principles of
noninterference. The essence of Pitt's and Canning's policy was not
a dread of revolution, as was commonly thought, but rather an
opposition to the tendency of aggressive nations to impose their will
on weaker neighbors. "Canning," Gardiner explained, " . . . was the
pupil of Pitt, not of Burke, and the element which Pitt brought with
him was resistance to the [French] Revolution as interfering with
other nations rather than . . . resistance to it as introducing new
forms of government. It was this view which Canning inherited.
When he saw the Holy Alliance interfering with the rights of
nations to settle their internal government in their own way, he
set himself against the Holy Alliance just as he had set himself
against the Revolutionary propaganda and the aggressive military
despotism of Napoleon."[34] At the time of Italian unification,
Palmerston and Russell extended Canning's liberal policy when
they condoned revolution in Italy in order to help found an Italian
state.[35]

Writing in 1880, the year of Gladstone's second Midlothian
campaign, Gardiner noted that the principles behind Canning's
policy still spoke directly to contemporary events: "The importance
of this side of Canning's activity is the greater because it connects
itself with all that is distinctive in those European international

[33] Ibid., 8: 323.
[34] Samuel Rawson Gardiner, "Modern History," *Contemporary Review*, 37 (June, 1880): 1057.
[35] Ibid., 1058.

relations of the present day."[36] He was plainly alluding here to the problems posed by the growth of militant nationalism in the Balkans. As an advocate of a liberal foreign policy, Gardiner would have rejected Disraeli's policy of backing the Ottoman empire in order to maintain Britain's interests in the Near East while extinguishing the revolutionary conflagration in the Balkans. Instead, he would have found congenial Gladstone's conviction that the Balkan insurrections were a legitimate attempt of oppressed nationalities to achieve their independence from the domination of the Turks. Indeed, during his first Midlothian campaign, Gladstone had portrayed himself as the representative of the same liberal tradition in foreign policy that Gardiner would endorse in 1880, associating it, as Gardiner would, with the names of Canning, Palmerston and Russell.[37]

Gardiner's decision to back Gladstone on Home Rule is perhaps the most telling indication of his political loyalties since no issue was more divisive in the 1880s and 1890s than Ireland. Like other Liberals, Gardiner developed his position gradually. Using a review of Justin McCarthy's *History of Our Own Times* in 1880 as an opportunity to discuss Home Rule, Gardiner expressed reservations about the measure. He acknowledged that the English had not always treated Ireland well, pointing out that they suffered from a "defect of imagination" which prevented them from understanding their Irish subjects. But he also believed that they were getting better at governing Ireland because they were becoming more sympathetic to Irish needs, and he referred to the Irish legislation enacted during Gladstone's first government as evidence of this improvement. More important, he thought that the English still had a crucial role to play in Ireland since only an outside authority could settle the fierce conflict between competing parties. "The advocates of Home Rule," Gardiner wrote, "assert that Ireland can best determine its own legislation because it best knows its own grievances. May it not be asked in return whether there are not divisions in Ireland which call for a disinterested mediator to heal them? Would the Irish landlords be likely to give to the tenant-farmers their due? Would the Irish tenant farmers be likely to give to the landlords their due? May it not turn out that the Parliament of the United Kingdom will be inclined to deal more fairly with both

---

[36] Ibid., 1057.    [37] See for example *The Times*, 26 November 1879, 10.

parties than any Irish Parliament, representing an overwhelming majority on one side, would be likely to do?"[38]

Gardiner's overriding concern, it seems, was to preserve the union of England and Ireland, and he was uncertain at the time whether Home Rule was the best way to achieve that end. Rather than establish two separate Parliaments, Gardiner called on his countrymen to govern Ireland conscientiously, something he felt would be done better if they would only view objectively the history of their dealings in Ireland. To this end, Gardiner used his reviews of books about seventeenth-century Ireland to emphasize the interpretation of the Anglo-Irish past that he had been developing in his histories since the 1860s. No matter how well intentioned the English might have been, their policies had failed in Ireland precisely because they had not taken into account the rights and needs of the Irish. "It must be acknowledged," Gardiner observed, reviewing a calendar of state papers for the *Academy* in 1877, "that no English Governor of Ireland ever fully appreciated the highest difficulties of his task. He was so convinced that English society was better than Irish society, so ready to imagine that Irishmen might be turned into Englishmen by the application of the proper means of compulsion, that it was only at rare intervals that facts would exercise some influence over him ... He was, therefore, always apt to fall back upon the old ways, and to treat Irish habits and Irish feelings with the bitterest contempt; at the same time that his English habit of respecting law embarked him in the pursuit of a technical legality which, in the eyes of those who suffered from it, went far to heighten the injustice which it clothed."[39]

This tendency to criticize his countrymen for their insensitivity was reflected in Gardiner's treatment of the Anglo-Irish past in those volumes of his *History* published during the years leading up to the Home Rule crisis. While arguing that the English had always intended to benefit Ireland, he readily acknowledged that they had failed because they had never adequately understood the Irish

[38] Samuel Rawson Gardiner, Review of Justin McCarthy's *History of Our Own Times*, *Academy*, 18 (9 October 1880): 251–252.

[39] Samuel Rawson Gardiner, Review of *Calendar of State Papers, Ireland*, *Academy*, 12 (15 September 1877): 261. See also Samuel Rawson Gardiner, Review of *Calendar of State Papers, Ireland*, *Academy*, 7 (26 June 1875): 654–655, Review of *Calendar of State Papers, Ireland*, *Academy*, 19 (14 May 1881): 347, Review of Hickson's *Ireland in the Seventeenth Century*, *Academy*, 26 (26 July 1884): 53.

nor taken their needs into account. In the *Personal Government of Charles I*, written between 1875 and 1877, Gardiner examined Wentworth's problematic tenure as Lord Deputy which laid the groundwork for the Irish insurrection of 1641. Wentworth's intentions, Gardiner pointed out, were laudable. He had set out to raise Ireland to a "higher level of civilization." By imposing the laws and religion of England on the recalcitrant Irish and by planting among them a Protestant and English population, which he hoped would provide a model worthy of emulation, Wentworth planned to transform Ireland into a prosperous nation loyal to its English benefactor. But Gardiner further admitted that Wentworth's plans were doomed from the start because they ignored the tenacity with which a nation "clings to its ancestral habits and modes of thought."[40] The Lord Deputy had no alternative but to coerce the Irish into accepting an alien faith and unfamiliar laws, which in the end generated the discontent expressed in the uprising of 1641. The lessons which Gardiner drew from this episode were clearly aimed at his own century: Wentworth had failed, Gardiner concluded, because he had ignored all "popular feeling," and instead of "guiding" the Irish, he had "driven" them against their will.[41]

By 1885, despite his earlier reservations, Gardiner had become an advocate of Home Rule. Late that year, Gladstone announced his own conversion to Home Rule, and in 1886 he submitted to Parliament the bill that would ultimately split his party, marking a watershed in Victorian politics. Unlike many Liberals who abandoned their leader over his Irish policies, Gardiner remained a Gladstonian throughout the crisis. His concern, in 1886 as in 1880, was how best to strengthen the union of the two nations, only now he had come to see that a measure of Home Rule was necessary in order to appease Irish nationalism. As he explained to James Bryce, "the modern tendency to amalgamation has only been rendered possible by the previous assertion of the rights of nationality."[42] Gardiner's plan was to establish two national Parliaments over

[40] Samuel Rawson Gardiner, *The Personal Government of Charles I: A History of England from the Assassination of the Duke of Buckingham to the Declaration of the Judges on Ship-Money, 1628–1637* (London: Longmans, Green and Co., 1877), 2: 122, 136, 146.

[41] Ibid., 2: 158–159.

[42] Samuel Rawson Gardiner to James Bryce (5 May 1886), MS. Bryce, UB 26, Bodleian Library, Oxford.

which a joint committee would preside. This joint committee, he explained, "would be offensive to nobody" and might eventually assume the responsibilities of a federal government.[43] Looking back on the crisis in 1889, Gardiner clarified his position, and expressed a willingness to grant a similar autonomy to Scotland and Wales as well. "I hold now," he wrote to E. A. Freeman, "as I held in 1885 that Irish Home Rule necessitates English, Scottish, and perhaps Welsh Home Rule very speedily after it is granted . . . I have always thought that there must be three or four Parliaments with a big united Parliament above them. If I had been an M.P. in 1886 I should have voted for the second reading of Gladstone's Bill because I had confidence in the common sense of Englishmen and Irishmen to add what was wanting, and I did not think men's minds were prepared to grasp the idea of federalism without considerable delay."[44]

Gladstone's decision to stand or fall on the issue of Home Rule in 1886 had profound consequences for the course of Victorian politics. It dealt a nearly fatal blow to the Liberal party as many Gladstonians who feared its consequences now deserted their leader, preparing the way for a prolonged period of Conservative government. Gardiner remained an advocate of Home Rule even after Gladstone's defeat in 1886, a decision he shared with other university trained liberals such as James Bryce, E. A. Freeman and John Morley. In 1887, for example, Gardiner subscribed to the Oxford University Home Rule League, established by the Shakespeare scholar E. K. Chambers, and became one of the organization's vice presidents.[45] The evidence also suggests that when Gladstone returned to office in 1892 and carried his second Home Rule Bill through the Commons, Gardiner gave the measure his backing.[46] The decision of the Lords to reject the Bill by an overwhelming majority provoked Gladstone, in his final speech before Parliament, to chastise the peers for defying the nation's representatives. Gardiner, who had once written that "it is

[43] Ibid.

[44] Samuel Rawson Gardiner to E. A. Freeman (21 October 1889), MS. Bryce, UB 26, Bodleian Library, Oxford.

[45] Samuel Rawson Gardiner to the Rev. E. K. Chambers (19 December 1887), MS. Autogr. e. 10, fols. 120–121, Bodleian Library, Oxford.

[46] Samuel Rawson Gardiner to James Bryce (24 June 1892), MS. Bryce 9, fols. 333–334, Bodleian Library, Oxford. [Samuel Rawson Gardiner], "New Light on the Common-wealth," *The Speaker*, 11 (27 April 1895): 469.

essential to the permanence of an Upper House that it should be unable to set at defiance the will of the nation expressed by its representatives," would no doubt have seconded Gladstone's parting harangue.[47]

As he reflected on the Irish question in both its past and present aspects, Gardiner noted its connection to other problems posed by the expansion of the Victorian empire. In particular, the difficulties that England had confronted in Ireland during the seventeenth century resembled closely those it was currently facing in its overseas possessions. "Many years ago," he recalled in 1875, "when I was attempting to understand the disturbances preceding the colonisation of Ulster, I found the greatest help in a Parliamentary Blue Book relating to certain troubles by which the native population of New Zealand was at that time agitated, while at the present day it is difficult to read about the flight of Tyrone without thinking of that unwieldy name which even South Africans do not always succeed in pronouncing without a slip – Langalibalele." Gardiner concluded that the Anglo-Irish past "ought to be studied by all who wish to know what light history has to throw on the relations between an English government and tribes in a lower stage of civilisation." The lessons he drew were suitably Gladstonian: peace in the empire could only be achieved if the rights of the colonized, particularly their right to the possession of their lands, took precedence over the needs of the colonists. The disturbances that preceded the plantation of Ulster in the early seventeenth century and the Maori wars of the 1860s, Gardiner discovered, had similar causes. In both instances, English governors had inadvertently created disorder by disregarding native customs and establishing an alien legal system based on English principles. In Ireland, these reforms were intended to break the independence of the native chiefs, but turned them into malcontents instead. Tyrone and Langalibalele were local chiefs, one Irish, the other African, who had fled their homelands because they would rather suffer exile than submit to foreign domination.[48]

Gardiner's outlook on imperial issues remained Gladstonian

---

[47] Samuel Rawson Gardiner, "England, History," *Encyclopaedia Britannica*, 8: 317.

[48] Samuel Rawson Gardiner, Review of *Calendar of State Papers, Ireland*, *Academy*, 7 (26 June 1875): 654. Gardiner, *History of England*, 1: 358–417.

throughout the troubled 1890s. Writing to James Bryce in 1896, as Kitchener began his advance down the Nile into the Sudan, and after the Jameson Raid had ended in a fiasco earlier in the year, Gardiner pronounced Lord Salisbury's foreign policy "miserable."[49] As British relations with the Boer Republics deteriorated at the end of the century and the prospect of a South African war loomed large, Gardiner continued to criticize the Conservatives' imperial policy. He confided to Bryce, just days before the outbreak of war in 1899, that he had "long felt that the [Uitlanders'] demand for the franchise was a mistake – an interference carrying with it the maximum of irritation with the least possible advantage." Rather than pushing the franchise issue to the point of war, as Chamberlain was intent on doing, Gardiner proposed a plan that he associated in part with John Morley. The position of the Uitlanders in the Transvaal, he suggested, was analogous to the position of the Irish in the United Kingdom, and consequently granting them a degree of local self-government, or "Home-rule" as he put it, might provide a peaceful solution to the problem. Though he doubted whether the arrangement would be acceptable to all parties, it would at least be a "policy which will satisfy our consciences," a distinctly Gladstonian consideration.[50]

One important area where Gladstone and Gardiner parted company was the Church of England. At issue was the Public Worship Regulation Act. Gardiner's comments on the measure, which comprise just about his only published observations on the Victorian Church, appeared in his review of Dean Hook's biography of Archbishop Laud. The initiative for the Public Worship Act, which was designed to eliminate ritualism in the Church, had come from Archbishop Tait with the backing of the Queen. Tait had tried at first to use the courts in order to curb ritualism, but when the ritualist clergy defied the legal judgments against them, Tait turned to legislation. The Public Worship Act was an attempt to arm the Church with the means to force recalcitrant clergymen to comply with the laws governing worship. Whereas Gladstone opposed the bill because he thought it infringed on religious

---

[49] Samuel Rawson Gardiner to James Bryce (30 May 1896), MS. Bryce, UB 21, Bodleian Library, Oxford.
[50] Samuel Rawson Gardiner to James Bryce (8 October 1899), MS. Bryce, UB 7, Bodleian Library, Oxford.

freedom within the Church, other Liberals supported it because, being Erastians, they felt the legislature had the right to regulate public worship to conform to the wishes of the nation.[51] In his biography of Laud, Dean Hook, a Tractarian fellow traveler, had blasted Tait, accusing him of acting more despotically than Laud. Where Laud had used his authority to enforce existing laws, Tait had disregarded those laws already in existence and had compromised the independence of the Church by calling on Parliament to legislate for it. Gardiner, in his review, accepted Hook's challenge and defended the authors of the Public Worship Act, pointing out that, unlike Laud, they had neither defied popular sentiment nor infringed on the religious freedom of their adversaries:

Is there any parallel to be drawn between his [Laud's] mode of dealing with Church questions and that which was accepted by the House of Commons in 1874? No candid person can fail to trace a resemblance reaching very deeply between Laud and the authors of recent legislation, especially those who were lawyers by profession. In both was a profound respect for the authority of the law; in both was a contemptuous dislike of the irregular manifestations of religious sentiment; in both was a desire to establish uniformity of ritual with a corresponding want of zeal for unity of doctrine. But it is seldom that comparisons run on all fours, and the main difference consists in this – that Laud became unpopular by appealing against use and wont to the unrepealed law, while his modern successors, having the legislative power in their hands, were able to produce a new law, the operation of which was intended to favour the popular use and wont. Nor must the great distinction between the seventeenth and the nineteenth centuries be left out of sight because Dean Hook deliberately closes his eyes to its existence. When Laud forbade the clergy to conduct the worship of their congregations according to a certain form of ritual, he forbade them to officiate anywhere within the King's dominions. At present the enforcement of the law leaves them perfectly free to continue any practices they please outside the limits of the Established Church.[52]

[51] For the controversy over ritualism, see: P. T. Marsh, *The Victorian Church in Decline: Archbishop Tait and the Church of England, 1868–1882* (Pittsburgh: University of Pittsburgh Press, 1969), 111–134, 158–192. G. I. T. Machin, *Politics and the Churches in Great Britain, 1869 to 1921* (Oxford: Clarendon Press, 1987), 4–7, 70–78. J. P. Parry, *Democracy and Religion: Gladstone and the Liberal Party, 1867–1875* (Cambridge: Cambridge University Press, 1986), 413–417.

[52] Samuel Rawson Gardiner, Review of Hook's *Lives of the Archbishops*, *Academy*, 8 (6 November 1875): 467.

In defending the Public Worship Act, Gardiner parted company with Gladstone. Where Gardiner spoke as a liberal Anglican who wanted the Establishment to appeal to the largest number of English men and women possible by removing practices that the majority found offensive, Gladstone's High Church sympathies led him to defend those practices on the grounds that they occupied a legitimate place within the Anglican Church. And where Gardiner spoke as an Erastian who believed that Parliament, representing the nation, had the right to regulate the practices of the Establishment, Gladstone upheld the spiritual independence of the Church.

Behind Gardiner's politics lay a liberal nationalism. His support for the emerging nations in the Balkans, his conviction that Irish, Welsh and Scottish nationalism deserved consideration within the political arrangement of the United Kingdom, his acknowledgment that sensitivity toward the rights and customs of subject peoples was one of Britain's paramount responsibilities as an imperial power all reflect his confidence that nations were legitimate political entities and that nations other than his own merited respect. His belief that English institutions, such as the Established Church and the universities, should be broadly based without restrictions so as to appeal to the largest section of the population reflects further his Liberal conviction that the nation as a whole, rather than special interests defined by class or religion, was the proper foundation of political life. Indeed, what Gardiner thought distinguished Liberalism, as it had emerged in England after the Reform Act of 1832, from other political creeds was precisely this awareness that the purpose of government was to achieve the good of the entire nation. "There is," he observed about early Victorian politics, "no mistaking the tendency of this great era of legislation under the influence of the reform by which the balance of power had swayed over to the middle classes by 1832. The idea which was steadily making its way was the idea of testing all questions by the interest of the nation as a whole, and of disregarding in comparison the special interests of particular classes."[53]

What had enabled statesmen finally to go beyond class or sectarian loyalties was the development of political and economic science. Where other politicians had acted according to narrowly defined interests, Liberals appealed to those objective laws of social

---

[53] Samuel Rawson Gardiner, "England, History," *Encyclopaedia Britannica*, 8: 328.

development that were the principal concern of the science of political economy. The younger Pitt, Gardiner concluded, was the first Liberal because he was the first statesman to appreciate the practical significance of Adam Smith's work. His ministry of 1784 – until, that is, the French Revolution threw English politics into disarray – was the first Liberal administration because it substituted a knowledge of "political and economic science for the influence of wealth and station." This early Liberalism continued in the free trade principles of Robert Peel and reached its final development – or so we can infer from the brief sketch of modern British history that Gardiner wrote for the *Britannica* – in the Liberal party of William Gladstone.[54] Good government, then, for Gardiner, meant intelligent government conducted by an administration educated in the latest theories of political science, and he was confident that this kind of government would persist in England because of the respect which the newly enfranchised working class had for intellect. The nineteenth century was a scientific age, he once observed, Darwin's discoveries were its most characteristic achievement, and a respect for men of intellectual accomplishment had spread to all classes. It was this "widespread reverence for science and practical capacity" that had finally "robbed of its terrors that democratic suffrage which our fathers regarded as certain to swamp all the virtue and intelligence of the nation."[55]

Most of these beliefs Gardiner held in common with that generation of Oxford and Cambridge-trained Liberals who had gained their first political experiences with the university reform movement of the 1850s and had entered national politics, often as journalists, in the 1860s. Like Gardiner, these university men can be described as liberal nationalists. They eagerly endorsed Italian unification and some of them, like the historians E. A. Freeman and James Bryce, later took up the cause of Balkan nationalism. Believing that a modern democracy could only function when the nation was more or less unified, they stressed the importance of eliminating those economic and religious divisions that disrupted

54 Samuel Rawson Gardiner, "George III," *Encyclopaedia Britannica*, 10: 382, Review of Lord Fitzmaurice's *Life of William, Earl of Shelburne*, *Academy*, 10 (9 December 1876): 558, "England, History," *Encyclopaedia Britannica*, 8: 322, 328.
55 Samuel Rawson Gardiner, Review of Justin McCarthy's *History of Our Own Times*, *Academy*, 18 (9 October 1880): 251.

the political life of the nation. An important impetus behind this Liberalism may have been the Broad Church movement which undertook to reconcile political, class and religious differences by uniting all groups within a tolerant and comprehensive Church. University Liberals justified enlarging the franchise in 1867 on the grounds that it would remove class divisions, create a unified political community and make Parliament a national institution. The opening of Oxford and Cambridge to Dissenters, which began with the reforms of the 1850s and culminated in 1871 with the abolition of religious tests for fellowships, would likewise transform the universities into national centers for higher education. Like Gardiner, these university Liberals advocated scientific government, conducted by an educated elite much like themselves, and they naively believed that the deference and common sense of the newly enfranchised working classes would lead them to vote for candidates of intellect, thereby bringing about John Morley's anticipated alliance of "brains and numbers."[56]

When these hopes failed to materialize in the election of 1868, many university Liberals grew disillusioned with democratic processes. Rather than representing an alliance of "brains and numbers," the election had returned a "chamber of mediocrity." As the reforming impetus behind Gladstone's first government dwindled in the early 1870s, many Liberals began to question whether in a democracy representative assemblies could ever overcome the apparent mediocrity of the electorate. These doubts seemed confirmed during the Bulgarian agitation and the Midlothian campaign as Gladstone, rather than leading the nation, stooped to demagoguery and allowed the uneducated opinion of the electorate to lead him. The Home Rule crisis provided the turning point for these Liberal skeptics. Gladstone, they feared, had taken up a dangerous and ill-considered policy merely to appease Irish opinion.[57]

[56] For university Liberalism, see: Christopher Harvie, *The Lights of Liberalism: University Liberals and the Challenge of Democracy, 1860–86* (London: Allen Lane, 1976). Christopher Kent, *Brains and Numbers: Elitism, Comtism, and Democracy in Mid-Victorian England* (Toronto: University of Toronto Press, 1978). Jeffrey Paul Von Arx, *Progress and Pessimism: Religion, Politics, and History in Late Nineteenth Century Britain* (Cambridge, Mass.: Harvard University Press, 1985). Parry, *Democracy and Religion*, 239–257.
[57] Von Arx, *Progress and Pessimism.* John Roach, "Liberalism and the Victorian Intelligentsia," *Cambridge Historical Journal*, 13 (1957): 58–81. G. R. Searle, *The Quest for National Efficiency: A Study in British Politics and Political Thought, 1899–1914* (Oxford: Basil Blackwell, 1971), 1–33.

Unlike many of his university colleagues, Gardiner never despaired of democracy. He acknowledged, to be sure, that Parliaments had their shortcomings. Reflecting all the commonplaces of the age, they were invariably conservative and therefore unlikely to adopt reforms that were ahead of their time. A long line of reformers, running from Bacon, Wentworth and Cromwell through advanced thinkers of his own day like the Positivist Frederic Harrison, had consequently doubted the readiness of Parliaments to adopt farsighted policies. But for Gardiner this was only half the picture. Representative assemblies were also indispensable because only they could ensure that reforms, though "slow in coming," would be "permanent" once they had been made. Nor, he thought, were Parliaments as likely to obstruct progressive legislation in the present as they had been in the past since modern-day cabinet government successfully combined a "very efficient administration with the supremacy of Parliament."[58]

### III

The same liberal nationalism that informed Gardiner's politics also shaped his conception of the historian's craft. For Gardiner hoped to write a national history that would transcend party divisions. "We have had historians in plenty," he observed in 1875, "but they have been Whig historians or Tory historians . . . I am not so vain as to suppose that I have always succeeded in doing justice to both parties, but I have, at least, done my best not to misrepresent either."[59] There was for Gardiner an essential similarity between statesmanship and the writing of history. What the statesman achieved in politics, the historian set out to accomplish in the realm of ideas. Bacon, Wentworth and Cromwell – Gardiner's most frequently cited exemplars of true statesmanship – all shared at one time or another the ability to stand above party conflicts and to reconcile competing interests in the name of the nation.[60]

---

[58] Samuel Rawson Gardiner, Note on Wentworth's unpublished speech, *Academy*, 7 (12 June 1875): 611, Review of A. Stern's *Milton*, *Academy*, 14 (14 December 1878): 558, "England, History," *Encyclopaedia Britannica*, 8: 315–316, 318.

[59] Samuel Rawson Gardiner, *A History of England Under the Duke of Buckingham and Charles I, 1624–1628* (London: Longmans, Green and Co., 1875), 1: vi.

[60] For Gardiner's views on statesmanship, see: [Samuel Rawson Gardiner], Item 21 of "Contemporary Literature," *North British Review*, American edition, 52 (April, 1870): 131. Samuel Rawson Gardiner, Review of Abbott's *Bacon and Essex*, *Academy*, 11 (23 June 1877):

Overcoming national divisions was also a principal concern for the historian, whose specific job was to remove the sources of conflict that arose from competing interpretations of the past. The historian must consequently understand all parties from the inside, he must empathize with them, even when he found their views uncongenial, and he must assess fairly the contribution each had made to the growth of the nation. "No history," Gardiner declared, "is ever properly written, unless the writer does his best to understand what people, of whose conduct or theories he disapproves, have to say for themselves."[61] Only in this way would an image of the past emerge that would reconcile rather than divide.

In his reviews, Gardiner repeatedly admonished the great Victorian historians – and many of the not so great as well – for their inability, or unwillingness, to judge fairly those parties whose views they did not find agreeable. Macaulay, Gardiner thought, had produced an "outrageous caricature of Strafford" because he lacked the "suppleness" and "broad-mindedness" necessary to "sympathize" with unfamiliar points of view.[62] David Masson, the Victorian biographer of Milton, may never have succumbed to Macaulay's "shallowness," but all the same he was unable to appreciate "the best points in Laud's character."[63] John Lothrop Motley, the American historian of the Dutch republic, likewise suffered from an "inability to enter into unfamiliar opinions."[64] Given the close association of politics and religion in both the seventeenth and nineteenth centuries, Gardiner believed that it was especially important for historians to empathize with all religious parties so as to write history from the standpoint of the nation, not of a particular sect. Here too his contemporaries often fell short. Macaulay may have recognized the "exterior shape" of

547, Review of Abbott's *Bacon, Academy*, 27 (13 June 1885): 411–412, "Bacon, Francis," *Dictionary of National Biography*, 1: 801–802, 808–809, Review of Traill's *Strafford*, *The Academy*, 36 (30 November 1889): 349–350. [Samuel Rawson Gardiner], "An English Republican," *The Speaker*, 10 (15 September 1894), 303.

61  Samuel Rawson Gardiner, Review of Mainwaring's *Religion and Allegiance, Academy*, 5 (3 January 1874): 4.

62  Samuel Rawson Gardiner, "Angleterre," *Revue historique*, 2 (October–December, 1876): 585.

63  Samuel Rawson Gardiner, Review of Masson's *Milton, Academy*, 5 (31 January 1874): 112.

64  Samuel Rawson Gardiner, Obituary of J. L. Motley, *Academy*, 11 (9 June 1877): 509. See also, Samuel Rawson Gardiner, "Modern History," *Contemporary Review*, 33 (October, 1878): 629, Review of Green's *History of the English People, Academy*, 15 (3 May 1879): 381.

the Puritans, but he could not "penetrate into their souls" because he was "incapable of understanding idealism or enthusiasm of any sort."[65] Even the great Ranke, whose works best represented the kind of "sublime and serene impartiality" that Gardiner was seeking, had failed to engage with the religious side of his subject.[66] Historians like David Masson or Peter Bayne, whose sympathies lay with Victorian Dissent, had also allowed their religious preferences to shape their interpretations of the past. The result was sectarian history. Masson, Gardiner complained, simply did not know how to write the history of England because he had failed to appreciate that the followers of Archbishop Laud had made as great a contribution to the development of the nation as had Milton and the Puritans. Masson's history was thus incomplete: it was merely "so much of the history as may concern a special sect of men."[67]

A scientific understanding of their craft, Gardiner believed, would provide historians with the means to transcend their prejudices and achieve a degree of impartiality. Just as the development of political economy had enabled statesmen to govern for the good of the nation as a whole, so the emergence of scientific history would put an end to the partisan approach to the past found in the works of Macaulay and others.[68] And yet it is not always clear what Gardiner meant by scientific history. In his obituary of Ranke, he criticized the German historian for not being sufficiently scientific: "Is it not possible," Gardiner asked rhetorically, "to do for history what Darwin did for science? Ranke, at all events, did not do it. He knew of the influence upon individuals of great waves of feeling and opinion; but he does not seek for the law of human progress which underlies them."[69] These comments suggest that Gardiner believed the growth of societies, like the evolution of species, to be governed by laws which it was the historian's business

65 Samuel Rawson Gardiner, "Angleterre,' *Revue historique*, 2 (October–December, 1876): 586.
66 Samuel Rawson Gardiner, Review of Ranke's *History of England*, *Academy*, 7 (20 March 1875): 285–286.
67 Samuel Rawson Gardiner, Review of Masson's *Milton*, *Academy*, 13 (30 March 1878): 277. See also Samuel Rawson Gardiner, Review of Bayne's *Chief Actors in the Puritan Revolution*, *Academy*, 13 (18 May 1878): 430, and "Modern History," *Contemporary Review*, 33 (October, 1878): 626.
68 Samuel Rawson Gardiner, Review of Spedding's *Life of Bacon*, *Academy*, 6 (10 October 1874): 393.
69 Samuel Rawson Gardiner, Obituary of Leopold von Ranke, *Academy*, 29 (29 May 1886): 381.

to discover. But in his own work, Gardiner never really set out to uncover these laws. His aim, he explained in the preface to his *History of England*, was not to "sketch out" the laws of social evolution, but rather to bring forth "the men and women in whose lives these laws [were] to be discerned."[70] For the most part, when Gardiner spoke of scientific history, he simply meant the thorough and objective analysis of facts, based on a first-hand use of documents culled from as many archives as possible. Here, for Gardiner, was the crucial distinction between the earlier historians of Stuart England and himself: where they had engaged in polemics, he was accumulating facts with the detachment of a naturalist. The honest, scientific disclosure of the factual record, Gardiner thought, would help ease sectarian conflict since most of the disagreements about the past that disrupted contemporary politics were only possible because party spokesmen deliberately obscured what had actually happened.

For Gardiner, the proper subject of history was the nation. "Facts," he once said, "are only of importance as they help us to understand the changes of thought, of feeling, or of knowledge which mark the growth of that complex social unity which we call a nation."[71] And the fundamental forces responsible for shaping the nation were primarily intellectual. The acts of individuals only became intelligible when seen in the context of the religious, political, scientific and artistic thought of the age. For this reason, Gardiner stressed in his own work the growth and conflict of ideas. To understand the making of England in the seventeenth century, one had to comprehend the interaction of Anglicanism and of Puritanism, of Royalism and Parliamentarianism. The historian's task was to rid himself of his modern biases and to become "instinctively familiar" with the "aims and ideas" of the period he was describing, "however strange they may seem."[72] To empathize with the thoughts of the past, whether one approved of them or not, was the way to attain historical knowledge, and it was precisely what Macaulay, Forster and others had been unable, or unwilling, to do. The problem with these previous historians was that they had

[70] Gardiner, *History of England*, 1: viii–ix.
[71] Samuel Rawson Gardiner, "Mr. Green and Mr. Rowley," *Academy*, 8 (11 December 1875): 604.
[72] Samuel Rawson Gardiner, Review of Abbott's *Bacon*, *Academy*, 27 (13 June 1885): 411.

judged the past according to the prejudices of the present. Failing to see the crucial differences between the seventeenth century and their own age, they had praised the Parliamentarians and condemned the Royalists as though these parties were little more than contemporary Whigs and Tories. To confuse past and present in this manner Gardiner considered methodologically unsound. He had learned from Ranke, "the father of modern historical research," and from Seeley that the frequent comparison of past and present was "altogether destructive of real historical knowledge."[73]

The desire for national unity lay at the heart of Gardiner's Liberalism and once this is understood the most important aspect of his famed impartiality becomes clear: while it owed something to Victorian ideas about science and something to a Rankean conception of the historian's craft, it was above all a Liberal historian's attempt to foster national unity by presenting a balanced interpretation of the Civil War. During the seventeenth century, two opposing views of Church and state had come into conflict as England had to choose between Anglicanism and Puritanism, between absolute monarchy and representative government. Gardiner's object was to describe this conflict and it was the measure of his impartiality that he saw within each of the contending parties a powerful and valid principle at work. Neither king nor Parliament, Laudian nor Puritan was in total possession of the truth; each had acted at times in error, but each had also made lasting contributions to England's greatness. "England," he once wrote, "sprang from a union between the Puritanism and the Churchmanship of the seventeenth century."[74] In presenting this image of the past, Gardiner knew that he must confront two sets of opponents. On one side were those Whigs and Dissenters whose fondness for representative government and religious freedom had led them to see only good in Puritanism and only evil in the Stuart cause. On the other side were those critics of Puritanism who seemed to value "culture" more than "liberty," a clear reference to Matthew Arnold, who had argued in *Culture and Anarchy* that Puritanism was akin to fanaticism and therefore disruptive of the

---

[73] Gardiner, *History of England*, 1: vi–vii.
[74] Samuel Rawson Gardiner, Review of Guizot's *L'Histoire de France*, *Academy*, 8 (28 August 1875): 214.

social order.[75] Gardiner hoped to place himself between these extremes and to the extent that he was successful, his history of England offered the Victorians a grand synthesis which demonstrated that both parties in the Civil War had contributed in a constructive way to the making of modern England.

IV

In evaluating the case against the Stuarts, Gardiner modified the usual notion of an English constitution. The result enabled him to interpret the Civil War as a legitimate revolt by a unified nation. Whereas in the past historians had considered the constitution a fixed body of law, to which they could appeal when determining the legality of a given act of government, Gardiner pointed out that it was in fact something much less definite: "The letter of the old statutes," he warned, "was singularly confused and uncertain." The laws of England had never been fixed, but had evolved over centuries as opposing ideas of government had come into conflict. Depending on where one looked, after all, precedent could be found for any number of conflicting practices.[76] Instead of focusing on the details of the constitution, Gardiner appealed to its "spirit." Throughout the ages, England's kings had attempted to rule in sympathy with their subjects. They had turned regularly to the representatives of the nation, either Lords or Commons, in order to seek the advice, meet the grievances and retain the confidence of the people. At all times it was this harmony between the king and his subjects that made good government possible, and any policy which promoted such harmony was, Gardiner implied, in accord with the constitution's "spirit."[77]

If, as Gardiner argued, the "responsibility of the Crown to the nation" formed the essence of the constitution, then from the earliest times onward, the mechanism ensuring this responsibility had been the crown's fear of rebellion. An English king who ran afoul of the nation's wishes risked the possibility that his subjects might rise against him, and Gardiner suggested that such acts of rebellion were a legitimate part of the constitution: "A view of the constitution," he explained, "which takes no account of these acts

[75] Gardiner, *Fall of Charles*, 1: vi–vii.
[76] Gardiner, *History of England*, 2: 76–77, 6: 83.     [77] Ibid., 2: 195, 3: 397, 4: 263–264, 6: 120.

of violence is like a view of geology which takes no account of earthquakes and volcanoes." More than a fixed body of law, the constitution was a "mass of custom and opinion" which included within it the use of force as a means of making sure "that a king who spoke for himself and acted for himself should not be permitted to reign."[78] Under Elizabeth's guidance, England had enjoyed particularly good government. A wise and sympathetic leader, she had shaped the fears and aspirations of her countrymen into successful policies, never once losing their trust.[79] Unfortunately for England, her Stuart successors lacked those qualities which had enabled Elizabeth to share in almost all the prejudices of her age. Unable to see that they, too, must make the interests of the country their own if they were to govern successfully, James and Charles pursued unpopular policies, lost the confidence of their Parliaments, and in due time drove them to rebellion.[80] Only after half a century of revolution, culminating in the events of 1688 and the establishment of cabinet government, was a new, more peaceful mechanism found to guarantee the responsibility of the crown to the nation.[81]

Gardiner conceded, however, that even under the best of circumstances the early Stuarts could not have governed as Elizabeth had. As a result of the emergency brought on by her struggle against Catholicism and especially by the threatened Spanish invasion, the Queen had amassed a considerable pre-rogative. James and Charles may have hoped to wield the same authority, but inevitably they were prevented from doing so. The crises of the sixteenth century warranting a strong executive were absent in the seventeenth, and Parliament began to deny the Stuarts those extraordinary powers which it had so willingly granted to Elizabeth.[82] England had also advanced steadily in wealth and civilization throughout the Elizabethan years and its representatives were now, under the Stuarts, beginning to demand a share in the direction of national affairs commensurate with their new standing. "It was impossible," Gardiner wrote, "that a people growing in intelligence and wealth, undistracted by vital differences of opinion, and trained to political action by the discipline of centuries, could long be kept back from taking a far more active

---

[78] Ibid., 6: 314–315.  [79] Ibid., 1: 191–194, 6: 315, 7: 79.
[80] Ibid., 1: 174, 193–194.  [81] Ibid., 9: 401–402, 10: 14.  [82] Ibid., 1: 42, 161–162.

part in public affairs than had been possible under the sceptre of Elizabeth." The disputes over purveyance, wardship, monopolies and impositions which had engaged the Parliaments of James I were signs of the nation's growing awareness of its capacity for self-government. For Gardiner, then, the quarrel between king and Commons, which would trouble England almost without interruption from the accession of James in 1603 until the Revolution of 1688, had its origins in the Elizabethan monarchy and most likely would have occurred no matter who occupied the throne.[83]

Gardiner, then, regarded the Civil War in its political dimension as the legitimate revolt of a unified country, increasingly aware of its capacity for self-government and jealous of its newly acquired wealth, against a king who had ignored and contravened its wishes. From the Tudors onward, Parliament had come to represent the will of the people. England, Gardiner argued, "had grown up into a harmonious civilization, so that its Parliament was the true representative of a united nation . . . The position which was occupied by the House of Commons at the close of the reign of Elizabeth, was due to the complete harmony in which it stood with· the feelings and even with the prejudices of all classes of the people."[84] And on the eve of the Civil War, this Parliament was unanimous in its denunciation of the type of government which Charles had practiced. Had the only issues at stake been constitutional, had the nation not also been divided on questions of religion, then Charles would have found no support among his subjects, except perhaps for a small and insignificant group of courtiers. In short, there would have been no Civil War because there would have been no Royalist party, just an isolated king, and "Charles would have been swept away by the uprising of a united people."[85]

When Gardiner depicted the political revolt against the Stuarts as the legitimate expression of the national will, he was affirming the liberal precept that executive government must listen to the voice of the nation as spoken by its representatives. The "principle," Gardiner wrote, "that, when new circumstances call for new modes of action, the course to be pursued must be resolved upon in concurrence with those men whom the nation chooses or allows to represent it," was the principle on which "the greatness of England had rested in past ages," and which the Parliaments of the

---

[83] Ibid., 4: 36.		[84] Ibid., 1: 159–160.		[85] Ibid., 10: 11–12, 32.

seventeenth century were engaged in vindicating for the "benefit of posterity."[86] The statesmen who best personified this precept were the two most prominent leaders of the Commons: Sir John Eliot, who "idealized" Parliament, considering it the "mirror" of the nation's "wisdom"; and John Pym, whose "mind teemed with the thoughts, the beliefs, the prejudices of his age," and who was "strong with the strength and weak with the weaknesses" of his generation.[87] But as his evaluation of Pym suggests, Gardiner also believed that no matter how indispensable the contribution of Parliament might be for good government, such an institution could never rule alone. The Stuart Parliament was inevitably conservative, closed to new ideas and often ignorant. Its ascendancy could have its "ugly side": Parliament might come to represent the "interests" of a few rather than the "wisdom" of the whole, and unless "aroused to reverence for justice," it might become "as arbitrary as Charles had ever been."[88] When confronted with new problems, the seventeenth-century Parliament was rarely capable of rising above the prejudices of the age and seeing that new remedies were required. Pym never appreciated the importance of toleration and for this reason Gardiner considered his leadership of the Commons to have been a failure in the end.

Gardiner's history, however, had the effect of reconciling party divisions by emphasizing the positive contribution made by both sides in the Civil War. The defenders of Parliament had stood for a noble ideal which eventually gained permanent recognition as the burden of government shifted to the Commons following the Revolution of 1688. But the supporters of the royal prerogative – statesmen such as Francis Bacon and Thomas Wentworth – were also, Gardiner affirmed, partly correct when they argued that only a strong executive would provide the means to overcome the narrow vision of Parliament. Bacon, a great reformer, looked to the king's prerogative as the instrument to carry through his reforms, knowing full well that the Commons would never consent to programs so far in advance of the age. According to his ideal of government, the executive should be as free as possible in order to implement the most far-reaching changes for the improvement of mankind.[89] But though Gardiner recognized a considerable degree

---

86 Ibid., 6: 211.    87 Ibid., 5: 187, 244.
88 Ibid., 5: 434–435, 6: 209–210.    89 Ibid., 2: 191–193.

of truth in Bacon's reasoning, he was also aware of its dangers: "[Bacon] left out of his calculation," Gardiner warned, " . . . the inevitable tendencies to misgovernment which beset all bodies of men who are possessed of irresponsible power."[90] In the end, Gardiner found neither the defenders of Parliament nor the champions of the royal prerogative wholly correct. Good government, he implied, would result only when the principles of Pym combined with those of Bacon, when a popular assembly joined forces with a capable executive. In essence, this was the modern arrangement: if Pym's ideals were embodied in the Victorian Parliament, then Bacon's were realized in the cabinet.[91]

V

The Civil War was undoubtedly the most divisive event in British history, and of all the discord it created the most damaging was the ecclesiastical split between Anglican and Dissenter which persisted well into the nineteenth century. During the years when Gardiner was writing his *History of England*, Protestant Nonconformity exercised a greater influence on national politics than ever before. Following the Reform Act of 1867, Nonconformists became an important force behind the Liberal party, working for a variety of causes, including Irish Church disestablishment, the abolition of Church rates, nondenominational state-funded education, the elimination of the remaining religious tests at Oxford and Cambridge, and the right of Nonconformist ministers to preside over burials in parish churchyards.[92] Not surprisingly, given the intensity of this sectarian discord, the religious dimension of the Civil War had a particular fascination for the Victorians. Like Carlyle, Gardiner regarded the conflict in large part as a religious struggle. What Carlyle had termed a "Puritan revolt," Gardiner called a "Puritan revolution." In his history, Gardiner repeated several times that England would never have gone to war in 1642

---

[90] Ibid., 2: 195.    [91] Ibid., 2: 194.

[92] For the role of Nonconformity in English politics, see among others: George Kitson Clark, *The Making of Victorian England* (Cambridge, Mass.: Harvard University Press, 1962), 147–205. D. W. Bebbington, *The Nonconformist Conscience: Chapel and Politics, 1870–1914* (London: George Allen and Unwin, 1982). Marsh, *Victorian Church in Decline*, 242–263. Machin, *Politics and the Churches, 1869–1921*, 1–167. Parry, *Democracy and Religion*, 200–228, 261–452.

over the crown's violation of the constitution. What brought the nation to arms was the emergence of two incompatible views on how the national Church should be governed, its theology defined and its worship conducted.[93] The Civil War was above all a conflict between Calvinists on one side and Laudians on the other.

For Gardiner, religious diversity was the inevitable outcome of the English Reformation as two tendencies came to characterize the nation's spiritual life following the breach with Rome. Whereas most English Protestants during Elizabeth's reign were Calvinists in theology, Episcopalians on matters of Church government and satisfied with the forms of worship prescribed in the Elizabethan Prayer Book, a small but significant group of Puritan clergy desired a simpler ritual and considered the Presbyterian system of ecclesiastical government of divine origin.[94] Faced with this diversity, Elizabeth had two options: either she could broaden the Church to encompass all varieties of Protestant belief, thereby making the Establishment truly national, or she could enforce a more narrow uniformity. Like his hero Sir Francis Bacon, Gardiner would have preferred the first, believing that a genuinely comprehensive Church would have put an end to sectarian strife.[95] Elizabeth, however, chose the second. Favoring an elaborate ritual, she set out to enforce uniformity to her ideal, and in so doing, sowed the seeds of future discord because her policy guaranteed that a body of Nonconformists, or Puritans, would exist outside the Establishment. "It was inevitable," Gardiner concluded, "that strife, and not peace, should be the ultimate result of what Elizabeth had done." She left, "as a legacy to her successor, an ecclesiastical system which . . . threatened to divide the nation into two hostile camps."[96] When James and Charles likewise chose uniformity instead of comprehension, the prospect of civil war became even more certain.

By the time Charles convened the Long Parliament in 1640, Puritanism had become a considerable force in both Church and state, and Gardiner attributed its steady growth during the early seventeenth century in part to the incompetent statesmanship of the Stuarts. Puritanism, he argued, was always strongest at those moments when England's Protestant faith seemed threatened. It was prominent at the end of the sixteenth century when invasion by

---

[93] Gardiner, *History of England*, 10: 11–13, 32.    [94] Ibid., 1: 17–27.
[95] Ibid., 1: 146–147.    [96] Ibid., 1: 27, 33.

Catholic Spain was imminent, and it became strong once again under the Stuarts when the outbreak of the Thirty Years War made the future of Protestantism appear uncertain both in England and on the continent. Faced with this crisis in foreign affairs, neither James nor Charles could carry through a successful anti-Catholic policy, and according to Gardiner this failure was a major impetus behind the spread of Puritanism. When, for most English Protestants, James should have been combating the spread of Popery, he was instead attempting to establish peaceful relations with the two most powerful Catholic nations by negotiating a marriage between Charles and either a Spanish or French bride. The significance for England of this proposed union was immense. Appearing to Englishmen at the time as a dangerous concession to Catholicism and a threat to the security of their own faith, it led directly to the increase of Puritanism: "When the [Spanish] marriage was first agitated," Gardiner wrote, "the leading minds of the age were tending in a direction adverse to Puritanism . . . When it was finally broken off, the leading minds of the age were tending in a precisely opposite direction, and that period of our history commenced which led up to the anti-episcopalian fervour of the Long Parliament."[97]

More important, however, for the development and spread of Puritanism were the efforts of a small number of Churchmen, led by William Laud, to challenge the predominance of Calvinism within the Church of England. A learned elite with little popular support, the Laudians looked to the crown as the instrument to carry through their reforms. They preached the divine right of kings, and in return Charles sanctioned their innovations in doctrine and worship and gave preference to their candidates in ecclesiastical appointments.[98] The rise of the Laudians to power in the Church and the willingness of the crown to encourage them was, Gardiner argued, one of the most significant forces leading the nation to war. For the Puritan opposition increased steadily as Laud and his followers transformed the Church of England, purging it of its Calvinist theology and practices. Puritanism, which began as a small opposition to certain rituals found in the Prayer Book, had come by 1640 to represent the Calvinism prevalent among the

[97] Gardiner, *Charles and the Spanish Marriage*, 1: v.
[98] Gardiner, *History of England*, 6: 203–204, 7: 127–128.

English nation. When the Civil War broke out in 1642, the parties largely divided on religious lines: on the Royalist side were the supporters of Laud, the Bishops, and the Book of Common Prayer; on the side of Parliament were the upholders of Calvinism.

The particular virtue of Gardiner's approach was that in assessing these two ecclesiastical parties he found something of value in each of them. Calvinism he considered above all a powerful moral force. It had emerged in Europe after the Lutheran Reformation had removed the Catholic Church as the center of authority, and it had restored order to the Protestant world by imposing a rigid discipline. The Calvinist advocated "self-restraint" and "self-denial," and he displayed a "stern dislike to even innocent pleasures." He proclaimed that man's purpose on earth was not to work for his own salvation, but to implement the will of God. Concerning forms of worship, the Calvinist rejected elaborate rituals. Emphasizing the need for sermons rather than sacraments, he believed that divine grace acted on the mind through the preaching of the Gospel, not on the senses through sumptuous ceremonies.[99] Calvinism, Gardiner wrote in a characteristic passage,

had done great things for Europe. At a time when the individual tendencies of Protestantism threatened to run riot, it had given to men a consistent creed and an unbending moral discipline, which was yet Protestant to the core . . . Wherever the struggle with Rome was the deadliest, it was under the banner of Calvinism that the battle had been waged. Wherever in quiet villages, or in the lanes of great cities, anyone woke up to the consciousness that a harder battle with sin was to be waged in his heart, it was in the strength of the Calvinistic creed that he had equipped himself for the contest. Alone with his God, the repentant struggling sinner entered the valley of the shadow of death.[100]

But if Gardiner valued Puritanism as a moral force, he was equally cognizant of its drawbacks. In the Calvinist scheme of society, the clergy were supreme, bound by neither the secular magistrate nor the law, and within this theocracy there was nothing to prevent them from exercising a tyranny which would destroy all meaningful liberty. Calvinists, Gardiner warned, "were not seldom narrow-minded and egotistical. In their hatred of vice, they were apt to be intolerant of pleasure . . . If ever they succeeded in acquiring

---

[99] Ibid., 1: 16–19, 3: 242.  [100] Ibid., 5: 355.

political power, they would find it hard to avoid using it for the purpose of coercing the world into morality."[101]

Laudianism arose in England as a reaction against the rigidity, narrowness and unreasonableness of Calvinism. For Laud himself, Gardiner had little sympathy or respect. But for the intellectual movement to which the Churchman's name was attached, Gardiner had considerable praise. The Laudians, he argued, represented the modern tendency in seventeenth-century theology:

They claimed to think for themselves . . . , and to search for goodness and truth on every side . . . They were offended with [Calvinism's] dogmatism, with its pretensions to classify and arrange men's notions of mysteries which eye hath not seen nor ear heard, and they claimed the right to say that there were things on which the popular religion had pronounced clearly, which were beyond the domain of human knowledge.

The Laudians, he concluded,

were intellectually the Liberal Churchmen of the age. They stood between two infallibilities – the infallibility of Calvinism and the infallibility of Rome – not indeed casting off entirely the authority of the past, but, at least in a considerable sphere of thought, asking for evidence and argument at each step which they took, and daring to remain in uncertainty when reason was not satisfied.[102]

For Gardiner, the Laudians represented the continuation of the Renaissance spirit into the seventeenth century. They were the intellectual descendants of one of the greatest thinkers of the English Renaissance, Hooker, who had likewise displayed a marked distrust of all dogmatic assertions.[103] It was not the Puritans who "inspired the progressive movement of the age," but rather the followers of Laud.[104]

Like the Puritans, the Laudians were also concerned with improving the moral tenor of their society. But where the Puritan hoped to influence men by preaching to their intellect, the Laudian sought to inculcate the habits of piety and morality by means of a uniform and repetitive appeal to the senses. By subjecting the churchgoer over and over again to the same suggestive ceremonies, he hoped to use "the senses . . . to reach the heart." As the Laudian understood it: "Men were to be schooled into piety by habitual

[101] Ibid., 1: 22–26, 3: 242–243.    [102] Ibid., 5: 357.    [103] Ibid., 1: 39, 41, 5: 359.
[104] Samuel Rawson Gardiner, Review of Lewis's *Life of Joseph Hall, Academy*, 29 (17 April 1886): 267.

attendance upon the services of the Church . . . Uniformity of liturgical forms and uniformity of ecclesiastical ceremony would impress upon every Englishman the lessons of devotion."[105] Moving from strengths to weaknesses, Gardiner also pointed out that the Laudian view was prone to certain dangers. Considering the Church supreme, this "new school" of ecclesiastics would not hesitate to use political power to impose it on everyone regardless of whether they approved of it or not.[106]

Gardiner's purpose was to heal the religious divisions which the Civil War had created. He wrote an even-handed narrative which indicated how national unity could arise out of so divisive an event. He suggested that both parties in the Civil War had, in truth, participated in something far greater than mere internecine strife. They had engaged in a struggle out of which emerged the idea of religious liberty. The freedom to think and speak as one chose in matters of conscience was, Gardiner argued, the noble consequence which ultimately gave meaning to that otherwise lamentable event. England had gone to war in 1642 because neither Puritan nor Laudian had understood the importance of toleration, neither Pym nor Hyde had realized that the ecclesiastical problem would not be solved until allowance were made for both conceptions of the Church.[107] With no understanding of toleration, war was inevitable. But it was precisely because both sides stood their ground and fought for their ideals, that the principle of toleration finally prevailed. "If it was in England," Gardiner wrote, "that the great problem of the seventeenth century was solved by liberty of speech and thought . . . , it [was] because at this crisis of her fate she did not choose to lie down and slumber."[108]

Gardiner agreed with those critics who argued that Laud himself was wholly ignorant of the value of religious liberty.[109] Though he may have opposed the two "infallibilities" of Geneva and Rome, Laud was nevertheless so confident in the truth of his own views that he imposed on the Church of England a rigid uniformity in which freedom of conscience played absolutely no role. Within the Laudian position, however, there were tendencies which would contribute to the latitudinarian ideas of a later age, and Gardiner

---

[105] Gardiner, *History of England*, 2: 124–125, 3: 243–244.
[106] Ibid., 3: 244.    [107] Ibid., 10: 32–34.
[108] Ibid., 10: 35.    [109] Ibid., 7: 125, 301–302.

suggested that a direct line of intellectual development could be traced from Hooker's *Ecclesiastical Polity*, through thinkers of the Laudian school, to Locke's *Letters on Toleration*.[110] Laud had looked with "contempt" on those "endless discussions about problems which it was impossible for the human intellect to solve," and Gardiner pointed out that it was only a small step from this dislike of "dogmatic controversy" to the latitudinarian thinking of Chillingworth. In his *Religion of Protestants*, Chillingworth had argued that men had no right to force their religious beliefs on others because human reason was too prone to error when considering the mysteries of Christianity. Instead of imposing dogmatic and most likely erroneous interpretations on others, the Church should require adherence to only the clearly revealed truths of Christianity while allowing for a variety of views on the more controversial points of doctrine. Thus, for Gardiner, the idea of comprehension first took hold within the Laudian school.[111]

The Puritans before 1642 were for the most part no more inclined toward liberty of conscience than was Laud. But after the outbreak of the Civil War, Puritanism fragmented and among some of its competing groups, especially among the Independents, ideas of toleration began to flourish. Independency had developed during the war as an alternative to Presbyterianism, which had become increasingly popular ever since Parliament turned to Scotland for military assistance, and as an alternative to the beliefs of the extreme Separatists. In response to these two groups, Gardiner argued, the Independents had "hit upon a wise middle course," holding that "no congregation ought to be subjected to coercive jurisdiction outside itself." Whereas the Presbyterians considered the clergy supreme in secular as well as spiritual affairs, the Independents wished to maintain the supremacy of the laity. And whereas the Separatists declared the Established Church to be apostate, the Independents were willing to accept the Church

[110] Samuel Rawson Gardiner, *History of the Great Civil War, 1642–1649*, new edition (London: Longmans, Green and Co., 1893–1894), 1: 276. Gardiner also made his position clear in a review of J. R. Green's *Short History of the English People*: "Mr. Green," Gardiner wrote, "misses the connexion of thought between Laud and the Latitudinarians, thus omitting the link which bound the men of the new learning in the sixteenth century to the Tillotsons and Lockes of a later day." *Academy*, 6 (5 December 1874): 602.
[111] Gardiner, *History of England*, 7: 20, 8: 262, *Great Civil War*, 1: 285, 2: 108.

on the condition that it would allow freedom to individual congregations.[112] During the war, Independency found its champion in Oliver Cromwell, who was willing to grant toleration to anyone providing he was determined to defeat the Royalists. As Gardiner pointed out, however, Cromwell's idea of toleration was actually limited since it did not extend to parties outside the Puritan camp. "How to get the best soldiers was the problem which made Cromwell tolerant, and tolerance built upon so material a foundation would to the end have something in it narrower than Chillingworth's craving for the full light of truth."[113]

The principle of religious freedom did not triumph in England until many years after the Civil War. But when it finally did gain official recognition following the Glorious Revolution in 1688, it was able to do so because the conflicts of the Civil War had already prepared the ground. Most important for Gardiner was the fact that liberty of conscience, as it developed in England, owed something crucial to the complementary notions of comprehension and toleration which had gained acceptance among the Royalists and Puritans respectively. Comprehension, Gardiner wrote, "would soften down asperities, and teach the assured dogmatist to put on something of that humility in which the controversialist of all periods is so grievously deficient." Toleration, on the other hand, "would prepare room for the unchecked development of that individuality which is the foundation of all true vigour in churches and in nations."[114]

Gardiner's view of the development of religious freedom in England brought together two distinct interpretations which the sectarian controversies of the Victorian period had tended to place in opposition. When he stressed the contribution that Puritanism had made to the growth of liberty and toleration, he was repeating the arguments that Nonconformist historians like William Godwin,

---

[112] Gardiner, *Great Civil War*, 1: 261–263.    [113] Ibid., 1: 312.

[114] Gardiner, *History of England*, 8: 268. Gardiner made a similar point in a review of A. Stern's *Milton und seine Zeit*: "His argument that religious liberty is impossible without liberty of Sectarian association is unanswerable, and it is equally clear that the Independents, and not the Latitudinarians, were the persons who first adopted the idea of sectarian association. But would the right of these sects to exist ever have obtained practical acknowledgement unless the Latitudinarians had diffused as widely as possible the idea that it was a good thing to leave as many open questions as possible, and had thus fostered the habit of regarding men of opinions opposed to one's own as persons with whom it was unnecessary to quarrel?" *Academy*, 11 (24 February 1877): 157.

John Forster or Robert Vaughan had been making since the 1820s, and that David Masson was popularizing in the 1870s in his massive biography of John Milton. Masson had once intended to become a minister in the Church of Scotland but, falling under the influence of Thomas Chalmers, he had walked out of the Church during the Great Disruption and embarked on a literary career in London. Masson's *Milton* was a work of considerable scholarship, based on an extensive use of documentary evidence and containing a complete history of England alongside a biography of its subject. Speaking in the voice of the Scottish Disruption, Masson traced the idea of toleration to the Independents, particularly the Baptists, and he saw its champions in Milton and Cromwell, its nemeses in Laud and Charles. For Masson, it was the Cromwell of the Protectorate who anticipated the liberal solution to England's religious difficulties when he advocated a comprehensive national Church and complete toleration for those Sectaries whose faith would not allow them to conform.[115] Gardiner's reaction to Masson's work is instructive for the insights it provides into his own designs. Though he agreed with one half of Masson's interpretation, he objected strongly to its partisan spirit. "The historian," Gardiner wrote, "may justly claim to have his preferences, but he may make no exclusions. He must take account of all the forces by which society is influenced, and this is precisely what Prof. Masson deliberately refuses to do." Masson's great shortcoming was that in praising – quite rightly – what Milton and Cromwell had done for the cause of religious freedom, he had failed to see that the Commonwealth and Protectorate were not the whole of English history. The opponents of the Puritans, after all, had triumphed at the Restoration and their impact on the development of the nation deserved an equally honest treatment.[116]

When Gardiner told the other half of the story, pointing out the contribution that the Laudian dislike of dogmatism had made to the idea of comprehension, he made use of an interpretation favored by liberal Anglicans. In *Saint Paul and Protestantism*, for

[115] David Masson, *The Life of John Milton: Narrated in Connexion with the Political, Ecclesiastical, and Literary History of His Time*, new and revised edition (London: Macmillan and Company, 1871–1894), 3: 99–109, 129, 166–171, 343–344, 525, 5: 54–72.

[116] Samuel Rawson Gardiner, Reviews of Masson's *Milton*, *Academy*, 5 (31 January 1874): 112, and 13 (30 March 1878): 277. Samuel Rawson Gardiner, "Modern History," *Contemporary Review*, 37 (June, 1880): 1056.

instance, Matthew Arnold alluded to a similar connection between the critical spirit of the Renaissance, the High Churchmen of the Laudian school and the latitudinarians of a later period. For Arnold, as for Gardiner, the Laudian Church rejected Calvinism because of its narrowness, rigidity and unreasonableness, preferring Arminian doctrines instead. The Arminianism of the Stuart Church, Arnold wrote, again echoing Gardiner, represented "an effort of man's practical good sense to get rid of what is shocking to it in Calvinism." Because it regarded doctrine as something broad and developing, Anglicanism kept its formularies open and indefinite, whereas Puritanism conceived of doctrine as narrow and fixed. Free inquiry, Arnold concluded, was therefore more congenial to Anglicanism than to Puritanism, and the "growth and movement" of religious thought was consequently found within the Church, not among the Puritans.[117]

The comparison with Arnold can be taken even further. In *Culture and Anarchy*, Arnold presented his classic analysis of the Hebraic and Hellenic traditions which he believed had shaped modern England. Where for Arnold, Hebraism emphasized proper conduct and strict obedience to moral rules, Hellenism stressed right reason and the play of intellect. Where Hebraism was found in the uncompromising moral earnestness of England's Puritan and Nonconformist heritage, Hellenism existed in the intellectual tradition of the Anglican Church and universities. *Culture and Anarchy* had appeared serially while Gardiner was completing *Prince Charles and the Spanish Marriage*, and Gardiner was certainly familiar with it. Like Arnold, he too saw the Dissenting and Anglican traditions as the principal forces behind the making of modern England. When Gardiner described Puritanism as being inflexible and dogmatic, and when he saw in Laudianism a continuation of Renaissance rationality, he was speaking in terms reminiscent of Arnold's essay. But here the similarity ended. Arnold, alarmed at the growth and political influence of Nonconformity, was attempting to prod the Nonconformists back into the Established Church by undermining the justification for their dissent. In *Culture and Anarchy*, he attacked Hebraism for its narrow vision and praised Hellenism for its "sweetness and light." In *Saint Paul and*

---

117 *The Complete Prose Works of Matthew Arnold*, ed. R. H. Super (Ann Arbor: University of Michigan Press, 1968), 6: 76–85, 91–92, 100–101.

*Protestantism*, he demonstrated how the Dissenters had based their separation from the Church on a misreading of Scripture. Gardiner, sharing none of Arnold's antipathy for Dissent and conceiving of the nation as something broad enough to contain both a Dissenting and a conforming tradition, was more even-handed. Both of these traditions, he suggested, were legitimate products of the Reformation. They had clashed, lamentably, in the Civil War, but ever since the establishment of toleration in 1689, they had exerted a healthy influence on one another as the "serious intelligence of the Puritan" combined with the "breadth of view and artistic perception of the Churchman."[118]

The one position to which Gardiner gave little credence was the High Church interpretation that regarded Laud as the preserver of a historic Christianity within the Anglican Church. Walter Farquhar Hook, the High Anglican Dean of Chichester, argued in his *Lives of the Archbishops* that Laud saved the true catholic Church in England from the corruptions of Rome on the one hand and the ravages of a Puritan minority on the other. When he strove for uniformity, he was ensuring that this truth would remain at the heart of English Christianity.[119] For Gardiner, however, this interpretation emphasized only one small part of Laud's endeavor. For Laud wanted to do more than simply hand down a body of doctrine and a form of ceremonial. His conception of the Church stressed a uniformity of worship which he was ready to use the coercive powers of the state to attain. But here, for Gardiner, was Laud's great failure. At no time had his conception of the Church taken hold. Neither during his own lifetime nor at the Restoration had the Anglican Church achieved the degree of uniformity for which Laud had stood. Indeed, the Toleration Act of 1689 had acknowledged the very opposite of uniformity. Even more important, this High Church interpretation failed to discern what was actually Laud's greatest legacy. In their dislike of latitudinarianism and their desire to see Anglican theology fixed for all time in the Prayer Book of 1662, High Churchmen like Hook were unable to see the contribution that Laud had

---

[118] Samuel Rawson Gardiner, *The First Two Stuarts and the Puritan Revolution, 1603–1660* (London: Longmans, Green and Co., 1876), 205.

[119] Walter Farquhar Hook, *Lives of the Archbishops of Canterbury* (London: Richard Bentley and Son, 1860–1884), II: vii–xiv, 389–390.

made to growth of latitudinarian sentiments within the Anglican Church.[120]

Reviewing the *Great Civil War* in 1887, Sir John Seeley argued that Gardiner was the first "serious" student of Stuart England because he was the first to write its history from a perspective free from political partisanship.[121] In one sense, Seeley's judgment was true enough. Gardiner certainly worked hard to be fair to all sides, he tried to avoid pronouncements not founded on documentary evidence, and he never exhibited the party spirit of earlier historians. But if Seeley meant to imply that Gardiner's history had no ideological dimension, then his judgment needs qualification. For Gardiner's attempt to unite Anglicanism and Dissent in one comprehensive interpretation of the seventeenth century was an expression of late Victorian Liberalism. As a nationalist, Gardiner used history as a tool for nation building, and as a Gladstonian, he envisioned building a nation characterized by religious equality. His experiences as an Irvingite in a society that was still predominantly Anglican had impressed on him the folly of religious discrimination and the wisdom of tolerating Dissent while incorporating the widest variety of Christian belief within the Established Church. Gardiner's desire to moderate sectarian discord was consistent with the aims of other Liberals who were attempting to create conditions conducive to modern democracy by easing those divisions that disrupted English political life. When he presented an interpretation of the Stuarts that brought together Anglicanism and Dissent, Gardiner thus gave expression to the same Liberalism that led him to endorse Balkan nationalism in the 1870s, opt for Irish Home Rule in the 1880s, and question the Boer War in the 1890s. The result of his life's labor was an image of the Stuart past that met the expectations of Victorian Liberalism.

---

120 Gardiner, *Great Civil War*, 2: 108. See also Samuel Rawson Gardiner, Review of C. H. Simpkinson's *Life and Times of William Laud* and W. H. Hutton's *William Laud*, *English Historical Review*, 10 (1895): 373.
121 J. R. Seeley, Review of Gardiner's *Great Civil War*, *Academy*, 31 (21 May 1887): 353.

# CHAPTER 5

# Cromwell and the late Victorians

The statue of Oliver Cromwell, which still stands outside the Houses of Parliament, has a troubled story behind it. In 1895, during the final weeks of Lord Rosebery's Liberal government, the cabinet decided to commemorate the tercentenary of Cromwell's birth, which would occur in 1899, by using public funds to commission a statue in the Protector's honor. But when the proposal was placed before the Commons, it provoked an uproar. "The Irishmen took fire," John Morley wrote later, describing the scene. "Drogheda, and all the other deeds of two centuries and a half before, blazed into memory as if they had happened yesterday. Nationalist wrath was aided by Unionist satire. Did peace Liberals then, we were asked, honour Oliver as the great soldier, or was it the jingo in international policy, or the founder of a big navy, or the armed destroyer of the House of Commons?" Eventually, the government was forced to withdraw its proposal in order to avoid the risk of alienating such an important Liberal constituency as the Irish. Rosebery, however, was not to be outdone. Taking on himself the cost of the statue, he commissioned Hamo Thornycroft to execute the work, and in 1899 the memorial to Oliver Cromwell appeared outside Westminster Hall as originally planned, angering once again the Irish and Conservatives.[1]

The decision to celebrate Cromwell's tercentenary with a statue, despite the outcry it occasioned, marks something of a watershed in England's appreciation of its Cromwellian past. A century earlier it would have been unthinkable to honor the Protector with a public

---

[1] John Morley, *Recollections* (New York: Macmillan, 1917), 2: 48. Lord Rosebery, "Cromwell," *Miscellanies, Literary and Historical* (London: Hodder and Stoughton, 1921), 1: 77–79. *The Times*, 31 October 1899, 8. *The Times*, 1 November 1899, 8, 9. Robert Rhodes James, *Rosebery: A Biography of Archibald Philip, Fifth Earl of Rosebery* (London: Weidenfeld and Nicolson, 1963), 381–382.

monument of any kind. In 1799, England was at war with the French Revolution, and the fear of radicalism, both abroad and at home, made any appeal to Cromwell appear subversive. For defenders of the Establishment, Cromwell epitomized that radicalism which in the seventeenth century had overturned the monarchy and the Church, and which now seemed to inspire Dissenters, Whigs and French revolutionaries. In his *Reflections*, Edmund Burke had emphasized this connection between the radical politics of the past and those of the present when he alluded to the regicides in order to point out the dangers inherent in contemporary Dissent. To have honored Cromwell's bicentenary would have meant endorsing those revolutionary forces that were tearing France apart and that threatened to do the same in England. Nor did Cromwell fare any better among the Establishment's opponents. Moderate Whigs accused him of destroying England's mixed constitution, radicals denounced him as the apostate who turned against the republic for which the Civil War had been fought, and both accused him of destroying English liberty for the sake of his own ambition.

By the 1890s, circumstances had changed. The threat of revolution had largely vanished, and the blend of radicalism and Dissent that Cromwell symbolized was no longer as worrisome as it had once been. Democracy had come peacefully with the three reform acts, while Dissent no longer posed a challenge to the fundamentals of the English constitution. Although radicalism still existed, it was now located within the labor movement, and spokesmen for the working-class had never seen in Cromwell a particularly inspiring hero. Even more to the point, new conditions had developed toward the end of the century that enhanced greatly Cromwell's appeal. The 1890s were a time of growing international anxiety, as the emergence of foreign rivals, particularly Germany, shook England's confidence in itself as a world power. The fact that interest in Cromwell coincided with England's poor performance in the Boer War suggests that the nation was searching for a historic myth that would restore its self-esteem. The Cromwellian past, now shorn of its revolutionary significance, seemed admirably suited for this kind of morale boosting since it had witnessed the growth of free institutions at home as well as the assertion of national power abroad. Speaking at the unveiling of the Protector's statue, Rosebery stressed the important themes. Englishmen, he declared should admire Cromwell because he was a soldier who never lost a battle, a ruler who fought for liberty and toleration, and an imperialist who made England respected overseas.[2]

The Cromwellian past, however, was not as suitable for mythic treatment as some might have thought. In order for a national or imperial myth to succeed, it must unite a wide variety of opinion behind a common image of the past, thereby defining the nation's purpose and strengthening its resolve. It was precisely here that Cromwell was bound to fail. As the controversy over his statue demonstrates, neither Conservatives nor the Irish were prepared to rally behind a vision of the past that was Cromwellian. Long dedicated to a tradition of Church and king, Tories would hardly endorse the man who had condoned the executions of Charles I and Archbishop Laud. No matter how strenuously Cromwell's defenders might apologize for his conduct in Ireland, the Irish would never forget the horrors of Drogheda and Wexford. Rosebery himself knew how divisive the Cromwellian past could be, for in his tercentenary address he deliberately sidestepped Cromwell's part in the king's death and his policies in Ireland.[3]

But if the Cromwellian myth failed to enlist the whole nation, it certainly appealed to a wide range of Liberal opinion. Unionists and imperialists, spokesmen for democracy and toleration. Nonconformists, broad Churchmen and free thinkers all agreed that modern England was in some way Cromwellian. When S. R. Gardiner declared in his Ford Lectures, delivered at Oxford in 1896, that Cromwell "stands forth as the typical Englishman of the modern world," he spoke for many of his Liberal contemporaries.[4] But even here, among Cromwell's admirers, invoking the Protector's name did not always produce unity of purpose. By equating Cromwellian and Victorian England, Liberals transferred to the past questions of national identity, ensuring that the debate over Cromwell's achievement would become inextricably linked to

[2] Rosebery, "Cromwell," 83–89. For the emergence of other myths during the late Victorian years, see David Cannadine, "The Context, Performance and Meaning of Ritual: The British Monarchy and the 'Invention of Tradition,' *c*. 1820–1977," in Eric Hobsbawm and Terence Ranger, eds., *The Invention of Tradition* (Cambridge: Cambridge University Press, 1983), 120–138.

[3] Rosebery, "Cromwell," 80–82.

[4] Samuel Rawson Gardiner, *Cromwell's Place in History*, second edition (London: Longmans, Green, and Co., 1897), 113.

a debate over the condition of England. Confusing past and present in this way could only produce discord, for Liberals were not only deeply split over contemporary issues, they were divided on history as well. Cromwell's Puritanism, his relations with Parliament and the army, his policies in Ireland and abroad were all controversial and not likely to occasion agreement.

I

The late Victorian appreciation of the Cromwellian past owed much to the spirit of international rivalry that flourished after Bismarck's unification of Germany, and to the enthusiasm for empire that followed Disraeli's decision to crown Victoria Empress of India. Reflecting back after almost twenty years on this cult of Cromwell, John Morley noted how it had grown out of the needs of an imperialistic age. Cromwell, he observed in his *Recollections*, "became a name on an Imperialist flag. It fell in with some of the notions of the day about representative government, the beneficent activities of a busy State, the virtue of the Strong Man, and the Hero for Ruler." Cromwell's memory, Morley continued, "diffused a subtle tendency to deify Violence, Will, Force, even War. It was the day of Bismarck." An editorial in *The Times*, written during the Boer War and commenting on the opposition to the Cromwell statue, corroborated Morley's observation: it was "scarcely credible," the columnist lamented, that Cromwell's "pre-eminent greatness as a ruler and a warrior should be contested in these days of militant Imperialism."[5]

The historian who best adapted the Cromwellian past to the needs of the imperialistic age was John Robert Seeley. Regius Professor of Modern History at Cambridge, Seeley wrote two influential works of international history: the *Expansion of England*, a series of lectures published in 1883 that did much to popularize the empire, and the *Growth of British Policy*, published posthumously in 1895. Seeley was both an imperialist and a defender of England's union with Ireland. An early member of the Imperial Federation League, he broke with Gladstone in 1886 over Irish Home Rule, joining the Liberal Unionist party and campaigning in support of its candidates. In many ways, Seeley was representative of those

---

[5] Morley, *Recollections*, 2: 49. *The Times*, 1 November 1899, 9.

intellectuals who grew disillusioned with Gladstonian Liberalism after the Home Rule debacle. The Unionist critique of Gladstone's statesmanship – a critique also shared by those Liberal Imperialists who coalesced around Rosebery in the 1890s – was more than a denunciation of Home Rule. At heart it reflected a deepening dissatisfaction with English democracy as it had developed following the Reform Act of 1867. According to these Liberal intellectuals, the true statesman should stand above sectional divisions and govern for the benefit of the nation as a whole. When it appeared that Gladstone was prepared to sacrifice the national interest simply to win the support of the Irish, they grew disillusioned. Liberalism, they now insisted, should move away from its Gladstonian preoccupation with sectional causes such as Welsh disestablishment, Irish Home Rule or franchise reform, and embrace issues of genuinely national importance. Imperialism and efficiency became their two most celebrated slogans. They advocated the consolidation of the existing empire, rather than its expansion, placing particular emphasis on the areas of white settlement, and they demanded "national efficiency," implying that the well-being of the state should take precedence over the rights of individual citizens.[6]

In the *Expansion of England*, Seeley argued strenuously for a new approach to the past that would be more appropriate for the age of empire. The study of English history, he urged, should connect past, present and future. It should identify large patterns of development, indicate the direction of England's destiny, and provide guidance for statesmen who were looking to the future. Reflecting back over the last three hundred years, Seeley declared that the expansion of England, the "extension of the English name into other countries of the globe, the foundation of Greater Britain," was the general tendency on which the study of history should focus.[7] With this claim, Seeley proposed nothing less than a radical

---

[6] Deborah Wormell, *Sir John Seeley and the Uses of History* (Cambridge: Cambridge University Press, 1980), 154–180. R. T. Shannon, "John Robert Seeley and the Idea of a National Church," in Robert Robson, ed., *Ideas and Institutions of Victorian Britain: Essays in Honour of George Kitson Clark* (New York: Barnes and Noble, 1967), 255–267. John Roach, "Liberalism and the Victorian Intelligentsia," *Cambridge Historical Journal*, 12 (1957): 58–81. H. C. G. Matthew, *The Liberal Imperialists: The Ideas and Politics of a Post-Gladstonian Elite* (Oxford: Oxford University Press, 1973), 125–149.

[7] John Robert Seeley, *The Expansion of England: Two Courses of Lectures* (London: Macmillan and Co., 1914), 9.

shift in the way English history was conceived. Previously, historians had concentrated on those domestic developments leading to the growth of liberty and democracy. But for Seeley, this conventional approach was wholly inadequate since neither liberty nor democracy could provide direction for the future. Liberty had already been acquired in the seventeenth century, while democracy was an insignificant development of the nineteenth. What was most instructive for the future was the growth of English power that had culminated in the Victorian empire. If England was to survive in the age of great powers, then Englishmen must come to regard this empire, especially Canada, South Africa and Australia, as an integral part of themselves, not as separate colonial possessions that could be discarded at will. In order to encourage this new appreciation of the empire, Seeley intended to show that the history of England was the story of its expansion.[8]

As Seeley conceived of English history, the hundred years stretching from the defeat of the Armada in 1588 to the Revolution of 1688 represented a period of transition, as the religious concerns of the Reformation gave way gradually to the commercial considerations of the contemporary world. The Elizabethan age marked the beginning of England's modern period, for it was Drake and Raleigh who first recognized their country's potential as a maritime power. The seventeenth century saw the consolidation of England's navy and the first movements toward colonization in the new world. After the Revolution, England finally emerged as the world's foremost commercial and industrial state, capable of accumulating a vast overseas empire. Interpreted within this framework, the Civil War took on new meaning: it was important not because it gave rise to free institutions, but because it pushed England along its modern course as a world power, and the momentous event of the period was not the execution of the king, but Cromwell's decision to wage war against Spain, which resulted in the conquest of Jamaica.[9]

Seeley's *Expansion of England* and *Growth of British Policy* contained perhaps the most innovative reinterpretation of the Cromwellian past that the Victorians would see. Cromwell's achievement was revolutionary, Seeley argued, because it transformed England into a military state that would become under the Protectorate a "first

---

[8] Ibid., 1–3, 8–10, 86–89, 138–140.    [9] Ibid., 91–102, 120–128, 130–137.

sketch of the British Empire."[10] For Seeley, Cromwell was the great
soldier whose victories in Scotland and Ireland fused the three
kingdoms together as the core of Greater Britain. He was the
ruler who dismissed the Long Parliament and established an
authoritarian regime capable of conducting a bold and decisive
foreign policy. He was the great European statesman who forged a
Protestant alliance against Spain and encouraged England's
colonial development. In contrast to the early Stuarts, whose
policies tended to be dynastic, Cromwell was a nationalist
concerned with promoting the greatness of England. His approach
to Europe and the new world thus developed further the modern
tendencies which first appeared during the Elizabethan age, and it
anticipated the imperial power that England would become in the
eighteenth century.[11] In making these claims, Seeley was charting
new ground. He rejected Carlyle's interpretation, which had
presented Cromwell as the Puritan hero building a Godly
Commonwealth, as well as Macaulay's, which had stressed
Cromwell's efforts to restore constitutional government. For
Seeley, Cromwell's Puritanism was important only because it gave
force and direction to his foreign policy, and his attempt at
constitutional government was important only to the extent that it
affected his ability to execute this policy.

Seeley believed that history should provide statesmen with
guidance, and by identifying Cromwell as one of the founders of
Greater Britain, he suggested that the Cromwellian past had
lessons to teach. Indeed, his interpretation of the Protectorate had
an unmistakable tendency to exalt the Cromwellian state along
with its authoritarian and military attributes. Cromwell, it implied,
would never have implemented his national policy, uniting the
three kingdoms and contributing to England's colonial expansion,
without the backing of an invincible army and navy, and without the
autocratic control necessary to formulate a consistent policy and
carry it out decisively. But Seeley never intended to set Cromwell
up as a model for emulation. Victorian England was not an empire
in the sense that the Protectorate was, and nowhere did Seeley
suggest that it should become one. Rather, he believed that

[10] John Robert Seeley, *The Growth of British Policy: An Historical Essay* (Cambridge: Cambridge
University Press, 1895), 2: 63.
[11] Ibid., 2: 1–100. Seeley, *Expansion of England*, 129–137.

Cromwell's imperialism was "unsound." Military states require war in order to survive; their armies must be satisfied, and their subjects must enjoy victory if they are to submit easily to dictatorship. These states might bring "glory" and "ascendancy," but only at the cost of "liberty" and "wealth." Had Cromwell lived longer, England might have embarked on a European war that would have postponed the development of constitutional liberty and impoverished the nation.[12]

But if Victorian England was in many ways more fortunate than the Protectorate, Seeley's history implied that in the future circumstances might possibly arise that would force the state to assume a more Cromwellian aspect. The seventeenth century had been an age of military states, of which Cromwell's was the best organized and most powerful. Under the old colonial system, war and commerce were indistinguishable since all the empires were closed monopolies and waging war was the only way a state could expand its trade.[13] The nineteenth century, on the other hand, was an age of economic liberalism in which states traded freely. War was no longer the indispensable counterpart of commerce, and the military state was no longer a necessity. But for Seeley, there was nothing permanent in this arrangement, and an age of commercial liberalism could degenerate into war. In such circumstances, England would be compelled once again to take on some of the characteristics of the military state in order to guarantee its preservation, even though individual and constitutional liberties might be sacrificed. Nor would readers in the 1890s, a time of heightened international tension, have considered this a remote possibility. Seeley had demonstrated clearly that England's standing as a great power depended on the consolidation of its empire. He had shown what the building of that empire had entailed from the Elizabethan age through the Victorian, and the example of Cromwell indicated how that empire might best defend its interests in the future.

The union of England and Ireland, which Cromwell had done much to secure, was a crucial step in the making of Greater Britain. But in neither of his works did Seeley actually argue the case for

---

[12] Seeley, *Expansion of England*, 51, 127, 132–134, 155–156, *Growth of British Policy*, 2: 87–88, 98–100.
[13] Seeley, *Expansion of England*, 127–130.

Cromwell's Irish policies. That task fell to another exponent of empire, James Anthony Froude. In his *English in Ireland*, Froude presented a defense of Cromwell that would have been familiar to any reader of Carlyle. The Cromwellian settlement was justifiable, he insisted, because it had benefited Ireland. For Froude, the Irish were simply incapable of governing themselves. War and anarchy had long been endemic to the land as the native chiefs routinely plundered their countrymen. The Irish insurrection of 1641 was only the most extreme instance of this anarchy, and its atrocities excused Cromwell's future conquest. Whereas the Irish rebels had slaughtered "the weak, the sick, and the helpless," Cromwell had complied with the rules of war when he executed the defenders of Drogheda and Wexford. Nor were Cromwell's actions without humanity. The examples of Drogheda and Wexford, horrible as they were, prevented further bloodshed by breaking Ireland's will to resist. The Cromwellian settlement finally put an end to Ireland's debilitating anarchy, laying the foundations for prosperity, depriving the Irish chiefs of their lands, and replacing them with industrious English and Scottish Protestants. Rebels were punished, an insurgent Catholicism was outlawed, a diligent Protestantism encouraged. For Froude, then, Cromwell represented the model governor of Ireland, one who "meant to rule Ireland for Ireland's good." He brought justice to the Irish people, established law and order, freed them from oppression, and brought prosperity. His methods may have been coercive, but, said Froude, the Irish "respect a master hand, though it be a hard and a cruel one." Had Cromwell's policies been given time, Froude predicted confidently, they would have solved England's Irish problem.[14]

This image of Cromwell as the statesman who dictated justice to Ireland complemented Seeley's interpretation of the Cromwellian past as one of the formative moments in the expansion of England, and together they appealed to an age when England's security seemed to depend on consolidating the empire and retaining the union with Ireland. When they held up Cromwell as a model, both Seeley and Froude were endorsing an alternative to the Liberal statesmanship that had become discredited after Gladstone's

---

[14] James Anthony Froude, *The English in Ireland in the Eighteenth Century* (London: Longmans, Green, and Co., 1887), I: 91, 133–134, 139–140, 145–149, 150–155.

decision to embrace Home Rule. For both Seeley and Froude, Cromwell was a nationalist who placed the interests of the state above the rights of its constituents, who stressed the primacy of executive authority, and who denied weak nations the right to govern themselves. For Seeley, Cromwell became one of the three great heroes of England's early expansion because he acted independently of Parliament, establishing a military dictatorship, while for Froude, Cromwell effectively governed Ireland because he chose to coerce the Irish rather than placate them. This image of Cromwell as the great statesman spoke directly to the anxieties of late Victorian England, its confident nationalism appealing especially to those imperialists and unionists who had rejected Gladstone's leadership, finding it excessively sentimental and inappropriate for an age of international politics based on relationships of power.

## II

Throughout the Victorian period, Cromwell's most devoted admirers were often found among the traditional Nonconforming denominations. William Godwin's *History of the Commonwealth*, John Forster's *Statesmen of the Commonwealth* and Robert Vaughan's many volumes on the Stuarts all attest to the persistent fascination which the Puritan past held for Nonconformity during the first half of the nineteenth century. Thomas Carlyle's edition of Cromwell's letters and speeches focused attention specifically on Cromwell, enabling Nonconformists to present the great Puritan as a Christian hero, a precursor of the contemporary Dissenter, one who had contributed significantly to the making of modern England. This tendency to look to the Cromwellian past for inspiration and guidance continued well into the 1890s. The major tercentenary celebrations, held at London, Cambridge and Huntingdon, were almost exclusively Nonconformist affairs. During the heavily attended London ceremony, David Lloyd George, Baptist member of Parliament for the Carnarvon Boroughs and future prime minister, declared that he "believed in Oliver Cromwell because he was a great fighting Dissenter," thereby emphasizing the connection between Cromwell and contemporary Nonconformity. Another Dissenting member of Parliament, the Methodist R. W. Perks, was even more explicit: "the modern equivalent of the 17th century

Puritan," he told his audience, "was the possessor of the Non-conformist conscience, who now raised his voice against the desecration of the Lord's Day, against the gambling saloon, the drink bar, the haunt of vice, and the overwhelming power of brute force in home and foreign affairs."[15]

Late Victorian Nonconformists, like their predecessors, routinely paid tribute to Cromwell's efforts to establish liberty in England. According to the Congregationalist divine E. Paxton Hood, Cromwell was the devout Puritan who led England in its battle against tyranny and persecution: "The sword of Cromwell," Hood declared in a popular biography, "alone gave victory to the people over the king . . . Had not those victories been obtained, this land would have been at the feet of a cold and cruel tyrant." R. F. Horton, a fellow Congregationalist, defined Cromwell's "task" in similarly liberal terms: "The power of an ancient throne had to be limited, and in order to be limited, it had first to be broken; the principle of religious liberty had to be brought from the region of abstract speculation, in which it had been born, into the field of practical politics."[16] But if these divines continued the Dissenting practice of celebrating the Puritan contribution to liberty, they now put it to a different use. The earlier generation of Nonconformists had used the Stuart past rhetorically to force open an exclusively Anglican political system and to transform a confessional into a nonsectarian state. By the end of the century, however, Dissenters were no longer so preoccupied with constitutional change, as the Burial Act of 1880 had redressed the last of their traditional grievances, and as their interest in English disestablishment began to diminish.[17] Instead of using the Puritan past to affirm their right to participate in national politics, late Victorian Nonconformists tended to exhibit Cromwell as a model of Christian morality in public life.

In contrast to earlier Dissenting historians, who had invoked the seventeenth-century past in order to convince a wide audience of the legitimacy of their claims, the late Victorians addressed their

---

[15] *The Times*, 26 April 1899, 12. *The Times*, 28 April 1899, 8.

[16] E. Paxton Hood, *Oliver Cromwell: His Life, Times, Battlefields, and Contemporaries* (New York: Funk and Wagnalls, 1883), 14–15, 225. R. F. Horton, *Oliver Cromwell: A Study in Personal Religion* (New York: Thomas Whittaker, 1897), 5.

[17] D. W. Bebbington, *The Nonconformist Conscience: Chapel and Politics, 1870–1914* (London: George Allen and Unwin, 1982), 18–36.

remarks mostly to fellow Nonconformists. As their leaders became more deeply involved in politics after the Reform Act of 1867, many Nonconformists began to question whether political activity, given its secular character, was appropriate for Christians who should be devoting their time to spiritual matters.[18] In answer to their critics, political Nonconformists appealed to Cromwell, the greatest activist in the history of Dissent, hoping to establish the legitimacy of their endeavors. Horton, for instance, dedicated his *Cromwell* to the "Young Free Churchmen of England," encouraging them to learn from his subject's example: "You need Cromwell. He is the man of the hour for you. Your work for England and the world, if it is to be done, must be done precisely as he did his." Sir Richard Tangye, Quaker industrialist and collector of Cromwelliana, directed his *Two Protectors* at the same "rising generation of Nonconformists," and with a similar intention of rousing them to action because "the spirit of Laud was still rampant in certain quarters."[19] A call to arms also featured in the speeches delivered at the Cromwell tercentenary. Adapting Wordsworth's sonnet to Milton, Horton declared, "Cromwell, thou shouldst be living at this hour; England hath need of thee," while the Methodist Silas Hocking asserted that "Cromwell was ahead of his time in insisting that religion had to do with politics . . . as much as with church-going." David Lloyd George, agreeing with Hocking, proclaimed Cromwell "the first statesman to recognize that as soon as the Government became a democracy the Churches became directly responsible for any misgovernment."[20]

---

[18] Ibid., 25–30. Stephen Koss, *Nonconformity in Modern British Politics* (Hamden, Connecticut: Archon Books, 1975), 21–23.
[19] Horton, *Cromwell*, v–vi. Sir Richard Tangye, *The Two Protectors: Oliver and Richard Cromwell* (S. W. Partridge and Co., 1899), 214–215.
[20] *The Times*, 26 April 1899, 12. Wordsworth's poem, entitled "London, 1802," began:

> MILTON! thou should'st be living at this hour:
> England hath need of thee: she is a fen
> Of stagnant waters: altar, sword, and pen,
> Fireside, the heroic wealth of hall and bower,
> Have forfeited their ancient English dower
> Of inward happiness. We are selfish men;
> Oh! raise us up, return to us again;
> And give us manners, virtue, freedom, power.

The poem, which calls on its muse – Milton in the original, Cromwell in Horton's rendering – to restore morality and strength to a spiritually barren England, captures nicely the mood in which late Victorian Nonconformists approached the seventeenth century.

In order to make the case that Cromwell's life justified political activity, Nonconformists had to demonstrate that his public career was an expression of his Christian piety. Taking their insights from Carlyle, they all stressed that Cromwell was a sincere Puritan drawn into political activity, often against his will, by the strength of his religious belief. Cromwell assumed a public role, his Nonconformist biographers maintained, not out of worldly ambition, nor out of a desire for temporal gain, but because of his duty to God. As Horton summed up Cromwell's life, quoting from his last Protectorate speech: Cromwell was "the most human of men, tender, passionate in his tenderness, who would have preferred to live 'under his own woodside,' cherishing wife and children, loved by rustic neighbours; but [he was] driven to 'tread the paths of glory, and to sound the depths and shoals of honour' by no choice of ambition but by the stern voice of God."[21] Cromwell's political activity, then, was a direct response to a divine call. For Cromwell to have turned his back on the public, remaining a private individual concerned only with saving his soul, would have been unthinkable. By implication, Horton's study of Cromwell's religion made it clear to his Nonconformist readers that they too risked disobeying the "stern voice of God" if they avoided the public responsibilities of their faith.

Spokesmen for Nonconformity went even further, invoking the Cromwellian past in their attempt to define the meaning of Christian politics. During the final decades of the century, as they moved beyond their earlier preoccupation with constitutional change, Nonconformists began to demand that purity in public life generally associated with the "Nonconformist conscience."[22] Believing that statesmen should be virtuous, they denounced Parnell's adultery and Rosebery's racehorses; believing that government should improve the nation's moral tone, they fought for social reform, such as the elimination of gambling, drunkenness and prostitution, and for a Christian policy abroad. In both these areas, the Cromwellian past became rhetorically useful since Cromwell could be portrayed as a virtuous statesman, the standard against which contemporary politicians could be measured and found wanting. Nonconformist biographers, taking their lead from Carlyle once again, tended to present Cromwell's religion in moral

---

[21] Horton, *Cromwell*, 200–201.    [22] Bebbington, *Nonconformist Conscience*, 11–17.

rather than doctrinal terms. According to the radical Congregationalist J. Allanson Picton, for example, what distinguished Cromwell's Puritanism from other varieties of Christian belief "was not so much a set of theological opinions as a spiritual temper and a moral tone."[23] In contrast to their vilification of the adulterer Parnell, Nonconformists praised Cromwell as the virtuous family man, "cherishing wife and children, loved by rustic neighbours."[24] When Salisbury refused to intervene on behalf of the Armenian Christians massacred by the Turks in 1896, Nonconformists referred to Cromwell, who had championed the Protestants of the Vaudois against the ravages of the Duke of Savoy, as the author of a truly Christian foreign policy: "if [Cromwell] had been with us these last ten years," declared the Quaker Rendel Harris at the Cromwell tercentenary at Huntingdon, "he would have stood a magnificent chance of being made 'Archduke of Armenia,' for he would never have stood still to see Christianity wiped out of Asia Minor whilst statesmen washed their hands of the responsibility."[25]

A Christian and a Nonconformist, a politician whose private faith and public conduct were compatible because they answered a single divine command, a leader who was morally incorruptible and committed to Christian policies at home and abroad – this Cromwell was ideally suited to the rhetorical needs of late Victorian Nonconformists. To them it made little difference that Cromwell dealt summarily with his Parliaments, that his government was no more than a military dictatorship, that his commitment to civil and religious liberty was imperfect, that his Puritanism was narrow and unpopular, that his foreign policies threatened to bankrupt the nation. These and the many other problems surrounding Cromwell's career were simply passed over in silence. Nonconformists saw in Cromwell a compelling figure capable of providing England with inspiration and guidance. But unlike the imperialist Cromwell, the Nonconformist version was narrowly sectarian and not likely to appeal to a wide audience. A Puritan above all, this Cromwell would never inspire those Victorians who found his moralistic Christianity distasteful, who

---

[23] J. Allanson Picton, *Oliver Cromwell: The Man and His Mission* (New York: Cassell, Petter, Galpin and Co., [1882]), 12.

[24] Ibid., 34. Hood, *Cromwell*, 42–43. Horton, *Cromwell*, 12–13, 44–45.

[25] *The Times*, 28 April 1899, 8.

regarded its demands on human nature as unreasonable, and who denied its applicability to contemporary politics. Not surprisingly, outsiders accused the Nonconformists of having monopolized the Cromwell tercentenary, of having "turned it into a sectarian instead of a national or even municipal movement."[26]

### III

No historian did more to shape the late Victorian understanding of the Cromwellian past than Samuel Rawson Gardiner. Whether they agreed with him or not, most contemporary biographers of Cromwell measured their interpretations against the standard of Gardiner's work. The imperialist J. R. Seeley valued Gardiner's opinion so highly that he asked Gardiner to comment on the early drafts of his *Growth of British Policy*, and the Nonconformist R. F. Horton thought the best biography of Cromwell could be found scattered throughout Gardiner's various works. Before turning his attention to the Puritan Revolution, Gardiner had spent nearly thirty years preparing himself for the task, studying the origins of the Civil War and presenting his research in a ten-volume *History of England* that began with the death of Elizabeth and ended with the outbreak of war in 1642. Gardiner had always intended to carry this narrative through the Restoration, and during the last two decades of his life, he worked steadily at his task. The *Great Civil War* and the *Commonwealth and Protectorate* brought the story up to 1656, but this was as far as Gardiner would get. A stroke in 1901, followed by his death in 1902, put an end to the project. Nor did these volumes represent the full extent of Gardiner's achievement as a historian of the Puritans. He was invited in 1896 to deliver the Ford Lectures at Oxford, where he spoke on *Cromwell's Place in History*, and he published a popular biography of Cromwell in 1900.

The work that exercised the greatest influence on Gardiner's conception of the Cromwellian past was Thomas Carlyle's edition of Cromwell's *Letters and Speeches*. Reviewing Carlyle's *Historical Sketches* when they appeared posthumously in 1898, Gardiner paid tribute to the earlier work. The *Letters and Speeches*, he declared, "was more than a book. It was an historical event, changing our whole conception of English history in its most heroic period."

We may [he continued] be somewhat weary now of the ejaculations inter-mixed amongst the Protector's speeches, or of the outbursts about apes of the Dead Sea and the like, which are served up as sauce for the letters. For all that, what Carlyle had to say was not only far more true than anything said before he arose, but even now – with all that we have learnt since, there is scarcely anything that needs to be swept away, though there is much that needs qualification.[27]

As his review made clear, Gardiner valued highly Carlyle's attempt to reappraise Cromwell's achievement and in particular to dispel popular myths and misconceptions by allowing the Protector to speak for himself. Like Carlyle, Gardiner too saw Cromwell as an honest and sincere Puritan, concerned more with religion than politics, whose chief motivation was not personal ambition, but rather the desire to place England's institutions on a Godly basis.[28] For both historians, Cromwell was above all the best example of English Puritanism in the seventeenth century. But while Gardiner may have agreed with Carlyle on many points of interpretation, he rejected his predecessor's hero-worship, considering it a "stumbling-block in [the] pursuit of historical truth."[29] If Gardiner found much to praise in Puritanism, he also knew that there was much to lament, and he acknowledged readily what Carlyle had admitted only with reluctance: that Cromwell and the Puritans had failed to remake England in their own image, and that Cromwell's attempt to settle the nation's institutions in a lasting way had not attained success.

Gardiner is often regarded as one of England's first objective historians, a professional immersed in the sources who refused to allow contemporary political debate to color his interpretations. And yet a reading of his work on the Cromwellian past shows that this was hardly the case. Despite his insistence that Cromwell should be judged only in the context of the seventeenth century, Gardiner himself was never wholly free from the vice of present-mindedness. As we might expect, Gardiner's historical judgments were consistent with the political positions he had developed over

---

27 [Samuel Rawson Gardiner], "A New Book by Carlyle," *The Daily News*, 28 November 1898, 7.

28 Samuel Rawson Gardiner, *History of the Great Civil War, 1642–1649*, new edition (London: Longmans, Green and Co., 1893–1894), 1: viii, x.

29 Samuel Rawson Gardiner, Review of F. Harrison's *Oliver Cromwell*, *Academy*, 34 (28 July 1888): 48.

the preceding thirty years. He was certainly aware of how spokesmen for Nonconformity and the empire were using Cromwell, and
being an advocate of neither cause, he dismissed the lessons they
drew from the past. In the first place, Gardiner's Liberalism led
him to reject the Cromwell eulogized by the Nonconformists. A
liberal nationalist like Gardiner, one who was seeking broad areas
of consensus on which to build national unity, could hardly approve
of Cromwell's attempt to impose a narrow Puritanism. No matter
how tolerant Cromwell himself might have been, his desire to
create a Godly Commonwealth could only produce the kind of
sectarian divisions that Gardiner was trying to overcome. Nor
should we expect an advocate of representative government like
Gardiner to disregard the way Cromwell defied the national will in
his determination to keep in power, by means of the army if need
be, an unpopular Puritan oligarchy. Gardiner's Liberalism also led
him to reject the Cromwell celebrated by the imperialists and
unionists. As an opponent of Disraeli's forward policy in the 1870s
and of Salisbury's in the 1890s, and as a supporter of Irish Home
Rule, Gardiner refused to see Cromwell's policies toward Ireland
and the continent as a success story inviting emulation.

Like the Nonconformists, Gardiner believed that Cromwell was
a Puritan above all. Carlyle, if nothing else, had convinced his
Victorian readers that Cromwell's piety had been sincere and that
his words should be taken at face value since an honest Puritan
would hesitate to prevaricate before his God. These insights into
Cromwell's religion allowed Gardiner to move beyond Hume's
assertion that Puritanism was simply a form of hypocrisy, a mask
behind which lurked base ambition. Taking Cromwell at his word,
Gardiner concluded that he had been an "honest man" whose chief
aim was "to serve God and the people of God." Addressing the
nature of Cromwell's Puritanism, Gardiner pointed out that it was
"moral" rather than "intellectual," a "spiritual emotion" rather
than a systematic creed. Cromwell was not a doctrinaire; he was
indifferent to the fine points of theology, and as a result he avoided
the bigotry that characterized so many of the Puritans. Indeed,
Cromwell would become one of the principal advocates of religious
toleration and it was the non-dogmatic quality of his faith which
would enable him to surmount the obstacles that theological
differences often placed between Protestants of opposing denominations. "It was sufficient for him," Gardiner wrote, "if he and his

associates found inspiration in a sense of personal dependence on God, issuing forth in good and beneficent deeds."[30] All these reflections bore the clear imprint of Carlyle's understanding: for Carlyle had spoken of Cromwell's Puritanism in simple moral terms as an awareness of heaven and hell, a belief in a soul to be saved, and an imperative to do good rather than evil.

By focusing on his Puritanism, Gardiner was able to solve some of the problems posed by Cromwell's apparent political inconsistencies. Religion, he insisted, not politics, provided the key to Cromwell's career. A devout man with little aptitude for speculative politics, Gardiner's Cromwell never took much of an interest in constitutional issues. He was not especially enamored of representative institutions and he certainly had never been a true republican. He opposed the monarchy of Charles I, not because he objected to monarchy in principle, but because Charles had thrown his support behind a persecuting Church.[31] Those interpretations that condemned Cromwell as a Parliamentarian who later betrayed the cause in order to promote his own ambition simply missed the point. Cromwell was a Puritan concerned most of all with achieving toleration for those Protestant sects that shared his religious convictions. He supported the Parliament in the Civil War not because he adhered to any particular theory of political rights, but rather because he saw that toleration could never be achieved so long as Laud and Charles dominated the Church. As Gardiner explained: "Cromwell was not the man to indulge in constitutional speculations, but he saw distinctly that if religion – such as he conceived it – was to be protected, it must be by armed force."[32]

But if Gardiner and the Nonconformists concurred on the importance of Cromwell's Puritanism, they were at odds over its impact on his statesmanship. Unlike the Nonconformists, Gardiner readily conceded that as a statesman Cromwell had failed. While he successfully destroyed one set of institutions, he was unable to create an alternative that would endure beyond the Restoration. Seeking an explanation for this failure, Gardiner parted company

---

[30] Samuel Rawson Gardiner, *Oliver Cromwell*, new impression (London: Longmans, Green and Co., 1925), 2, 7, 64–67, *Great Civil War*, 1: 310.

[31] Gardiner, *Cromwell*, 8, 10, 16–17, 89, *Cromwell's Place in History*, 23, 27, 46.

[32] Gardiner, *Cromwell*, 25–26.

with the Nonconformists and pointed to Cromwell's faith. Though Puritanism may have been the source of Cromwell's strength and inspiration, it was also his greatest liability. For Gardiner recognized that Puritanism could never provide an adequate basis on which to reconstruct the nation. To the extent that Cromwell remained a Puritan, he was destined to fail as a statesman since the Puritanism of the Independents was too narrowly conceived to secure the support of the English people. Its ideas about liberty, democracy and toleration, while admirable from the Victorian point of view, were too far ahead of their time to win popular approval. It was culturally narrow, and it was often ignorant and fanatical. But most of all, its moral earnestness demanded too much from its adherents and failed to take into account the limitations of human nature. In his *History of England*, Gardiner had warned that one of the dangers with Puritanism was its willingness to coerce the world into morality. Cromwell, animated by an urge to transform England into a Godly Commonwealth, was a case in point. His attempt to enforce a Puritan morality infuriated his contemporaries and converted the royalist opposition into a national movement.[33] Puritanism, as royalists like Hyde realized, was simply "incapable of giving permanent guidance to the nation."[34]

Though Gardiner's Cromwell was capable at times of rising above this vulgar Puritanism, he was never wholly free of it. In an article on "Cromwell's Constitutional Aims," written for the *Contemporary Review* in 1900, Gardiner argued that Cromwell's Puritanism provided the one constant factor that rendered intelligible the bewildering variety of his constitutional experiments. When he turned against the monarchy and the Church, Gardiner now suggested, Cromwell had something more constructive in mind than eliminating absolutism and persecution. He hoped above all to convert the nation to Puritanism by maintaining in power a "Puritan oligarchy" that would win the support of the people by its beneficent reforms. Once it was acknowledged that the creation of a Godly Commonwealth was Cromwell's principal objective, then

---

[33] Gardiner, *Great Civil War*, 2: 329–330, 3: 119–120, 4: 327, *Cromwell*, 161, 164, 262–263, 316–318. Samuel Rawson Gardiner, *History of the Commonwealth and Protectorate, 1649–1656*, new edition (London: Longmans, Green and Co., 1903), 4: 40.
[34] Gardiner, *Great Civil War*, 3: 123.

all his constitutional experiments made sense.[35] Cromwell dismissed the Long Parliament not merely because it had ceased to represent the will of the nation, but because its members had come to place their interests before the cause of God. He agreed to replace the Long Parliament with a new governing body, chosen by the army from among the Godly, in order to put his Puritan oligarchy into power. When the Nominated Parliament failed to rule as he wished, Cromwell gave his consent to the Instrument of Government. This constitution, which provided the basis for the Protectorate, guaranteed that Cromwell's Puritan oligarchy, now embodied in the Protector and his council, would exercise almost unlimited executive authority. Attempting to replicate this oligarchic arrangement on the local level, Cromwell established a system of Major Generals, Puritan officers who imposed Godly rule on the counties. When the Humble Petition and Advice returned power to Parliament, Cromwell urged the creation of an upper house, hoping that his oligarchy might endure within its ranks.[36]

The lasting consequence of this effort to create a Godly Commonwealth was to increase Cromwell's dependence on the army. The Puritan Revolution, extending from the Long Parliament through the Protectorate, transferred power to a smaller and smaller group of Puritans as supporters of a modified Anglicanism gave way to Presbyterians, Independents and finally, during the Nominated Parliament, Fifth Monarchists. As the government became increasingly elitist and unpopular, it was driven to rely on the army, the one steadfastly Puritan force in England, in order to ensure its survival.[37] For Gardiner, England's transformation into a military state during the Commonwealth and Protectorate was the one development that refuted absolutely all those who pronounced Cromwell's Puritan statesmanship a success. Although the army might destroy tyranny, it could not replace tyranny with a government founded on liberty. Its notorious disregard for Parliamentary procedures, its willingness to interfere in politics at the slightest provocation, and the unpopular levels of taxation necessary for its upkeep all guaranteed that Cromwell's government would never

[35] Samuel Rawson Gardiner, "Cromwell's Constitutional Aims," *Contemporary Review*, 77 (January, 1900): 134.
[36] Ibid., 133–142. Gardiner, *Commonwealth and Protectorate*, 2: 228–231, 251–265.
[37] Gardiner, *Great Civil War*, 3: 352, 289–290, 304–305, *Commonwealth and Protectorate*, 2: 266–267, 329, 339–341.

relinquish power to the freely elected representatives of the nation.[38] On numerous occasions, Gardiner pointed out in Cromwell's defense that he had never desired military rule and that he had always planned to restore civilian government.[39] But the unpopularity of Puritanism made this impossible. Despite Cromwell's best intentions, the Protectorate began as and remained a military despotism.

Of all Cromwell's policies, it was his exploits overseas that appealed to the imagination of an imperialistic age and won the greatest respect from Gardiner's contemporaries. And yet, for Gardiner, the admiration of the imperialists was as misplaced as that of the Nonconformists. Like Seeley, whose *Expansion of England* he drew on, Gardiner believed that Cromwell's foreign policy was balanced uneasily between the old and the new, between a Puritan idealism better suited to the age of religious war that had ended with the Treaty of Westphalia, and a materialism appropriate for the age of commercial rivalry that was just beginning.[40] At its best, Cromwell's religious enthusiasm could lend his policies a nobility that was truly admirable – as when he championed the Protestants of the Vaudois against their oppressor, the Duke of Savoy – but when religious and commercial interests coincided, they laid Cromwell open to the charge of hypocrisy. As an example of this, Gardiner pointed to the proposal to wrest America from Spain. To promote such a policy, as Cromwell did, on the grounds that it would advance the Protestant cause seemed more than a little disingenuous once it became clear that English commerce, and not religion, stood to gain.[41] Still more important, Cromwell's Puritanism was an obstacle to the formulation of a meaningful policy. Its anachronistic assumptions, more appropriate to the age of Elizabeth, led him to misread diplomatic realities and in particular to place undue emphasis on the struggle between Protestantism and Catholicism, which was no longer a decisive factor in European diplomacy.[42] But what disturbed Gardiner most

38 Gardiner, *Commonwealth and Protectorate*, 1: 1–2, 160, 2: 21, 338–339, *Cromwell*, 164, 316.
39 Gardiner, *Great Civil War*, 3: 226, 246, 328–329, *Commonwealth and Protectorate*, 2: 284, 3: 191, 209, 247, 4: 77, *Cromwell*, 88–89, 108, 196–197, 213–215, 227, 247–248, *Cromwell's Place in History*, 104–105.
40 Gardiner, *Commonwealth and Protectorate*, 2: 150–152, 3: 164–166, 4: 120–121, *Cromwell*, 265–266.
41 Gardiner, *Cromwell*, 269–272, 296–297, *Commonwealth and Protectorate*, 2: 150–151, 3: 48–51.
42 Gardiner, *Commonwealth and Protectorate*, 2: 151–152, 181, 3: 161, 4: 122, *Cromwell*, 265, 297–298.

about Cromwell's foreign policy was its domestic consequences. By committing England to such expensive ventures overseas, Cromwell was in fact undermining his attempt to restore civilian government. To wage war against Catholic Europe was an immense undertaking, and the high levels of taxation needed to finance such a policy would only add to the Protectorate's unpopularity, making it all the less likely that Cromwell would ever transfer authority to a freely elected Parliament.[43]

Turning to Cromwell's Irish policies, Gardiner found even less to applaud. In answer to Froude, whose work on the Irish past he thought riddled with "misrepresentations,"[44] Gardiner argued that the Cromwellian settlement could never have brought about a successful resolution of the Anglo-Irish problem. After the campaigns of Cromwell and Ireton had restored England's supremacy in Ireland, the Long Parliament passed the Act of Settlement, which provided the basis for Cromwell's future policies. Had the Act been implemented thoroughly, Gardiner pointed out, it would have entailed the execution of approximately one hundred thousand Irish and the forced relocation of countless others. To say the least, Gardiner found the act abhorrent: "No such deed of cruelty," he declared, "was ever contemplated in cold blood by any State with pretence to civilisation."[45] Even if the Act had been enforced beyond the Restoration, Gardiner denied that it would have produced the desired result. Indeed, it too would have failed for the very reason that all of England's policies in Ireland had failed – by relying on coercion and by displaying nothing but contempt for the Irish and their traditions, it fed an Irish nationalism that would someday become unconquerable.[46] Nor was the fault Cromwell's alone. The Long Parliament had passed the Act of Settlement in 1652, "before Cromwell was in a position to make his weight felt," and though he implemented the Act with a zeal that was truly his own, the actual settlement had "little in it that was new," for it was largely a continuation of the policies of Elizabeth

[43] Gardiner, *Cromwell*, 235–237, 264, 273, 295–296, 306–307. Samuel Rawson Gardiner, Review of J. R. Seeley's *Growth of British Policy*, *English Historical Review*, 11 (1896): 160.
[44] Samuel Rawson Gardiner, "Modern History," *Contemporary Review*, 33 (October, 1878): 629.
[45] Gardiner, *Commonwealth and Protectorate*, 4: 82.
[46] Ibid., 2: 129–130, 4: 80, 90. Gardiner, *Cromwell's Place in History*, 58–59.

and Wentworth. It was not Cromwell who failed in Ireland, but rather three generations of English statesmen.[47]

When Gardiner showed how Cromwell had failed to reconcile Puritanism with free institutions, becoming increasingly dependent on the army, he was demonstrating how unsuitable the Puritan past was as a model for contemporary politics. When he showed how the cost of Cromwell's foreign policy hindered the return to a freely elected civilian administration, he was pointing out the dangers to democracy inherent in all empires. When he condemned the Cromwellian settlement in Ireland because of its disregard for Irish traditions, he was making it clear that a resolution of the Irish problem could only be based on a respect for Irish national aspirations. But Gardiner's intention was not to present a purely negative portrait of the Protector, an example of the misguided statesmanship a Liberal should avoid. It was Gardiner, after all, who had termed Cromwell the "typical Englishman of the modern world," implying the presence of strengths as well as weaknesses. At his best, Cromwell could also provide a model of what Liberal statesmanship should entail. The capacity to comprehend what was best for the nation as a whole, to see beyond the personal or dynastic, the local or sectarian, distinguished Cromwell from Charles and represented a crucial element in any successful state-craft, past or present.

Victorian Liberals had always placed religious toleration at the top of their agenda. Confronted with a society fragmented by sectarian strife, they stressed that a Christianity shorn of its inessentials could provide the groundwork for national unity by bringing together opposing denominations. That Gardiner shared this ideal is clear enough. One of the purposes behind his earlier *History of England* had been to promote national unity by demon-strating how the liberal tendencies within England's Anglican and Nonconforming traditions had worked together to create the tolerant atmosphere of modern-day England. Toleration played an equally important role in his interpretation of the Commonwealth and Protectorate. When he described Cromwell as a Puritan whose faith was moral rather than dogmatic, Gardiner was advancing an interpretation consistent with the aims of Victorian Liberalism.

[47] Gardiner, *Commonwealth and Protectorate*, 2: 130, 4: 79–80, 90–91, *Cromwell's Place in History*, 57–58.

Indeed, with his portrait of Cromwell, Gardiner placed before the Victorians a precursor of the modern Liberal, one whose faith had been reduced to the bare essentials of a belief in God and good conduct, and one who consequently found denominational distinctions of little importance. By Victorian standards, Cromwell's idea of toleration may have been inadequate since it embraced only Protestants, but it was as perfect as the circumstances of the seventeenth century would allow. Nondogmatic in matters of religion and as tolerant as was historically conceivable, Gardiner's Cromwell was, in the best sense of the term, a visionary because he had understood long ago what the nineteenth century had only just realized: that only toleration would end sectarian discord.

Cromwell also promoted the national interest by renouncing the dynastic considerations that had led Charles to look abroad for protection. A desire to defend England against foreign influence, Gardiner suggested, informed all Cromwell's shifts in policy from the outbreak of the Civil War through his campaigns in Ireland and Scotland. Whereas Parliament and the Presbyterians looked to Scotland for help and the king turned indiscriminately to Scotland, Ireland and the continent, Cromwell and the Independents were determined to rely only on themselves. From the outset, Cromwell had been uncomfortable with Parliament's decision to call on the Scots, considering it at best an unpleasant expedient for beating the king. Then, as he dealt with the army, Parliament and the king after the first Civil War, his concern for the national interest remained dominant. He negotiated first with Parliament and then with the king, hoping in each instance to arrange a settlement that would bring peace to England. Only when these efforts failed did he join the radicals in the army and agree to the execution of the king. Where Cromwell's detractors saw in these maneuvers hypocrisy and opportunism, Gardiner discerned a consistent national purpose. In each instance Cromwell gave up on negotiations once he discovered that first Parliament and then the king had conspired with the Scots for a second invasion. It was not republican sentiment that prompted Cromwell to demand the king's trial, but rather his anger that Charles had been ready to "vassalise" the nation to Scotland in order to save his crown.[48] Much certainly could be inveighed against the Cromwellian revolution, but this much

---

[48] Gardiner, *Great Civil War*, 2: 23, 120, 177, 3: 265, 281–282, 287–290, 319–321, 4: 250–253, 328.

Gardiner felt had to be said in its defense; with Cromwell and the Independents, "England had in truth entered into possession of herself."[49]

In his discussion of these events Gardiner stressed not only Cromwell's nationalism, but also his essential conservatism. For Cromwell, as Gardiner represented him, shared with most Englishmen a traditionalism that was reflected in his respect for the nation's age-old institutions. As he struggled to settle the nation's affairs after the first Civil War, Cromwell endeavored to retain as much of the old constitution as possible so as to avoid the radical implications of a military government. When the Levellers put forward their *Agreement of the People*, a revolutionary proposal for an English republic based on democratic principles, Cromwell found it "distasteful" on account of its total disregard for past practice. "Without any constitutional learning," Gardiner wrote, and "still more without any philosophical training, [Cromwell] instinctively turned against a proposal to cast the institutions of the country into the melting pot, after the fashion practised by the makers of modern France a century and a half later." By linking the Levellers with the French Revolutionaries of 1789, Gardiner implied that Cromwell and traditionalists like Burke stood together in condemning radical innovation based on abstract principles. The Levellers may have been a revolutionary group operating outside national traditions, but Cromwell, the epitome of Puritanism, was in fact an advocate of that "policy of bit-by-bit reform" which was the "characteristic feature in English political history."[50]

Even Cromwell's contempt for representative government could be reconciled with a liberal nationalism. In Cromwell's defense, Gardiner suggested that behind his apparent despotism a valid political principle was at work – a principle that connected Cromwell's statesmanship to the earlier practices of Bacon and Strafford, and to the later views of Victorian thinkers like Frederic Harrison. "If the morality of Oliver's political actions are ever to be judged fairly," Gardiner explained, "it must never be forgotten that the right of an honest Government to prevent the people from injuring themselves by out-voting the saner members of

[49] Ibid., 3: 191.
[50] Gardiner, *Cromwell's Place in History*, 24, 37–41, *Cromwell*, 112–123, *Great Civil War*, 3: 328, 380–391.

the community was . . . the predominant note of his career."[51]
Cromwell, as Gardiner often noted, had always been indifferent
to representative government, and the intransigence of his
Protectorate Parliaments transformed this indifference into
distrust. Determined at all costs to preserve the gains of the Civil
War, and aware that the unpopularity of Puritanism ensured that a
freely elected Parliament would reverse everything he had
achieved, Cromwell put his trust in government by an elite.[52]
Interpreted in this way, Cromwell became one in a series of statesmen who rejected democracy on the grounds that the multitude,
or its freely elected representatives, could not be trusted to do
what was best for the nation. Bacon and Strafford, discouraged by
the myopia of representative assemblies, had both looked to a
strong executive as the only way to carry through beneficent and
farsighted reforms. Similarly, Victorian critics like Frederic
Harrison shared with Strafford and Cromwell a suspicion that
democracy might prove incapable of governing in the nation's
interest.[53]

Taken as a whole, Gardiner's interpretation demonstrates how
thoroughly Cromwell's reputation had changed over the Victorian
years, for Gardiner's Cromwell was no longer the radical Dissenter
who, a century earlier, had inspired such fear. He was not an out-
sider to English institutions intent on their destruction, nor was he
the hypocritical fanatic who used the language of Puritanism to
conceal a carefully laid plan of self-aggrandizement. Rather, he was
an English patriot sympathetic to the nation's traditions, a devout
man whose sense of what was important in religion had allowed him
to discern the outlines of the future solution to England's sectarian
dilemma. The tragedy of his career was that, despite his best
intentions, he was never able to free himself from dependence on
the army. And yet, despite his shortcomings, Cromwell was a
statesman of considerable ability, one who tried to do what was best
for the nation as a whole. Where Cromwell failed – as he did in
Ireland – he failed in ways in which the English had always failed.
Cromwell was thus representative of the English nation: strong

[51] Gardiner, *Cromwell*, 309–310.
[52] Gardiner, *Commonwealth and Protectorate*, 2: 283–284, 339–340, 3: 169–170, 253–254, 4: 46–47, 77–78.
[53] Ibid., 3: 253–254. Samuel Rawson Gardiner, Note on Wentworth's unpublished speech, *Academy*, 7 (12 June 1874): 611.

where it was strong, weak where it was weak, the typical
Englishman of the modern world. By presenting Cromwell in
these terms, Gardiner reversed much of the hostile rhetoric that
had tarnished Cromwell's reputation. Conservatives had long
condemned the line of Dissenters which began with Cromwell and
the Puritans on the grounds that they had opposed England's
fundamental institutions. The Puritan Revolution of 1649, Burke
had argued, like the French Revolution of 1789, stood condemned
because of its total break with the past. With his interpretation of
the Commonwealth and Protectorate, Gardiner effectively turned
this argument around, stressing the essential continuity of
Cromwell's achievement with the course of English history, thereby
making the case for including the Puritan episode within the
acceptable past.

But if the Puritan Revolution was an integral part of England's
past, Gardiner recognized that it was neither the whole of that past
nor its most important part. In his earlier work, Gardiner had
conceived of English history as the product of two competing
currents, one Anglican and the other Puritan, that had collided in
the seventeenth century. Of these two, he knew that Puritanism
was the weaker. Like Carlyle, he realized that the Puritans had
failed to remake England in their own image. After the Restoration,
the Anglican current, representing the constructive side of
the Laudian movement, would come to dominate, exerting the
formative influence on England's historical development.[54]
Gardiner readily conceded that Puritanism was not the progressive
movement of the age, and at times he referred to it as a "back-
water," a figure of speech remarkably similar to Matthew Arnold's
characterization in *Culture and Anarchy*: "Puritanism," Arnold wrote,
"was no longer [by the seventeenth century] the central current of
the world's progress, it was a side stream crossing the central
current and checking it."[55] Like Gardiner, Arnold regarded English
history as the product of competing Anglican and Puritan
traditions. In terming Puritanism a "side stream," he clearly

[54] Gardiner, *Cromwell's Place in History*, 3, 6–8.
[55] *The Complete Prose Works of Matthew Arnold*, ed. R. H. Super (Ann Arbor: University of
Michigan Press, 1965), 5: 175. Compare Arnold's description of Puritanism with
Gardiner's: "the Puritanism of the seventeenth century may fairly be regarded as a back-
water, taking its course in a contrary direction to the general current of national
development." *Cromwell's Place in History*, 108–109.

intended to discredit the Puritan achievement. That Gardiner made a similar point suggests that he was in fact closer to liberal Anglicans like Arnold than to those Dissenters who, from mid-century onward, were describing Puritanism as the constructive force responsible for all that was best in English history. Gardiner's understanding of the Puritan past, whatever else we might think of it, was never narrowly sectarian.

Gardiner believed that much like the statesman, whose job it was to transcend sectional divisions and govern in the interest of the nation, the historian should forge an interpretation of the past that was national in scope. For one whose formative years as a professional were the 1860s and 1870s, when sectarian controversies divided the nation, the reconciliation of Anglicanism and Dissent was regarded as a precondition for the successful operation of democracy. To remove the historical roots of those controversies by writing a history of the Civil War that was broad enough to comprehend England's Anglican and Puritan legacies became the principal impetus behind Gardiner's work as well as an essential characteristic of his Liberalism. In his work on Cromwell, then, Gardiner set out to assess the Puritan achievement and to assign it a place in the making of modern England. It may have been less than its Dissenting champions claimed, it may in the long run have been less influential than the Anglican achievement, but all the same Puritanism did accomplish something constructive for England. As an especially intense form of Protestantism, it had, in the first place, made an enduring mark on the development of the English character. Puritanism, Gardiner concluded, had impressed on English men and women "high spiritual and moral aims," a "contempt . . . for outward formalities," and it had given them the strength to obey the "dictates of their consciences" even when they contradicted the commands of the established authorities in Church and state. These national traits were the great legacy of the English Reformation. They had survived into Gardiner's own Victorian age, and he "fervently" hoped they would endure forever.[56]

Gardiner also concluded that Cromwell and the Puritans had exerted a largely "negative" force on England's constitutional development because it was their work of destruction, not creation,

---

[56] Gardiner, *Cromwell's Place in History*, 4.

that continued beyond the Restoration. "It is impossible to resist the conclusion," Gardiner declared in his Ford Lectures, "that [Cromwell] effected nothing in the way of building up where he had pulled down, and that there was no single act of the Protectorate that was not swept away at the Restoration without hope of revival."[57] His victory in the Civil War and the execution of Charles I ensured that an English monarch would never again exercise absolute authority. Charles II may have returned to the throne at the Restoration, but as Gardiner pointed out, "he sat on it under conditions very different from those of his father, and when James II reverted to his father's conception the Stuart monarchy fell, past recall." It was Cromwell and the Puritans, more than anyone else, who set the precedent that prevented the triumph of absolutism in England. Nor, according to Gardiner, were Cromwell's efforts directed solely at the crown. When he and the army dismissed the Long Parliament because it insisted on remaining in power even though it had long since ceased to represent the nation, they made sure that England would never "tolerate a Parliament which . . . set the constituencies at defiance."[58] And when the Puritans overturned the Anglican Establishment of Archbishop Laud, they guaranteed that "a persecuting Church supporting itself on royal absolutism" would never appear again.[59] These were Cromwell's achievements and although Gardiner considered them "negative actions,"[60] he believed none the less that they occupied a crucial place in England's political development. Between the seventeenth and nineteenth centuries, the basis of the constitution would shift from the supremacy of the king to the supremacy of the nation. That this transition occurred at all was due in large measure to Cromwell.

IV

The reform acts of 1867 and 1884, which ushered the Victorians into the age of democracy, raised the question of whether Britain's political institutions were capable of meeting the needs of time. Would the newly enlarged electorate return representatives of sufficient caliber to pass the farsighted legislation required by

---

[57] Ibid., 103–104.    [58] Ibid., 104.
[59] Ibid., 45.    [60] Ibid., 102.

the new age? Would an executive dependent on a majority in the Commons be able to provide effective leadership? For many Liberals, dissatisfaction with Gladstone's early legislation fed a growing disillusionment with democracy as it had developed in Britain. The Liberal leader's apparent surrender to the mass electorate in his Midlothian campaigns and his desire to placate the Irish constituency during the Home Rule crisis seemed to confirm that efficient and farsighted government was incompatible with British democracy. On this issue of democracy, the Cromwellian past had lessons to teach. Carlyle, no friend to representative assemblies, had already used the authoritarian element in Cromwell to offer a critique of Parliamentary government, contrasting the efficiency of the army to the incapacity of Parliament, a do-nothing talking apparatus.

Another biographer who used the life of Cromwell to comment on democracy was the Positivist Frederic Harrison. Having embraced the Religion of Humanity as his Christian faith waned, Harrison employed the teachings of Auguste Comte as the basis for a critique of Victorian society that placed him on the radical wing of Liberal politics. Trade-union rights, franchise extension, secular education, the separation of Church and state, defense of the Parisian Communards and Irish Home Rule were among the causes that Harrison supported during his long career as a political journalist.[61] A longstanding admirer of Oliver Cromwell, Harrison put the Protector to a suitable political use. In many ways, his biography of Cromwell, published in 1888 as part of John Morley's Twelve English Statesmen series, was typical of other Liberal interpretations. Post-Carlylean in its appreciation of Cromwell as an honest Puritan, it avoided Carlyle's hero-worship. Harrison's Cromwell was a friend of the poor, an advocate of toleration – indeed, "the most tolerant statesman of his time" – and a consummate soldier. While his Irish policies were lamentable, they were, Harrison claimed, no worse than those of any other English statesman. In contrast to Gardiner, who would later emphasize the "negative" quality of Cromwell's work, Harrison stressed its positive achievement. Cromwell was a statesman who destroyed the feudal monarchy, laid the groundwork for England's future

---

61 For Harrison's politics, see Martha S. Vogeler, *Frederic Harrison: The Vocations of a Positivist* (Oxford: Clarendon Press, 1984).

constitutional development, and as Protector, provided England with the best domestic administration it had ever known.[62]

What was most distinctive, however, about Harrison's *Cromwell* was the way he used the Protectorate to criticize British Parliamentary democracy and to argue the case for strengthening the executive. After the Reform Act of 1867, Harrison developed a critique of Parliamentary government that he sustained through the remainder of the Victorian period. A nominal supporter of the Gladstonian Liberal party, Harrison was constantly dissatisfied with the inadequacies of its legislation, which he believed had never gone far enough to redress the problems of modern society. Harrison based his critique on the republican ideal, which he defined as government by a qualified minority, sustained in power by the consent of a politically educated community, governing not in the interest of a particular party or class, but in the interest of the whole community. The problem with Britain's Parliamentary democracy was that it failed to meet the standards of this ideal. In the first place, Parliament was not representative of the nation and Harrison doubted that it would ever become so. Despite three reform acts, it was still a body composed of the rich and the powerful, the lawyers and the journalists, which would never work in the interest of the entire nation. In the second place, the Victorian constitution had confused the legislature and the executive. Having developed over the centuries as an alternative to a despotic monarchy, Parliament had assumed all the powers of government, including those executive functions for which it was totally unsuited. A deliberative assembly intended for discussion and debate, Parliament simply lacked the unity of purpose necessary to rule decisively. As a result, Britain's Parliamentary democracy was incapable of providing efficient government. Harrison's solution to this problem was to strengthen the executive by placing government in the hands of a single statesman who would receive the sanction of the public and act decisively in the national interest.[63] In this way the republican ideal would be

---

[62] Frederic Harrison, *Oliver Cromwell* (London: Macmillan and Co., 1888), 21–32, 44–45, 49, 57–64, 71–73, 128–129, 132–133, 139–140, 167, 208–209. Frederic Harrison, "Recent Biographies of Cromwell," *George Washington and Other American Addresses* (London: Macmillan and Co., 1901), 144–148.

[63] Frederic Harrison, *Order and Progress* (London: Longmans, Green and Co., 1875), 3–122. Frederic Harrison, "Republicanism and Democracy," *Washington and Other Addresses*, 165–187.

fulfilled, efficient government restored, and the people would "find a hand to do their will, a voice to express their thoughts, and a brain to give effect to their purpose."[64]

In Cromwell, Harrison found an example of the strong executive he desired, one who embodied the will of the nation and was able to govern decisively in its interest. For Harrison, Cromwell was a "conservative revolutionist," a remarkable leader who brought England through a difficult period by reconciling the revolutionary forces in the army with the traditional inclinations of the rest of the country. Cromwell was the reformer whose new modeling of the army had unleashed the radical tendencies within English Puritanism, and yet he was also a traditionalist who realized that in settling the nation's affairs something of the old monarchical constitution must be retained. As a statesman, Cromwell thus stood above parties, using them in the interests of the nation as a whole, rather than being led by them. As a powerful executive, Cromwell also overcame the problems of representation and indecision that Harrison thought characterized Parliamentary government. During the debates over the Self-Denying Ordinance, all the qualities that would later distinguish Cromwell from other Parliamentarians became apparent: he was a "statesman," Harrison wrote, "impressing his policy on Parliament and the nation," a "man in authority," not an "orator addressing a senate." Following the execution of the king, it was Cromwell who instinctively represented the will of the nation, not the Rump Parliament, which only represented itself, and it was Cromwell who acted decisively, not the Rump, which became mired in endless debate.[65]

In the debates over the constitution that followed the expulsion of the Rump, Cromwell – as we might expect – stood for the very position that Harrison was proposing for his own age. As Harrison explained: "His whole soul rejected the idea of a mere Parliamentary executive," of a "government vested in a single elective chamber." Instead, Cromwell wanted a strong executive, represented by a single person, independent of Parliament. Indeed, for Harrison the "whole future history of England lay in this struggle, – the alternative of the American system with its distinct personal

---

[64] Harrison, *Order and Progress*, 41.
[65] Harrison, *Cromwell*, 80–87, 101–103, 106–107, 114–116, 170–176.

executive, or the modern British system of a single supreme Parliament having the executive as a part and creature of itself." On Cromwell's side, Harrison placed those English statesmen like Elizabeth, Wentworth and William III, as well as the American Federalists, Washington, Hamilton, Jay and Madison. On the side of Parliamentary government were republicans like Vane. To be sure, Harrison admitted that in the long run Cromwell had lost and that the Parliamentary solution had eventually triumphed in England. But, he went on, this victory did not mean that Cromwell was necessarily wrong. In all of these discussions, Harrison insisted that neither he nor Cromwell were advocating a simple dictatorship. To the contrary, Cromwell always intended that the executive, though vested in a single person, should be limited by an elected Parliament that would consent to taxation and pass the laws.[66]

Not all historians of the Stuart past, however, were ready to accept Harrison's diagnosis of his government's ills and his prescription for their cure. Gardiner acknowledged that Harrison's interpretation of the Protectorate contained a degree of truth. Cromwell, distrustful of an unlimited Parliament, did advocate a strong and independent executive much as Harrison claimed, which lent a certain legitimacy to his conduct as Protector. But Gardiner shared few of Harrison's misgivings about Parliamentary democracy and was not inclined to see in Cromwell a solution to a problem which he felt did not exist. Besides, there were too many other complications surrounding Cromwell's statesmanship to make him a suitable model for contemporary government. The unpopularity of his Puritanism and his reliance on the army, if nothing else, discredited the prescriptive usefulness of the Protectorate.

Building on Gardiner's interpretation of the Puritan past, John Morley argued even more strenuously that Cromwell was an inappropriate model for democratic statesmanship. Friends from the 1860s, Morley and Harrison shared much in common. The teachings of Auguste Comte had influenced them both early on, but whereas Harrison remained committee to the Religion of Humanity, Morley eventually outgrew it. Both were attracted to radical causes, but were unsure whether Parliamentary government was the best way to balance order and social progress in an

[66] Ibid., 174–176, 187, 193–197.

age of mass politics. As a response to democracy, both were attracted to strong men, seeing them as the leaders of political elites capable of providing progressive government in the national interest. But as Morley was drawn into a political career, representing Newcastle in 1883, their attitudes to Parliamentary government began to diverge. While Harrison remained a critic of Parliament, Morley became committed to the system, having fallen under the tutelage first of Joseph Chamberlain and then Gladstone. Throughout his political career, Morley would continue to look to strong leaders, practical statesmen who balanced order and progress by shaping public opinion.[67] Judged by this standard, Gladstone was a success and Cromwell a failure.

For Morley, Cromwell succeeded only in those areas where force was effective. He was a "consummate" soldier, one of the "foremost masters of the rough art of war," whose military victories destroyed the Stuart monarchy and united the three kingdoms of England, Ireland and Scotland. After the anarchy of the Civil War, he maintained order, becoming in his own quaint phrase the "constable of the parish," but he could not provide progressive leadership. Cromwell had no aptitude for speculative politics, and all of his attempts to create a lasting political settlement failed. The Protectorate was all expediency, Morley complained, containing nothing that was systematic. Indeed, for Morley, Cromwell's impact on England's political development was insignificant. When a permanent revolution came in 1688, it bore no resemblance to Cromwell's achievement: "it was aristocratic and not democratic, secular and not religious, parliamentary and not military, the substitution for the old monarchy of a territorial oligarchy supreme alike in Lords and Commons."[68] The lasting consequence of the Glorious Revolution was in fact a Parliamentary supremacy that Cromwell would have abhorred. Nor did Cromwell have an enduring influence on England's religious development. When the Church returned after the Restoration, it was as powerful and oppressive as ever. Nor was Cromwell, so often described as the epitome of English Puritanism, an effective conduit for the transmission of Puritan ideals to later generations. That Puritanism

67 For the development of Morley's political views, see D. A. Hamer, *John Morley: Liberal Intellectual in Politics* (Oxford: Clarendon Press, 1968).
68 John Morley, *Oliver Cromwell* (New York: The Century Co., 1900), 5.

made its mark on English culture was due to Milton and Bunyan, not the Protector. The triumph of toleration, which Morley acknowledged Cromwell had stood for, was due not to the Puritans, but rather to the growth of rationalism.[69]

As he recounted the struggles between the army and Parliament from 1647 to 1653, Morley's sympathies lay with the remnant of the Long Parliament, the notorious Rump which most Cromwellians denounced as an intolerant, impractical and unrepresentative minority. In pursuing such an individual interpretation, Morley indicated clearly his own preference for Parliamentary institutions. The Civil War had been fought in large part to safeguard constitutional liberty, and Morley believed that once the war was over, the best chance of preserving that liberty lay with Parliament. The problem with armed interference in politics was that one act of political violence tended to lead to another. Thus it was all but inevitable that the army's march on London in 1647, Pride's Purge in 1648 and Cromwell's dispersal of the Rump in 1653 had terminated in the military dictatorship of the Protectorate. Nothing demonstrated better the dangers which the army posed to constitutional liberty than its efforts to purge the Commons of its Presbyterian members. When the army marched on London in 1647, and conducted Pride's Purge in 1648, it violated constitutional liberty as grossly as Charles had when he tried to arrest the leaders of the Commons in 1642.[70] Those like Harrison, who defended the army on the grounds that it had become the real representative of the nation, were simply mistaken. It was Parliament, after all, not the army, which understood that the nation wanted a settlement with the king. "When we think that the end of these heroic twenty years was the Restoration," reflected Morley, "it is not easy to see why we should denounce the pedantry of the Parliament, whose ideas for good or ill, at last prevailed, and should reserve all our glorification for the army, who proved to have no ideas that would either work or that the country would accept."[71]

To establish Cromwell as a model statesman was to legitimate the use of force and the power of the state. Morley, who had long opposed imperialism because he believed it would erode the liberal foundations of British politics, suspected that the authoritarian state of the imperialists was among the "false directions" in which

[69] Ibid., 4–6, 414, 465–472.    [70] Ibid., 215–216, 330–333.    [71] Ibid., 216.

Cromwell's example would lead. "It can hardly be accident," he wrote "that has turned [Cromwell] into one of the idols of the school who hold, shyly as yet in England, but nakedly in Germany, that might is a token of right, and that the strength and power of the state is an end that tests and justifies all means." On more than one occasion, Morley suggested that the ideal of a strong executive which informed the political practice of both Wentworth and Cromwell would have led to the "qualified absolutism of modern Prussia."[72] Rather than eulogize the Wentworths, Cromwells and Bismarcks, Morley turned to the great Parliamentary leaders, the Pyms of the past and the Gladstones of the present.[73] After completing his biography of Cromwell, Morley began working on his monumental *Life of Gladstone*, who more than anyone defined his ideal statesman. Where Cromwell relied on the force of arms to achieve his ends, Gladstone shaped public opinion. At all the important crises in his career – moments when a Cromwell would have been tempted to call on his soldiers – Gladstone succeeded by convincing the cabinet, Parliament and nation that his policy was best.[74] We may admire Cromwell as a soldier who fought in an honorable cause and who did his best in circumstances that were often beyond his control. We may respect him because he wrestled honestly with the "ever-standing problems of the world."[75] But when we elevate his statesmanship, Morley warned, we do so at our own peril.

Of all Cromwell's late Victorian biographers, Morley was among the most critical, and yet, in the end, even he found the Cromwellian enterprise appealing: it had left behind, he reflected, "some noble thoughts, the memory of a brave struggle for human freedom, and a procession of strenuous master spirits, with Milton and Cromwell at their head."[76] Despite their differences, most Liberals would have agreed with Morley that Cromwell was one of the "master spirits" of English history, and if we allow for the nuances generated by the controversies within Liberalism, we can discern in their collective work a more or less coherent interpretation of the Cromwellian past. For most late Victorians, Cromwell

---

[72] Ibid., 5, 35, 359, 469–470.    [73] Ibid., 39–41.
[74] John Morley, *The Life of William Ewart Gladstone* (London: Macmillan and Co., 1903), 3: 536–537.
[75] Morley, *Cromwell*, 5–6.    [76] Ibid., 471–472.

was a great soldier, as Morley had asserted, but he was a great statesman as well. They generally accepted Carlyle's verdict that Cromwell was a sincere Puritan whose statesmanship was motivated by religion more than politics. At its best, Puritanism gave his politics an idealism rarely found among statesmen, but at its worst it opened Cromwell to the charge of sectarianism. He valued toleration more than political freedom, and attempted to maintain in power a Puritan oligarchy.

But for the late Victorians, Cromwell was also an English patriot. He successfully united England, Scotland and Ireland, though the severity of his Irish policy was lamentable. Abroad, Cromwell's policy was bold and adventuresome. It secured England against foreign intervention, advanced commerce and contributed to prosperity. Cromwell was a zealous proponent of colonial expansion and his policies laid the foundations of England's future empire. At home, Cromwell desired to rule constitutionally and tried to free himself from dependence on the army, though circumstances prevented him from succeeding. He believed in popular sovereignty, the principle for which the Civil War had been fought, but tempered that principle with the conviction that the people might not always do what was in their best interest. When his Parliaments thought differently than he did, particularly when they began to question the foundation of his government, Cromwell was not afraid to dispense with them and govern by himself. With or without Parliament, however, his leadership was always an honest attempt to serve the national interest. Though the unpopularity of his Puritanism ensured that many of his accomplishments would disappear after his death, he nevertheless achieved great things. "Thanks to his sword," wrote the Oxford historian Charles Firth, "absolute monarchy failed to take root in English soil. Thanks to his sword Great Britain emerged from the chaos of the civil wars one strong state instead of three separate and hostile communities."[77] Truly, Cromwell and the Puritans had entered the acceptable past.

---

[77] C. H. Firth, *Oliver Cromwell and the Rule of the Puritans in England*, third edition (London: G. P. Putnam's Sons, 1929), 486.

EPILOGUE

# Beyond the Victorians

In 1904, G. M. Trevelyan published his *England under the Stuarts*, the first important interpretation of the seventeenth century to appear since S. R. Gardiner had completed his life's work, and one containing an eulogy on the English national character appropriate for Macaulay's grandnephew. Of all England's achievements, Trevelyan wrote, "there is one, the most insular in origin, and yet the most universal in effect":

While Germany boasts her Reformation and France her Revolution, England can point to her dealings with the House of Stuart. Our Tudor Reformation, although it affected greater changes in the structure of English society and the evolution of English intellect, was but one part of a movement general throughout Europe. But the transference of sovereignty from Crown to Parliament was effected in direct antagonism to all continental tendencies. During the seventeenth century a despotic scheme of society and government was so firmly established in Europe, that but for the course of events in England it would have been the sole successor of the mediaeval system . . . But at this moment the English, unaware of their destiny and of their service, tenacious only of their rights, their religion, and their interests, evolved a system of government which differed as completely from the new continental model as it did from the chartered anarchy of the Middle Ages.[1]

To emphasize England's singularity, to point out its good fortune at having preserved its free institutions at a time when continental regimes were turning to absolutism, to describe England's destiny in messianic terms as the savior of European liberty – all were attitudes common to English historical writing. In spirit at least, Trevelyan's claims added little to Hallam's belief, articulated almost a century earlier, that England's constitution was "the most

[1] George Macaulay Trevelyan, *England under the Stuarts*, thirteenth edition (London: Methuen and Co., 1926), 1–2.

beautiful phaenomenon in the history of mankind."[2] But in one important respect, Trevelyan's emphasis was different: "the English under the Stuarts," he wrote, "had achieved their emancipation from monarchical tyranny by the act of the national will."[3] By interpreting the seventeenth century as an expression of national unity, Trevelyan proved himself the heir of the Victorians. That he could state the proposition as a matter of fact, as received wisdom, indicates how thoroughly the Victorian achievement had been internalized.

For Trevelyan, the seventeenth century was a crucial step in the building of a free and tolerant English nation. Divided in the 1640s, England came together in the 1680s in order to defend its religion and its freedom. The Civil War had raised the problem of liberty at a time when neither Roundhead nor Cavalier was prepared to solve it, though Cromwell and the Puritans went far toward understanding the value of toleration. When James II raised the question again, England had learned from forty years of strife the importance of civil peace. The result was the Glorious Revolution, a political compromise that placed the monarchy beneath the law and guaranteed individual liberty. Most important, however, it united the nation. The Revolution settlement, Trevelyan concluded, "stanched for ever the blood feud of Roundhead and Cavalier, of Anglican and Puritan . . . Under it, England has lived at peace within herself ever since." Because the Revolution finally united the nation, it provided the permanent foundation on which all future liberal reform would be built. The Revolution settlement, Trevelyan continued, "stood almost unaltered until the era of the Reform Bill of 1832. And throughout the successive stages of rapid change that have followed, its fundamentals have remained to bear the weight of the vast democratic superstructure which the nineteenth and twentieth centuries have raised upon its sure foundation."[4] For Trevelyan, then, the Stuart past became the pivotal moment in England's constitutional development.

The Victorians, preoccupied with sectarian controversy, had stressed the religious dimension of the seventeenth century, and

---

[2] Henry Hallam, *View of the State of Europe during the Middle Ages*, seventh edition (Paris: Baudry's European Library, 1840), 2: 1.

[3] Trevelyan, *England under the Stuarts*, 516.

[4] George Macaulay Trevelyan, *The English Revolution, 1688–1689* (New York: Henry Holt and Company, 1939), 4–5.

Trevelyan incorporated their insights into his own interpretation. Like Carlyle, he conceived of the period as one of conflict between Catholicism and Protestantism. Like Gardiner, he saw that religious issues ultimately divided the parties that fought the Civil War. The Catholic policies of the Stuarts, particularly Laud's attempt to impose an Anglo-Catholic uniformity on the Church, alienated the nation from the court, while disputes over Episcopacy and the Prayer Book finally separated Anglican from Puritan, Cavalier from Roundhead. For Trevelyan as well as for Gardiner, the emergence of the principle of toleration conferred nobility on the otherwise lamentable internecine strife of the 1640s. Though born prematurely during the Civil War, this principle finally triumphed forty years later with the Glorious Revolution. Like Macaulay, Trevelyan saw in William's latitudinarian sentiments the solution to England's sectarian difficulties as freedom of conscience became embodied in the Toleration Act of 1689, "one of the most lastingly successful measures ever passed by Parliament," and one which "closed for ever the long chronicle of religious persecution and religious war."[5]

But unlike the Victorians, whose involvement in sectarian controversy prevented them from settling the issues raised by the Stuart past, Trevelyan brought these issues to a kind of national resolution. Nowhere was this more apparent than in his treatment of Puritanism. For most of the Victorian period, the subject of Puritanism had divided historians along denominational lines. In the early nineteenth century, Nonconformists like William Godwin, John Forster and Robert Vaughan had championed the Puritans, while spokesmen for the Establishment had condemned them as subversives. Even Establishment liberals like Macaulay, who were attracted to the Puritan cause in the Civil War because it was also the Parliamentarian cause, were uncomfortable with its excesses. This tendency to equate Puritanism with Dissent persisted throughout the century to such an extent that Gardiner found it necessary to mediate between sectarian parties in the interest of historical accuracy and national unity. By Trevelyan's time, however, the denominational disputes that once politicized discussions of Puritanism had largely abated as England accommodated Dissent and as the growth of secularism united Churchman and

---

[5] Ibid., 166.

Dissenter in a common struggle against unbelief. Trevelyan accepted the claim, made repeatedly by Victorian Dissenters, that the Puritans had rescued English liberty from Stuart absolutism. But he addressed the issue in a way that demonstrated how thoroughly sectarian controversy had subsided. For the Puritanism that Trevelyan described was truly national, the property of no one denomination. It was the serious, thoughtful Christianity of all Protestants from Anglicans to Quakers. Drawing on Carlyle, Trevelyan described this Puritanism as an emotion, a spiritual intensity, free from those doctrinal, ceremonial or ecclesiastical considerations that distinguished one denomination from another.[6]

If, as Trevelyan suggested, England in the early seventeenth century was Puritan, then the Churchmen who opposed the Puritans must have been mistaken. Just as the accommodation of Dissent in the nineteenth century represented a victory for liberal Anglicanism and a defeat for the High Churchmanship that resolutely opposed concessions to Dissent, so in the historiography of the Stuarts the triumph of Puritanism entailed the defeat of the Laudians. As part of their campaign against the Establishment, Dissenters routinely contrasted the intolerance of the Stuart Church to the appreciation of religious freedom that eventually took hold among the Puritans. Hallam and Macaulay, Whigs who supported concessions to Dissent, similarly disapproved of the persecuting policies of the Laudians and used their histories to promote a liberal Anglicanism that was comprehensive and tolerant. Even Gardiner, who was more charitable than most to the Laudian school, noting its contribution to the latitudinarian thinking of a later generation, found little to praise in the policies of Archbishop Laud. Trevelyan, a descendant of the Macaulays and the Arnolds who once identified himself as an "Anglican agnostic," was immersed in the tradition of liberal Anglicanism.[7] For him, the Laudians were an unpopular Anglo-Catholic minority within the Church. Illiberal in their politics and religion, they supported the absolutism of the Stuarts and opposed the right to private judgment that lay at the heart of English Protestantism.[8]

---

[6] Trevelyan, *England under the Stuarts*, 58–66.
[7] Noel Annan, *Leslie Stephen: The Godless Victorian* (New York: Random House, 1984), 234.
[8] Trevelyan, *England under the Stuarts*, 150–153.

For the Victorians, Roman Catholicism posed a problem in large part because of its association with Ireland. The Stuart past spoke directly to the contemporary Irish problem because for much of the Victorian period the Cromwellian settlement provided the basis for England's supremacy in Ireland. Just as the demands of Dissent politicized treatments of Puritanism, so the question of Irish reform conferred an ideological dimension on discussions of the Anglo-Irish past. Hallam, Macaulay and Gardiner, Whigs and Liberals who hoped to maintain England's connection with Ireland by reforming its abuses, all used the Anglo-Irish past to identify England's prior mistakes and to propose remedies for the future. Only Carlyle and his unionist followers argued the paradoxical position that England's injustice to Ireland was its decision to discontinue the full extent of the Cromwellian settlement. With the creation of the Irish Free State in 1922, however, the history of England's relations with Ireland could be placed in more national context. In his celebration of the Glorious Revolution, written in 1939 to commemorate its two hundred and fiftieth anniversary, Trevelyan remained true to his liberal heritage and condemned the Cromwellian settlement as unjust. Its legacy, he pointed out, was more than two centuries of Anglo-Irish animosity. But the subjection of Ireland was also a prerequisite for England's security. William's reconquest of Ireland, Trevelyan declared, "which meant slavery for Ireland, meant freedom and safety for England, and in the long run for Europe" because it was "part of the great European struggle for religious and international freedom against France."[9]

To search for sources of unity in the turmoil of the seventeenth century was an enterprise common to the Victorians and their successors. And yet an important distinction separated the two. The Victorians were still feeling the effects of the sectarian controversy which everyone regarded as the consequence of the Stuart past, whereas their twentieth-century successors for the most part were not. When Macaulay or Gardiner spoke of the Glorious Revolution or the Civil War as a national event, they were doing so in order to encourage a unity that later generations would take for granted. Both Macaulay and Gardiner developed their interpretations at moments when denominational conflict was a dominant and

---

[9] Trevelyan, *English Revolution*, 242–262, 249.

potentially disruptive factor in national politics. Macaulay began work on his history during the twenty years following the repeal of the Test and Corporation Acts in 1828, a time when the Dissenters' demands for the elimination of their remaining disabilities clashed with the Whigs' traditional support for the Anglican Church, and when peace in Ireland required concessions to Roman Catholicism and reform of the Irish Establishment. Responding to these concerns, Macaulay used the Stuart past to free liberalism as much as possible from its religious preoccupations and to lay the groundwork for a comprehensive religious settlement that would include Protestant Dissent as well as Irish Catholicism. Gardiner, too, conceived his view of the Stuart past at a time of heightened sectarian conflict. During the 1860s and 1870s, as Dissent became an increasingly influential force behind the Liberal party, Gardiner came to believe that applying the scientific method to the past would enable the historian to overcome sectional interests and create an interpretation that was truly national.

By Trevelyan's time, these religious battles were mostly over, and in his history there were already indications of the new controversies to come. Now that sectarian discord no longer divided English society, now that the disruptive forces released by the Reformation seemed reconciled, the Stuart past could be interpreted as an example of organic unity. Trevelyan approached the seventeenth century much as the Victorians had approached the Middle Ages – as a time of harmony before industrialization disturbed social peace, pitting class against class. "England," he wrote, "was a land of local government, local armaments, local feeling, where the life of the shire, the parish and the city was vigorous, yet where no feud existed between country and town; where ranks were for ever mingling; where the gentry intermarried with the middle class, and shared with them the commercial and professional careers."[10] And just as the Victorians' idealization of the Middle Ages masked their anxieties about the rifts in their own society, so Trevelyan's image of a socially integrated England suggests growing fears about the impact of economic forces on twentieth-century England. Indeed, the tone of the coming age was captured not so much by Trevelyan as by Tawney, whose

[10] Trevelyan, *England under the Stuarts*, 71.

*Protestantism and the Rise of Capitalism* appeared in 1926, the year of the General Strike, and assessed the contribution of Puritanism not in the Victorian terms of liberty, toleration or piety, but in the new terms of economic development. The next generation of scholars, building on the labors of the Victorians, would ultimately leave their predecessors' concerns behind.

# Index

Althorp, Lord, 28, 56, 57, 58
Arnold, Matthew, 77, 167, 180–182, 210–211
Atterbury, Francis, 87

Bacon, Francis, 69, 114, 163, 171–172, 173, 208, 209
Bagehot, Walter, 77
Baxter, Richard, 78–79
Bayne, Peter, 134, 135, 136, 137, 165
Belsham, William, 96
Bentham, Jeremy, 77, 136
Benthamites, 32, 59, 60, 63, 122
Bismarck, Otto von, 187, 219
Boer War, 158, 185, 187
Bolingbroke, 1st Viscount, 32
Bonaparte, Napoleon, 23, 27–29, 96
Boyle, Robert, 138
Brady, Robert, 32–33
Brent, Richard, 26n, 56, 64
Brodie, George, 97, 98
Broglie, Duc de, 23, 47–48
Brougham, Henry Peter, 25, 27, 28
Browning, Robert, 104
Bryce, James, 155, 156, 158, 161
Bunyan, John, 218
Burke, Edmund, 2, 7, 13–14, 16, 29, 38, 77, 95, 96, 115, 152, 185, 208, 210
   use of the Stuart past, 14–16
   and Hallam, 20, 35, 36–37, 47, 49

Canning, George, 152, 153
Cardale, John Bate, 142, 143
Carlyle, Thomas, 23, 104
   his politics, 121, 122, 123, 128–130
   his religion, 118–120, 126
   reception of his *Cromwell*, 21, 77, 132–138, 190, 192, 193, 196, 213, 220, 223, 224, 225
   writing of his *Cromwell*, 117–118, 124
   on Cromwell, 20, 55, 119, 120, 122–132
   on Ireland, 131–132

on Puritanism, 19, 118, 120–122, 123–128, 134
and Gardiner, 172, 198–199, 200–201, 210
Catholic Apostolic Church, *see* Irvingites
Cavaliers, 61–62, 63
Chalmers, Thomas, 142, 180
Chamberlain, Joseph, 158, 217
Chambers, E. K., 156
Charles I (king of England), 30
   Carlyle on, 123, 125, 127
   Croker on, 38
   Dissenters on, 94
   Gardiner on, 169–170, 173–174, 206, 207
   Hallam on, 40, 42–43
   Hume on, 9–10, 41
   Catharine Macaulay on, 39
   T. B. Macaulay on, 59
   Masson on, 180
   Morley on, 218
   Vaughan on, 111
   Victorians on, 1, 55
Charles II (king of England), 102, 212
Chillingworth, William, 46, 47, 178, 179
Civil War, English, 2–3
   Burke on, 15
   Carlyle on, 120, 122, 123, 124–125, 126–128, 129
   Croker on, 38
   Fox on, 19
   Gardiner on, 167–168, 170–173, 175, 177, 178, 179, 182
   Godwin on, 99–100, 103
   Hume on, 7
   Hallam on, 42–43, 49, 51
   T. B. Macaulay on, 21, 51–52, 59–62
   Morley on, 218
   Seeley on, 189
   Trevelyan on, 222, 223
Coke, Edward, 35
Commonwealth, English, 13
   Belsham on, 96

228